Nature's Frontiers

ENVIRONMENT
AND
SUSTAINABLE DEVELOPMENT

The Environment and Sustainable Development series covers current and emerging issues that are central to reducing poverty through better management of natural resources, pollution control, and climate-resilient growth. The series draws on analysis and practical experience from across the World Bank, partner institutions, and countries. In support of the United Nations Sustainable Development Goals (SDGs), the series aims to promote understanding of sustainable development in a way that is accessible to a wide global audience. The series is sponsored by the Environment and Natural Resources Global Practice at the World Bank.

Titles in this series

The Changing Wealth of Nations: Measuring Sustainable Development in the New Millennium

Convenient Solutions to an Inconvenient Truth: Ecosystem-Based Approaches to Climate Change

Environmental Flows in Water Resources Policies, Plans, and Projects: Findings and Recommendations

Environmental Health and Child Survival: Epidemiology, Economics, and Experiences

International Trade and Climate Change: Economic, Legal, and Institutional Perspectives

Poverty and the Environment: Understanding Linkages at the Household Level

Strategic Environmental Assessment for Policies: An Instrument for Good Governance

Strategic Environmental Assessment in Policy and Sector Reform: Conceptual Model and Operational Guidance

The Sunken Billions Revisited: Progress and Challenges in Global Marine Fisheries

Nature's Frontiers: Achieving Sustainability, Efficiency, and Prosperity with Natural Capital

ENVIRONMENT AND SUSTAINABLE DEVELOPMENT

Nature's Frontiers

Achieving Sustainability, Efficiency, and Prosperity with Natural Capital

*Richard Damania, Stephen Polasky, Mary Ruckelshaus, Jason Russ,
Markus Amann, Rebecca Chaplin-Kramer, James Gerber,
Peter Hawthorne, Martin Philipp Heger, Saleh Mamun, Giovanni Ruta,
Rafael Schmitt, Jeffrey Smith, Adrian Vogl, Fabian Wagner, Esha Zaveri*

 WORLD BANK GROUP

Contents

Maps

Tables

Foreword

What an exciting World Bank report, breaking new ground! *Nature's Frontiers: Achieving Sustainability, Efficiency, and Prosperity with Natural Capital* is timely, given the explosion of interest in bringing nature into decision-making. It is also urgently needed. With the focus on natural capital as central for prosperity, the report makes abundantly clear that this is about so much more than nature-based or nature-positive solutions. Accounting for the work of nature is about accounting for the very foundation for sustainable futures—that is, the capacity of nature and its biodiversity to provide the essential ecosystem services that economic progress and societal development, as embedded parts of our living planet, ultimately rest upon.

This essential interplay is beautifully captured in the report's analyses of the efficiency gap: the difference between the set of goods and services that could be provided in a sustainable way and what is currently provided, without sacrificing other benefits. By combining innovative science, new data sources, and cutting-edge biophysical and economic models, the highly innovative NatCap team and colleagues from the World Bank derived, in an impressive manner, sustainable resource efficiency frontiers. Through these frontiers they assessed how as many as 146 countries can use their natural capital in more efficient and sustainable ways. This work is highly innovative, impressive, and significant!

They found that closing efficiency gaps in relation to biodiversity, carbon storage, agriculture, grazing, and timber returns can account for many of the world's pressing economic and environmental problems, like health, food and water security, climate change, and economic productivity. The report is truly encouraging and inspirational.

Science plays a vital role in making sense of the world, now more than ever in these turbulent times. Here, leading scientists forming the research front, in collaboration with leading policy experts, have generated stunning results of great value for guiding the urgently needed transformation toward biosphere stewardship and sustainable futures. Their novel and pathbreaking approach clearly shows that this way forward is not only environmentally and economically feasible but also hugely desirable.

Carl Folke
Professor and director, Beijer Institute,
Royal Swedish Academy of Sciences
Founding director and chair of the board,
Stockholm Resilience Centre

Stockholm, December 2022

Acknowledgments

This report is the product of a partnership among the World Bank Group, the Natural Capital Project, and the International Institute for Applied Systems Analysis (IIASA). It was initially led by Marianne Fay, at the time chief economist of the Sustainable Development Practice Group at the World Bank and currently country director for Bolivia, Chile, Ecuador, and Peru. It was subsequently led by Richard Damania, chief economist, and Jason Russ, senior economist, Sustainable Development Practice Group, together with a World Bank team comprising Marianne Fay; Martin Philipp Heger, senior environmental economist; Amjad Khan, economist; Giovanni Ruta, lead environmental economist; and Esha Zaveri, senior economist.

The landscape modeling, analysis, and drafting were carried out by the Natural Capital Project team, led by Stephen Polasky (University of Minnesota) and Mary Ruckelshaus (Stanford University) and comprising Kate Brauman, Jinfeng Chang, Rebecca Chaplin-Kramer, Adam Charette-Castonguay, Gretchen Daily, James Douglass, James Gerber, Peter Hawthorne, Matthew Holden, Justin Johnson, Ginger Kowal, Ian Madden, Saleh Mamun, Lisa Mandle, Eve McDonald-Madden, Issoufou Ouedraogo, Deepak Ray, Rafael Schmitt, Jeffrey Smith, Brent Sohngen, Adrian Vogl, Paul West, and Stacie Wolny.

The air quality modeling, analysis, and drafting were carried out by a team from IIASA led by Markus Amann and Fabian Wagner and comprising Gregor Kiesewetter, Zbigniew Klimont, and Wolfgang Schöpp.

The report has greatly benefited from strategic guidance from Laura Tuck, former vice president, and Juergen Voegele, vice president, Sustainable Development Practice Group. The authors received incisive and helpful advice and comments from World Bank colleagues, including Benoît Blarel, Rafaello Cervigni, Steve Danyo, Thomas Farole, Erik Fernandes, Madhur Guatam, Stephane Hallegatte, Shafick Hoossein, Aart Kraay, Urvashi Narain, Julie Rozenberg, Juha Siikamäki, Mona Sur, Kibrom Tafere, Mike Toman, Ede Ijasz Vasquez, and Marcus Wishart.

Finally, Sreypov Tep provided impeccable administrative support and Shenghui Feng provided excellent graphic design, for which the team is grateful. The team also extends its appreciation to the editorial production team: Caroline Polk, production editor; Sabra Ledent, copyeditor; and Ann O'Malley, proofreader.

About the Authors and Contributors

Authors

Markus Amann, consultant to the World Bank, served at the International Institute for Applied Systems Analysis (IIASA) as director of its air quality and greenhouse gases program. He led the Centre for Integrated Assessment Modeling of the UNECE Air Convention and coordinated scientific policy analyses to support international clean air policies in Asia and Europe, including for the National Emission Ceilings Directive of the European Union and the climate policy proposals of the European Commission. He holds a PhD in economics from the University of Karlsruhe, Germany.

Rebecca Chaplin-Kramer is a principal research scientist at the University of Minnesota and a senior fellow at Stanford University with the Natural Capital Project. She leads research programs on global ecosystem service assessment, linking earth observations and ecosystem service modeling, and accelerating the development of products and tools to integrate the values of nature into decision-making. Chaplin-Kramer is co-founder and executive director of the tech nonprofit SPRING, which builds software solutions for environmental research and problem solving. She was a coordinating lead author on the Values Assessment for the Intergovernmental Science–Policy Platform on Biodiversity and Ecosystem Services (IPBES) and is a lead author on the upcoming IPBES Nexus Assessment. She holds a PhD in environmental science, policy, and management from the University of California, Berkeley.

Richard Damania is the chief economist of the Sustainable Development Practice Group at the World Bank. At the World Bank, he has served as senior economic adviser to the Water Global Practice and lead economist in the Africa region's Sustainable Development Department. He also has worked in the South Asia and Latin America and the Caribbean regions of the World Bank. Damania's work has spanned multiple sectors, and he has helped the World Bank become an acknowledged thought leader on matters relating to environment, water, and the economy. Before joining the World Bank, he held positions in academia and has published extensively in scientific journals. Damania holds a PhD in economics from the University of Glasgow.

James Gerber is a principal research scientist at the University of Minnesota's Institute on the Environment. His research develops solutions for improving global food security while minimizing agriculture's impact on earth's ecosystems. He has published broadly on the topic of agriculture's impact on earth's ecosystems, food security, and the interrelationship of climate variability, crop yields, and systemic trends in food security. Gerber was a lead author for the *Sixth Assessment Report* of the Intergovernmental Panel on Climate Change, with a focus on development pathways. He holds a PhD in physics from the University of California, Santa Cruz.

Peter Hawthorne is the head of Hawthorne Spatial, an independent consultancy specializing in environmental modeling, decision support, and spatial optimization. Previously he was a lead scientist with the Natural Capital Project, where his work focused on developing approaches to modeling and improving co-benefits in environmental decision-making, including through optimization and policy analysis. He holds a BA in mathematics from Harvard University and a PhD in ecology, evolution, and behavior from the University of Minnesota.

Martin Philipp Heger is a senior environmental economist at the World Bank, where he currently focuses on environmental and natural resource issues in South Asian countries. He has previously worked in several regions of the World Bank, including Europe and Central Asia, and the Middle East and North Africa. Heger works closely with governments and development partners on policies and projects aimed at improving air quality, marine health, coastal resilience, forest management, and climate resilience. He maintains a rigorous evidence-based focus in his country policy work. Prior to joining the World Bank, he worked for the UN Development Programme, the European Commission, and a nongovernmental organization in Panama. He holds master's degrees in economics and natural resource management from the University of Vienna and the University of Hawaii, respectively, and a PhD in environmental economics from the London School of Economics and Political Science.

Saleh Mamun is a postdoctoral associate at the University of Minnesota. He is jointly appointed to the Applied Economics Department and Natural Resources Research Institute. Mamun's research interest is natural resource economics and ecological economics, and his research focuses on optimizing decision-making on managing natural resources while considering nature's contribution to people. He uses a nonmarket valuation approach to quantify behavioral and market responses to environmental amenities and hazards. Mamun is a team member of the Natural Capital Project. He holds an MBA in finance from the Institute of Business Administration at the University of Dhaka and a PhD in economics from the University of New Mexico; he also worked in construction, marketing, and government for six years in Bangladesh.

Stephen Polasky is Regents Professor and Fesler-Lampert Professor of Ecological/Environmental Economics at the University of Minnesota. His research focuses on issues at the intersection of ecology and economics, including the value of ecosystem services and natural capital, biodiversity conservation, land use, sustainability, common property resources, and environmental regulation. Polasky is a co-founder of the Natural Capital Project, a collaborative initiative between Stanford University and the University of Minnesota. He has served as senior staff economist for the environment for the President's Council of Economic Advisers. He was a coordinating lead author for the Global Assessment of the Intergovernmental Science–Policy Platform on Biodiversity and Ecosystem Services. He is a member of the US National Academy of Sciences and a fellow of the Association of Environmental and Resource Economists, the American Academy of Arts and Sciences, and the American Association for the Advancement of Science. He holds a PhD in economics from the University of Michigan.

Mary Ruckelshaus is executive director of the Natural Capital Project and a senior research associate at Stanford University. She previously held leadership positions with the US National Oceanic and Atmospheric Administration and served as assistant professor of biological sciences at Florida State University. Her recent work has been devoted to developing standard approaches to valuing nature and mainstreaming the results into high-leverage decisions globally. Ruckelshaus was a lead author and reviewer for the 2013 and 2017 US National Climate Assessments. She has served on many boards and is past chair of the Science Advisory Board of the US National Center for Ecological Analysis and Synthesis. She holds a master's degree in fisheries and a doctoral degree in botany from the University of Washington.

Jason Russ is a senior economist in the Office of the Chief Economist of the Sustainable Development Practice Group at the World Bank. His professional interests center on using econometrics and data analytics to diagnose development challenges and to quantify the economic and social impacts of environmental externalities. His tenure at the World Bank includes five years in the Water Global Practice where he helped to develop and coordinate the analytical work program of the Economics Global Solutions Group, including authoring many of its global flagship reports. Russ has published extensively in academic journals largely related to environmental and development economics. Before joining the

World Bank, he was an analyst at PricewaterhouseCoopers. He holds a PhD in economics from George Washington University.

Giovanni Ruta is lead environmental economist in the Environment, Natural Resources and Blue Economy Global Practice at the World Bank, East Asia and Pacific region, where he coordinates the operational and analytical agenda on green growth, climate change, biodiversity, and natural resource management. He joined the World Bank in 2001 and has worked on the economics of sustainability, green growth, and natural capital accounting. He has experience working on projects in East Asia and the Pacific, Latin America, and Africa. Ruta holds a master's degree in environmental economics from University College London and a PhD in environmental and natural resource economics from the London School of Economics and Political Science.

Rafael Schmitt is a lead scientist at the Natural Capital Project and the Woods Institute for the Environment at Stanford University. His work is centered on the role of built and natural infrastructure for the water-energy-food (WEF) nexus from global to local scales. Because rivers are central connectors in natural ecosystems and the WEF nexus, much of his work focuses on large rivers, such as the Mekong and the Amazon. Schmitt has been driving the development of new models—for example, for global sediment transport, landslides, and water quality—and spearheads their integration into frameworks for strategic decision and robust decision-making under climate change. He previously was a postdoctoral researcher at the University of California Berkeley College for Environmental Design, where he worked on trade-offs between climate mitigation and adaptation for the Mekong. He holds a PhD in information technology from Politecnico di Milano.

Jeffrey Smith is a postdoctoral research associate at Princeton University working on understanding how nature-based climate solutions are likely to affect biodiversity. During his academic studies, he has investigated the effects of climate change and land use change on biodiversity, sought to determine how New England old-field arthropod food webs varied along a suburban forest gradient, and undertaken research on the biological control of invasive weeds and on restoration ecology. Smith holds a BS in ecology and environmental science from the University of Delaware, a master's degree in environmental science from the Yale School of Forestry and Environmental Studies, and a PhD in biology from Stanford University.

Adrian Vogl is a lead scientist for Stanford University's Natural Capital Project and a consultant with the World Bank. Her work engages researchers, policy makers, and civil society groups worldwide, advancing the science and practice of nature-based solutions for water security. Her focus is on how land management affects water and other ecosystem service co-benefits, particularly in the face of changing and uncertain climatic conditions. At the World Bank, Vogl co-leads the Biodiversity, Ecosystems, and Landscape Assessment initiative, working with policy makers, technical staff, and consultants to produce analytical tools and build capacity for integrated landscape management with the goal of enhancing the durability of investments in infrastructure, agriculture, and the environment. She holds a BA in cultural anthropology from the University of Arizona and a PhD in aquatic resources from Texas State University–San Marcos.

Fabian Wagner is a senior research scholar in the Energy, Climate, and Environment Program, as well as dean for capacity development and academic training at the International Institute for Applied Systems Analysis (IIASA). He is also editor-in-chief of the journal *Mitigation and Adaptation Strategies for Global Change* (Springer Nature). Between 2014 and 2016, Wagner was the Gerhard R. Andlinger Professor for Energy and the Environment at Princeton University. Before joining IIASA in 2004, he was a researcher with the Intergovernmental Panel on Climate Change located at the Institute for Global Environmental Strategies in Hayama, Japan. Postdoctoral, he joined the International Energy Analysis Group at the Lawrence Berkeley National Laboratory. Wagner holds master's degrees in mathematics and in the history and philosophy of science and a PhD in theoretical physics from Cambridge University.

Esha Zaveri is a senior economist with the World Bank's Water Global Practice. She has professional interests in water resource management, climate impacts, environmental health, and the use of geospatial data with statistical analysis to study interactions between the environment and social and economic systems. She has published on these topics in leading scientific journals and has authored World Bank flagship reports on water scarcity (*Uncharted Waters,* 2017), water pollution (*Quality Unknown,* 2019), and migration (*Ebb and Flow,* 2021). Prior to joining the World Bank, Zaveri was a postdoctoral fellow at Stanford University's Center on Food Security and the Environment where she remains an affiliated scholar. She holds a PhD in environmental economics and demography from Pennsylvania State University.

Contributors

Adam Castonguay is a postdoctoral research fellow at the University of Queensland working on modeling and mapping climate-sensitive zoonotic diseases in South Asia. His research consists of developing spatial models to explore human-environmental systems and inform decisions at the interface of water, food, health, and climate systems. Castonguay joined the University of

Queensland in 2018 to develop a spatial optimization to assess trade-offs between sustainable development goals in global beef production. He holds a PhD in water and sanitary engineering from Monash University.

Gretchen Daily is the Bing Professor of Environmental Science in the Department of Biology and the director of the Center for Conservation Biology at Stanford University. She is co-founder and faculty director of the Stanford Natural Capital Project. Daily's work is focused on understanding human dependence and impacts on nature and the deep societal transformations needed to secure people and nature. Her work spans fundamental research and policy-oriented initiatives to open inclusive and green development pathways. She has published several hundred scientific and popular articles, along with a dozen books, including a seminal publication on ecosystem services: *Nature's Services: Societal Dependence on Natural Ecosystems* (1997). Daily holds a PhD in ecology from Stanford University.

Marianne Fay, an economist specializing in sustainable development, is the World Bank country director for Bolivia, Chile, Ecuador, and Peru. She has 25 years of experience in different regions of the world, contributing to knowledge on and the search for development solutions in the areas of infrastructure, urbanization, climate change, green growth, and poverty reduction. Fay has published and edited several books and articles, including the World Bank publications *World Development Report 2010: Development and Climate Change* and *Infrastructure in Latin America and the Caribbean: Recent Developments and Key Challenges.* She holds a PhD in economics from Columbia University.

Justin Johnson is an assistant professor of applied economics at the University of Minnesota. He works closely with the Natural Capital Project at the Institute on the Environment at the University of Minnesota and Stanford University. His research focuses on how the economy affects the environment, and vice versa, on global to local scales. Johnson leads a project that links the Global Trade Analysis Project (Purdue University) with the Integrated Valuation of Ecosystem Services and Trade-Offs model from the Natural Capital Project, aiming to build strong quantitative evidence on how changes in ecosystem services affect economic performance at the macroeconomic level and how global policies can be designed to sustainably manage our natural capital. He holds a PhD in applied economics from the University of Minnesota and a BA in economics from St. Olaf College.

Amjad Khan is an economist at the World Bank providing evidence-based insights to inform policy design and investment projects, particularly in developing country contexts. His work has focused on issues of human capital formation, urbanization, regional development, conflict, and natural resource management. Khan specializes in building analytical narratives that engage with contextual nuances through large amounts of quantitative and spatial data and economic theory. Much of his research interest also lies at the intersection of political economy, economic history, and institutional economics. Khan holds a PhD and MA in economics from the George Washington University and a BSc (Hons) in economics and mathematics from Lahore University of Management and Science.

Virginia Kowal is a geospatial data scientist and research fellow. With a background in ecology and ecological modeling, she currently works on modeling sector transition pathways for businesses and philanthropic organizations to align their emissions with global climate ambition. She contributes technical analysis to diverse research groups and advocates, including groups focused on the power sector, the buildings sector, and steel and cement sectors. Kowal holds an MSc in ecology from the University of Calgary and a BSc in biology from the University of North Carolina–Asheville.

Lisa Mandle is a lead scientist with the Natural Capital Project at Stanford University. Her research sheds light on how the environmental impacts of land management and infrastructure development affect ecosystem services, social equity, and human health. Mandle works with governments, multilateral development banks, and nongovernmental organizations to incorporate this understanding into development decisions, particularly in Latin America and Asia. She is also lead editor of the book *Green Growth That Works*, which provides a practical guide to policy and finance mechanisms from around the world for securing benefits from nature. Mandle holds a PhD in botany from the University of Hawaii at Manoa and a combined AB/ScB in anthropology and biology from Brown University.

Deepak Ray is a senior research scientist at the Institute on the Environment at the University of Minnesota. He builds high-resolution global agricultural datasets and conducts model simulations to answer questions on the impact of land use / land cover change and global climate change on food security and sustainability. Ray holds a PhD in atmospheric science from the University of Alabama–Huntsville.

Brent Sohngen is an environmental and natural resource economist at the Ohio State University. He conducts research on climate change and forests, including development of integrated assessment models linking dynamic vegetation models and forest land use and management models, modeling the marginal costs of forests as a natural climate solution, and conducting policy analysis. He served as lead author on the Intergovernmental Panel on Climate Change 2022 Working

Group III (Mitigation) Report. Sohngen holds a PhD from the Yale School of Forestry and Environmental Studies.

Paul West is a senior scientist at Project Drawdown (https://drawdown.org/) researching and sharing how climate solutions can create win-wins and trade-offs for conserving biodiversity and creating sustainable food systems, water, and many other aspects of planetary health and human well-being. He also holds a research appointment at the University of Minnesota. Before joining Project Drawdown in 2021, West worked at the University of Minnesota's Institute on the Environment and at The Nature Conservancy, where he led local and global land and freshwater projects. West holds a PhD in limnology and marine science from the University of Wisconsin–Madison, where he developed new methods for quantifying the trade-offs of food production, climate, biodiversity, and water.

Main Messages

The great expansion of economic activity since the end of World War II has caused an unprecedented rise in living standards, but it has also caused rapid changes in earth systems. Nearly all types of natural capital—the world's stock of resources and services provided by nature—are in decline. Clean air, abundant and clean water, fertile soils, productive fisheries, dense forests, and healthy oceans are critical for healthy lives and healthy economies. Mounting pressures, however, suggest that the trend of declining natural capital may cast a long shadow into the future.

Recognizing the essential services provided by natural capital, *Nature's Frontiers: Achieving Sustainability, Efficiency, and Prosperity with Natural Capital* **proposes a novel approach to address these foundational challenges of sustainability.** A methodology combining innovative science, new data sources, and cutting-edge biophysical and economic models builds *sustainable resource efficiency frontiers* to assess how countries can sustainably use their natural capital in more efficient ways. The analysis provides recommendations on how countries can better utilize their natural capital to achieve their economic and environmental goals.

The report indicates that significant efficiency gaps exist in nearly every country in the world. Closing these gaps can address many of the world's pressing economic and environmental problems—economic productivity, health, food and water security, and climate change. The following is a summary of the key results:

- **Key finding 1: Significant efficiency gaps exist in the use of land in countries at all income levels and in all regions.** For most low-income countries, significant increases in net economic returns are possible without sacrificing environmental quality. In fact, there are opportunities to improve both economic output and environmental outcomes in most countries. On average, countries can almost double their performance in terms of either economic returns or environmental outcomes by improving on one dimension without a sacrifice in the other outcome.

- **Key finding 2: More efficient use of land could sequester an additional 85.6 billion metric tons of carbon dioxide equivalent with no adverse economic impacts.** This outcome is equivalent to about two years of global emissions at current rates and would give the world much-needed time to decarbonize before atmospheric greenhouse gas (GHG) concentrations reach critical levels. Because most tropical low-income countries have a comparative advantage in sequestering carbon through forests, they gain significantly more than any other group of countries from policies that reward land-based GHG sequestration initiatives.

- **Key finding 3: Better allocation and management of land, water, and other inputs could lead to increases in agriculture, grazing, and forestry annual income by approximately US$329 billion—and enough food production increases to feed the world until 2050—without net loss of forests and natural habitats.** Global populations are expected to reach 10 billion by 2050, and more food will be needed to meet global demands. Better cultivation strategies that close yield gaps, along with smarter spatial planning, can reduce the land footprint of agriculture while increasing global calories produced by more than 150 percent.

- **Key finding 4: Existing policies for reducing air pollution and the resulting mortality could be achieved with a 60 percent cost saving.** The 63 countries examined for air quality spent a total of US$220 billion—0.6 percent of their collective gross domestic product—on air pollution controls per year. These expenditures prevented 1.9 million premature deaths per year. If more economically efficient policies were adopted, the same results could be achieved at an even lower cost—only US$75 billion, or less than US$40,000 per life saved.

- **Key finding 5: More efficient air pollution policies could have saved significantly more lives with the same level of spending.** Had countries spent the same amount of money to abate particulate matter but implemented the most efficient policies instead of the abatement policies they actually implemented, they would have prevented an additional 366,000 premature deaths each year—a 20 percent improvement over the current level of avoided premature deaths.

- **Key finding 6: Although richer countries are more efficient at abating air pollution, there are examples of good performers and underperformers across all income groups.** Most high-income countries perform relatively well in terms of pollution abatement and, consequently, reducing negative human consequences, but being a high-income country does not automatically ensure good performance.

No one-size-fits-all solution exists, given the differences in endowments, needs, and capacities among countries. Instead, this report identifies what changes are needed and where these changes need to occur in a country. It also develops a policy filter for choosing the most appropriate policy mix for the country. The result is a detailed roadmap that can assist in the selection of approaches that are most feasible and affordable in each country. The report also drills down into specific country examples of priority reforms to illustrate how to put these tools into action.

Given countries' competing needs and stretched budgets, tackling ineffi-ciencies remains among the more cost-effective and economically attractive ways to achieve global sustainability goals. As global populations expand and the climate changes, pressures on common property natural resources will inevi-tably escalate, and economic consequences will worsen. This report demonstrates that there are significant opportunities for using the world's scarce and valuable natural capital more efficiently. Although the approach outlined in this report will entail demanding policy reforms, the costs of inaction will be far higher.

Executive Summary

Introduction

The great expansion of economic activity since the end of World War II has lifted billions of people out of poverty and raised living standards around the world, but it has also produced rapid changes in the earth's environment. Air pollution kills more people than all wars and forms of violence combined. Deforestation, degradation of soils, and destruction of wetlands have diminished the fertility of land and the functionality of watersheds. And natural habitat conversion is accelerating the loss of flora and fauna and having impacts on biodiversity and critical ecosystem services such as pollination, water purification, and pest control that support healthy economies and healthy populations.

To some observers, the decline in natural capital, like the canary in the coal mine, is a sign of unsustainable economic activity that could undermine the foundations of human well-being (Folke et al. 2021). Others note that economic growth continues unabated, despite mounting environmental stresses. According to this view, environmental degradation may be the price to be paid for economic progress, implying that trade-offs are inevitable for greater human prosperity. However, because nature provides essential services for life, health, and the economy, mounting evidence suggests that the trend of declining natural capital may cast a long shadow into the future (Dasgupta 2021). Thus there may be scope for achieving both growth and well-being by enhancing the environment instead of destroying it. A recent World Bank analysis found that the partial collapse of some ecosystem services globally could bring a decline in global gross domestic product (GDP) of US$2.7 trillion by 2030 (Johnson et al. 2021).

A decline in natural capital is typically a result of market failures. Most natural capital is in the form of common property. Thus, too often no price is paid for utilizing ecosystem services, no reward is given for maintaining natural capital, and no costs are incurred for actions that destroy natural capital. Because natural capital is routinely unpriced or underpriced, it is used wastefully, and unsustainably. Moreover, seldom are renewable natural resources allocated in ways that maximize the full benefits they could produce. Inefficient and unsustainable use of these resources for private gain impose local, national, and global costs that are paid by society at large.

Recognizing the essential services provided by natural capital, this report proposes a novel approach to address these foundational challenges of sustainability. Innovative science, new data sources, and cutting-edge biophysical and economic models are combined to devise *resource efficiency frontiers* to assess how countries can sustainably use their natural capital in more efficient ways. These new models evaluate ecosystem services and economic production to estimate a country's efficiency gap—that is, the difference between the set of goods and services currently provided and those that could be provided in a sustainable way without sacrificing other benefits. Recommendations are also offered on how countries can better utilize their natural capital to achieve their economic and environmental goals. In doing so, this report provides countries with a road map for improving on economic and environmental objectives by delivering more efficient and more sustainable outcomes.

This approach is used for two of the most significant natural capital assets, land and (clean) air. The report begins by examining three potentially competing land-based outputs: economic production (agriculture, grazing, and forestry), greenhouse gas (GHG) sequestration, and biodiversity. Metrics for the joint efficiency of all three outputs, as well as individual efficiency measures, are generated. Box ES.1 shows an example of the landscape resource efficiency frontier comparing economic production and GHG sequestration. The report then takes a look at the level of efficiency applied to the control of air pollution. The air pollution efficiency frontier measures the additional health benefits (lives saved) from more effective spending on the abatement of fine particulate matter ($PM_{2.5}$). $PM_{2.5}$ is the air pollutant that claims the majority of lives, while also causing respiratory infections, cognitive disorders, and impairments in worker productivity. It is therefore a key pollutant to target for abatement.

The findings of the study reported here indicate that nearly every country has significant efficiency gaps. Closing these gaps can address many of the world's pressing economic and environmental problems—economic productivity, health, food and water security, and climate change. What follows is a summary of the key findings.

Key findings of this study

Finding 1: Land use is inefficient in countries at all income levels and in all regions. For most low-income countries, significant increases in net economic returns are possible without sacrificing environmental quality. In fact, the vast majority of countries have opportunities to improve both economic output and environmental outcomes. On average, countries can almost double their performance on at least one outcome without a sacrifice in any other outcome.

BOX ES.1
An example of an efficiency frontier from West Africa

Figure ES.1.1 shows an efficiency frontier for Liberia, a West African country. The blue curve traces the maximum attainable combinations of greenhouse gas mitigation and biodiversity conservation (vertical axis) and income from farming, forestry, and grazing (horizontal axis) that is achievable on a sustainable basis. Points on the frontier represent efficient land use and land management, where environmental outcomes cannot be increased further without economic losses (and vice versa). Point A is the current steady-state outcome. Were the country to maximize economic returns from land without any sacrifice of environmental services, it would reach point D. Were the country to maximize environmental returns without economic sacrifice it would reach point C. The colors in the map show the changes in land use and land management needed to achieve these transitions.

Very few countries are found to be operating near their efficiency frontiers. Most countries can make significant gains in at least one dimension. A contribution of this report is to provide the first quantification of the magnitudes of efficiency gains and policy shifts needed to achieve frontier efficiency.

FIGURE ES.1.1
Example of an efficiency frontier, Liberia

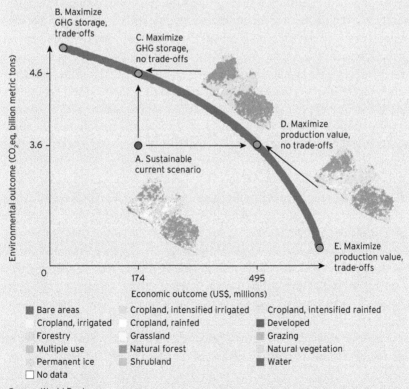

Source: World Bank.
Note: CO_2eq = carbon dioxide equivalent; GHG = greenhouse gas.

Finding 2: With more efficient use of land, an additional 85.6 billion metric tons of carbon dioxide equivalent (CO_2eq) could be sequestered with no adverse economic impacts. This amount is equivalent to about two years' worth of global emissions at current rates and would give the world much-needed time to decarbonize before atmospheric GHG concentrations reach critical levels. Because most tropical low-income countries have a comparative advantage in sequestering carbon through forests, they gain significantly more than any other group of countries from policies that reward land-based GHG sequestration initiatives.

Finding 3: If maximizing income is the objective, better allocation and management of land, water, and other inputs alone could lead to increases in the annual income from agriculture, grazing, and forestry by approximately US$329 billion (and enough additional food production to feed the world until 2050) without loss of biodiversity or GHG storage and sequestration provided by forests and natural habitats. Because the global population is expected to reach some 10 billion by 2050, more food will be needed to meet that demand. Better cultivation strategies that close yield gaps and smarter spatial planning can reduce the land footprint of agriculture while increasing global calories produced by more than 150 percent. These efficiency gains would produce more calories than estimates suggest are needed to meet growing per capita consumption and rising populations. Evaluated at current prices, this increase in production translates into an 82 percent increase in net value from agriculture, grazing, and timber production without adverse consequences for GHG storage and sequestration or biodiversity. Notably, most low- and middle-income countries are currently achieving less than half of their potential agricultural output, whereas high-income countries are reaching, on average, 70 percent of their potential output.

Because there are large efficiency gaps in the production of food and most GHG sequestration occurs on land that is rich in biodiversity, these results suggest that development need not come at the cost of a nation's biodiversity. For most countries, strategic planning and improving the efficiency of production can be achieved without a fatal strain on biodiversity. And as the world implements the new Post-2020 Global Biodiversity Framework,[1] the resource efficiency frontiers described in this report can become a useful evidence-based tool to optimize the use of land so that income generation and multiple environmental goals are achieved simultaneously. The last chapter of this report illustrates for three countries how this could be achieved.

Finding 4: Existing policies for reducing air pollution (and the resulting mortality) could be achieved with a 60 percent cost saving. The 63 countries examined for air quality spent a total of US$220 billion—0.6 percent of their collective GDP—on air pollution controls per year. These expenditures prevented 1.9 million premature deaths a year. Even before accounting for inefficiencies, they are a remarkably cheap way to save lives—approximately US$115,000 per life saved. However, if more economically efficient policies were adopted, the same results could be achieved at an even lower cost—only US$75 billion, or less than US$40,000 per life saved.

Finding 5: More efficient air pollution policies could have saved significantly more lives with the same level of spending. Had countries spent the same amount of money to abate $PM_{2.5}$ but implemented the most efficient policies instead of the abatement policies they did put in place, they would have prevented an additional 366,000 premature deaths each year—a 20 percent improvement over the current level of prevented premature deaths.

Finding 6: Although richer countries are more efficient at abating air pollution, there are examples of good performers and underperformers across all income groups. Most high-income countries perform relatively well at reducing pollution and consequently its negative human consequences, but being a high-income country does not automatically ensure good performance. Some high-income countries do not place a priority on pollution abatement, whereas others have invested in abatement but not efficiently so. In general, lower-income countries do not spend much on pollution abatement, but a few do spend efficiently what little they devote to pollution abatement even as most do not.

The way forward

For landscapes

Policy makers seeking to achieve the efficiency gains identified in this report face significant headwinds. Indeed, if change were easy it would already be achieved, especially in view of the magnitude of the potential gains. Nevertheless, powerful examples from around the world are reminders that natural resource reallocation and restoration are not only a path out of poverty, but also a necessary step toward sustainable prosperity (Box ES.2). Landscape efficiency gaps typically emerge because the allocation of renewable natural resources is related neither to the full environmental benefits they could confer, nor to the full economic benefits they could generate. As a result, most natural capital is allocated inefficiently and degraded and depleted beyond what is economically justifiable.

There is no one-size-fits-all solution for inefficiencies because of countries' different endowments, needs, and capacities. Instead, this report identifies *what* changes are needed and *where* these changes need to occur in a country. It also

BOX ES.2
The Loess Plateau: A transformational landscape

Reaching the efficiency frontier by making better use of environmental resources while enhancing economic growth and multiplying livelihood opportunities is possible. Perhaps the most salient example of this possibility comes from the Loess Plateau in north-central China. After thousands of years of agricultural exploitation and limitless grazing, this region of China—which extends over 640,000 square kilometers—became a barren dust bowl. The degraded vegetation only accelerated the dilapidation process because nothing was left to prevent the flow of rainfall from turning into silt-filled floods and further eroding the landscape. Few would have believed that restoration of such a barren, infertile landscape would have been possible.

Over the last 40 years, however, funding from the Chinese government and the World Bank has successfully reversed this vicious cycle and restored close to 4 million hectares in the Loess Plateau. Restoration involved a three-tier strategy: (1) planting trees on the tops of hills to filter the rain and increase biodiversity; (2) building terraces for agriculture along the center of the plateau, which would then benefit from increased moisture and natural irrigation; and (3) building reservoirs to help collect excess water in the valleys. The transformation was truly revolutionary. Once dry, barren, and depleted, the land is now green, fertile, and abundant.

The economy has benefited as well. Agricultural yields have risen markedly and continuously since the restoration began, and the land is producing not only more yields but also greater quality and variety. Meanwhile, farmers and vendors have seen higher incomes, which have improved the living standards of the entire region (Guo et al. 2014).

presents a *policy filter* to choose the most appropriate policy mix for a country. The result is a detailed road map that can assist in the selection of approaches that are the most feasible and affordable for each country. This report also drills down into specific country examples of priority reforms to illustrate how to put these tools into action.

The road to greater efficiency calls for three fundamental shifts:

- *Reallocating resources among sectors to their most productive uses.* Resource reallocation is often a complex, difficult process, but it is also among the most powerful engines of economic progress and growth. Land and freshwater are widely misallocated due to multiple market and policy failures. Thus policies such as forest restoration, where the services of forests are most needed, or reallocation of water to where it is most valuable will often generate especially large benefits.
- *Changing the composition of resources within a sector.* Inefficiency may arise because of less productive land uses within sectors. For example, production patterns often do not reflect the suitability and comparative advantage of land across different agroecological dimensions.
- *Improving the efficiency of resource use.* Even when the *allocation* of resources between and within sectors is efficient, resources may still be used inefficiently.

On average, 55 percent of gains in the value of agricultural production are from sustainable intensification—using resources more efficiently. These gaps are especially large in low-income countries, suggesting that there is a significant potential to close productivity gaps without compromising environmental outcomes.

A wide array of policies is available to achieve these objectives. The suite of policies to induce such shifts has been extensively documented and comprehensively analyzed. They include payments for ecosystem services and conservation tenders (bids) that provide the incentives needed to reallocate resources to better uses. Other approaches involve zoning, planning, and support for both environmental and economic benefits through regenerative production and sustainable and nonconsumptive forest utilization. Often, misallocation is a consequence of misaligned incentives caused by policy failures such as poorly designed taxes or subsidies that should be repurposed and rendered less harmful. Market-based instruments such as "cap-and-trade" schemes or pricing can discourage profligacy in resource use. In low-income countries where agricultural yields are often far below their potential, the mix of required policies might include tackling the credit constraints facing smallholders, lack of inputs, lack of access to markets, informational constraints, lack of insurance, skill deficits, and lack of secure land tenure. Investments in infrastructure such as irrigation, transport, and communications—to better connect farmers to markets in both a physical sense and an informational sense—may also pay large dividends for intensifying agriculture without encroaching on the forest frontier. A nonexhaustive menu of policy options and how to choose between these using a policy filter is described in the report with country examples.

For air pollution

Because of the vital role that air quality plays in protecting human lives and the economy, it is critical that policies and investments prevent its degradation. Countries vary in terms of how ambitious they are in protecting air quality, as well as how efficient they have been in the policies and investments that they have put in place. Thus solutions to improving air pollution abatement will differ based on these factors:

- More complex approaches are needed in countries that are already highly efficient at abating pollution and are also highly ambitious. Despite the admirable performances of several wealthy economies, important cost-effective gains can still be made by further reducing $PM_{2.5}$. These countries generally have strong institutions and large capacities for monitoring and can use more cost-effective policy instruments such as pollution taxes. Cost-effective remedies may call for addressing pollution abatement in upwind jurisdictions where marginal abatement costs may be lower.

- Expanding the scope of pollution abatement is necessary in the lower-income countries that are highly efficient in reducing pollution but have low ambition. The current focus in these countries tends to be on the lower-hanging fruits of pollution control (such as particle filters for large point sources burning coal), where pollution abatement is relatively less expensive. Expanding ambition will require looking outside of these sectors to things such as solid-fuel cook-stoves, agricultural residue burning, and waste management. Large data and knowledge gaps also often exist in these countries, which makes monitoring and efficient program implementation difficult.
- Most low-income countries are not ambitious in their spending or ambitious in their pollution reduction policy goals. They need to invest systematically in pollution control, starting with the lowest-cost options. Typically, countries in this group have taken only very basic measures to control air pollution, despite their serious pollution levels and the resulting significant burden on public health and economic performance. As with the previous category, they will have to expand pollution control measures to a wider set of sectors, revisit energy subsidy systems, and fill critical data and knowledge gaps. Nevertheless, these countries often face additional challenges due to lack of funds, enforcement capacity, and even basic information on sources of emissions. In such cases, technical assistance, budget support, and identification of co-benefits—with, for example, climate change mitigation and adaptation objectives—will be required to lower the costs of taking action.

Conclusions

With competing needs and stretched budgets, tackling inefficiencies remains among the more cost-effective and economically attractive ways to achieve global sustainability goals. As global populations expand and the climate changes, pressures on common property natural resources will inevitably escalate, with worsening economic consequences. Using state-of-the-art techniques and new data, the study reported here demonstrates that there are significant opportunities for using the world's scarce and valuable natural capital more efficiently. Doing so would stimulate increases in economic productivity and improvements in environmental outcomes. Such a transformation is shown to be both feasible and environmentally and economically desirable. It will entail policy reforms that will be demanding, but the costs of inaction will be far higher.

A guide to this report

Readers wishing to explore land-based applications of the tools can proceed directly to the country case studies and illustrations in chapter 6. Those seeking an understanding of the land-based resource efficiency frontier and the differences found across countries would find chapters 1, 3, 4, and 6 useful. The air pollution results are covered in chapters 1 and 5. Chapters 1 and 2 provide a nontechnical overview of the analytical foundations, data, and underlying assumptions and serve as an adjunct to the online technical appendix.[2]

Notes

1. Convention on Biological Diversity, "Preparations for the Post-2020 Biodiversity Framework," https://www.cbd.int/conferences/post2020.
2. The online technical appendix (appendix B) is available with the text of this book in the World Bank's Online Knowledge Repository, https://openknowledge.worldbank.org /handle/10986/39453.

References

Dasgupta, P. 2021. *The Economics of Biodiversity: The Dasgupta Review.* Abridged Version. London: HM Treasury.

Folke, C., S. Polasky, J. Rockström, V. Galaz, F. Westley, M. Lamont, M. Scheffer, et al. 2021. *Ambio* 50 (4): 834–69. https://doi.org/10.1007/s13280-021-01544-8.

Johnson, J. A., G. Ruta, U. Baldos, R. Cervigni, S. Chonabayashi, E. Corong, O. Gavryliuk, J. Gerber, T. Hertel, C. Nootenboom, and S. Polasky. 2021. "The Economic Case for Nature: A Global Earth-Economy Model to Assess Development Policy Pathways." World Bank, Washington, DC.

Abbreviations

BMP	best management practice
CGE	computable general equilibrium
CLE	current legislation emissions
CO_2eq	carbon dioxide equivalent
ESA	European Space Agency
EU	European Union
FAO	Food and Agriculture Organization
GAEZ	Global Agro-Ecological Zones
GAINS	Greenhouse Gas–Air Pollution Interactions and Synergies
GBD	Global Burden of Disease
GDP	gross domestic product
GHG	greenhouse gas
GTAP	Global Trade Analysis Project
HIC	high-income country
IFAD	International Fund for Agricultural Development
IPCC	Intergovernmental Panel on Climate Change
LIC	low-income country
LMIC	lower-middle-income country
MFR	maximum feasible reduction
NbS	nature-based solution
NDC	nationally determined contribution
NDVI	Normalized Difference Vegetation Index
NOC	no control
NO_x	nitrogen oxides
PES	payment for ecosystem services
PM	particulate matter
SCR	selective catalytic reduction
SLMP	sustainable land management project
SO_2	sulphur dioxide
TFP	total factor productivity
UMIC	upper-middle-income country
WHO	World Health Organization

CHAPTER 1

Introduction:
Down to Earth

Destroying a rainforest for economic gain is like burning a
Renaissance painting to cook a meal.
E. O. Wilson, American biologist[1]

Key messages

- Natural capital is declining at an unprecedented rate. Diminishing land fertility, lost flood protection benefits, reduced water filtration, and an increased risk of zoonotic diseases such as COVID-19 are just some of the ways this effect is being felt by people and economies.

- Misaligned incentives are largely to blame for the decline in natural capital. As a result, it is not used as efficiently as it could be and is not allocated in ways that maximize its many possible benefits.

- Reversing this decline and using natural capital more efficiently are opportunities to dramatically increase both economic productivity and environmental benefits such as health, carbon sequestration, and biodiversity, with limited trade-offs.

- This report presents the results of a new study that explores and quantifies the scope for win-wins and the magnitude of trade-offs. It proposes policy solutions to help countries achieve them.

Introduction

Nature provides essential inputs for human life, health, and prosperity. Indeed, the web of life nurtures and supports humanity in innumerable ways. People depend on nature for food, medicines, and materials. They depend on functioning ecosystems to filter pollutants, provide clean air and water, regulate flows of water and nutrients, modulate climate, and provide protection from storms. Nature also provides inspiration and meaning, adding richness to human culture. Efforts to sustain nature will give future generations the opportunity to enjoy these benefits. Because nature provides essential inputs for human life, health, and prosperity, both now and in the future, economists treat it as an asset, or *natural capital*.

The unraveling web of life

The great expansion of economic activity since the end of World War II has lifted billions of people out of poverty and raised living standards around the globe, but it has also produced rapid changes in earth systems. Emissions of greenhouse gases (GHGs) from burning fossil fuels, cement production, agriculture, and land uses are driving climate change (IPCC 2014, 2018, 2021). Pollution from industrial and household activity degrades local air and water quality, with negative consequences for human health (Damania et al. 2019; Landrigan et al. 2018). Meanwhile, the loss of natural habitats from the expansion of crops, pastures, managed forests, infrastructure, and urbanization are driving a loss of habitat for biodiversity, leading to a rapid decline in species populations. Indeed, it is estimated that one in eight species may be extinct within the next 100 years (IPBES 2019). The loss of habitat has been particularly severe in wetlands, with over 85 percent loss in area since 1700 (IPBES 2019), contributing to increased flooding, erosion, water quality degradation, reduced groundwater recharge, and biodiversity loss (Woodward and Wui 2001; Zedler and Kercher 2005).

Natural capital provides tangible economic benefits known as *ecosystem services*. These benefits include the provision of material goods (such as food, fiber, fuel, and fodder); nonmaterial services (such as recreation, aesthetic enjoyment, and cultural and spiritual values); and regulating services (such as carbon storage, pest and pathogen regulation, pollination, water and air purification, and storm protection)—see IPBES (2019). The decline in natural capital over the last 50 years has led to a decline in a majority of ecosystem services, with particularly severe declines in regulating ecosystem services (Brauman et al. 2020). For example, the loss of pollinators poses a threat to agricultural crop production, estimated at US$200–US$600 billion annually (IPBES 2019). Land degradation from soil erosion, loss of carbon and soil nutrients, salinization, and waterlogging threatens agricultural productivity and negatively affects the well-being of large numbers of people, primarily in low- and middle-income countries.

Estimates range from 1.3–1.5 billion (Bai et al. 2008; Barbier and Hochard 2016) to over 3 billion people (IPBES 2019).

COVID-19, a zoonotic disease that spreads from wildlife to humans, is a stark illustration of the interdependence among natural capital, human health, and the economy. The pandemic led to the most dramatic decline in the gross domestic product since the Great Depression and a collapse in investment. It also pushed over 100 million more people into extreme poverty in 2020, and worsened inequality (World Bank 2021a). On average, two new viruses spill each year from wildlife into human populations, typically a consequence of deforestation driven by expanding agriculture and livestock production, trade in wildlife, and consumption of wild meat (Dobson et al. 2020; Woolhouse et al. 2012).

This trend of declining natural capital, if continued, may cast a long shadow into the future. Human actions are causing the complex web of life to unravel with declines in natural capital that may have profound consequences for planetary systems and humanity (Díaz et al. 2019; IPBES 2019; UNEP 2021). Some effects such as loss of species through extinction are irreversible. Loss of habitat and increases in greenhouse gas concentrations can be reversed, but it will take a long time. A dramatic reduction of natural capital can also have nonlinear effects, including the potential for crossing thresholds leading to a rapid collapse of planetary systems (Lenton et al. 2008, 2019; Rockström et al. 2009; Scheffer et al. 2001; Steffen et al. 2015). Natural capital and climate change are linked— that is, reductions in natural capital stocks have feedback loops with the climate system (Bastien-Olvera and Moore, forthcoming; Drupp and Hänsel 2021). It is difficult, if not impossible, to reverse such changes and restore the flow of benefits because ecosystems often display history-dependent (hysteretic) effects (box 1.1).

For some observers, these trends, like the canary in the coal mine, are signs of unsustainable economic activity that could undermine the foundations of human well-being. Others note that economic growth continues unabated and that living standards have improved significantly since the Industrial Revolution, despite mounting environmental stresses (Raudsepp-Hearne et al. 2010). According to this view, environmental degradation may be the price of economic progress, and trade-offs with natural capital are inevitable along the path to greater human prosperity.

The decline in natural capital would be less problematic if there were close substitutes available for it. Where there is sufficient substitutability, the loss of natural capital could be *offset* by investments in other forms of capital. There would, then, be little reason for concern because another resource or human-made capital could replace the loss of natural capital. Indeed, if all forms of natural and physical capital were perfect substitutes, then a fishing vessel would replace fish stocks and a chain saw could replace a rainforest, whereas in practice these are complements. Examples of complementarity between natural capital and other forms of capital abound. For example, clean air protects health

BOX 1.1
Critical natural capital and tipping points

Complex dynamic systems such as ecosystems (or economic systems) can undergo rapid changes in behavior (*regime shifts*), which can lead to major changes in the desired outcomes. For example, shallow lakes can undergo a regime shift from clear (oligotrophic) to algae-dominated (eutrophic) with the addition of nutrient inputs. This shift may happen in dramatic fashion once the lake reaches a critical level of nutrient inputs (*tipping point*). Such lakes may remain eutrophic even after nutrient inputs are reduced (*system hysteresis*). The shift to a eutrophic lake can cause large declines in water quality, fishing, recreation, aesthetics, and other benefits derived from the lake.

Figure B1.1.1 illustrates graphically regime shifts and tipping points. The figure shows that, for a midrange of conditions such as nutrient inputs into a lake, an ecosystem can fall into three different equilibrium states, ranging from high water quality (top solid line) to low water quality (lower solid line), and an unstable intermediate equilibrium (dashed line). If the lake starts with high water quality but the nutrient inputs are increased (movement to the right), there will initially be small declines in water quality. However, once nutrient inputs go to the right of F_2, there will be a rapid drop in water quality moving toward the equilibrium state of low water quality. It will not be possible to return to the state of high water quality unless nutrient inputs fall below F_1.

Crossing tipping points in larger ecological systems could cause dramatic declines in ecosystem services, biodiversity, and other valued outcomes. One potential tipping point with large regional to global consequences is in the Amazon Basin (Lovejoy and

FIGURE B1.1.1
Illustration of tipping points and hysteresis

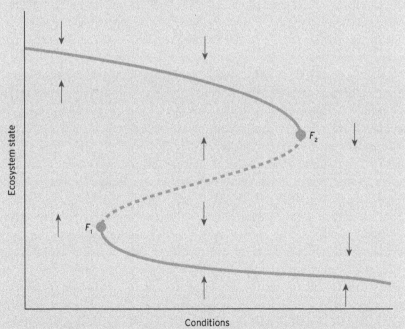

Source: Scheffer et al. 2001.

Continued

BOX 1.1
Continued

Nobre 2019; Nobre and Borma 2009). Most of the water in a tropical rainforest is recycled through the vegetation. Cutting too many trees can interrupt the water cycle and result in dramatic shifts in precipitation that no longer support the forest. Other potential tipping points induced by climate as well as land use change have been identified in earth systems (Lenton et al. 2008, 2019).

Crossing tipping points can cause massive environmental change, with potentially large disruptions in the flow of benefits from nature. Disregard of the potential for regime shifts may result in overlooking one of the major costs of declining natural capital. Including tipping points and regime shifts in a quantitative analysis presents two problems: (1) determining the location of potential tipping points and (2) identifying the consequences of crossing a tipping point and triggering a regime shift. Little knowledge is available to address these problems. A recent article by Moore (2018) summarized the state of affairs as follows:

> Seeing the tipping point after the fact and ascribing mechanisms to the change is one thing; predicting them using empirical data has been a challenge. The difficulty in predicting tipping points stems from the large number of species and interactions (high dimensionality) within ecological systems, the stochastic nature of the systems and their drivers, and the uncertainty and importance of initial conditions that the nonlinear nature of the systems introduce to outcomes.... For certain types of ecological systems an analysis of the model and real-world time series reveals that there are indeed leading indicators of regime shifts in the form of increases in the variance of populations or process variables (for example, decomposition and mineralization) or changes in the underlying dynamics of the system. Other types of models, particularly those that have multiple attractors or the potential for chaos, exhibit abrupt changes with no advanced warning in the time series.

The challenge for researchers is how to include possible tipping points in an empirically realistic and defensible way to inform decision-making. Recognizing the paucity of information and data, this report notes the challenges created by tipping points, but the study was unable to reliably model them.

and human capital. Protecting soil fertility and avoiding erosion are critical for sustaining agricultural yields. And conserving natural areas can boost yields of pollination-dependent crops.

In other cases, limited substitutability may be possible. For example, a levee can provide flood protection in lieu of wetlands that were destroyed, and a water filtration facility can substitute for the water purification services of ecosystems in providing clean drinking water. A common, though not isolated, example of the latter is in New York City, which receives much of its water from a forested watershed in New York State's Catskill Mountains. Had the watershed been converted to other land uses, the city would have needed to build filtration plants at a cost of about US$6 billion in capital expenditures and a further US$250 million per year for operations and maintenance costs. By contrast, protecting the watershed comes at a fraction of that cost of approximately US$167 million in expenditures per year (Ashendorff et al. 1997; Chichilnisky and Heal 1998).

Even when replacement of natural capital is possible, it comes at a cost, as illustrated by the New York City water supply example. Moreover, often the produced capital does not provide all the benefits of natural capital, and for some forms of natural capital that are essential for life, there are no viable substitutes. For example, there are no substitutes for clean air, which is why premature mortality and morbidity rates are higher in airsheds with high levels of air pollution.

Ultimately, it comes down to an empirical question: are natural capital and other forms of capital close enough substitutes? The answer will depend on the type of capital and the goods and services under investigation, as well as the level of aggregation (firm, sector, national, or global) under consideration. At the level of a farm, a tractor is clearly no substitute for a depleted aquifer. However, if one were to aggregate to the country level, it may be possible to compensate for the revenue lost from a decline in crop yields stemming from drought by investments in crop production in other regions or in other economic sectors such as manufacturing. For other environmental services—such as clean air, climate regulation, and planetary systems—there are no substitutes. These are critical issues, with far-reaching implications for promoting more sustainable growth. However, little empirical evidence on the degrees of substitutability between natural capital and other forms of capital is available to help policy makers establish priorities and identify assets critical for sustaining development.[2] This lack of evidence contrasts with the growing literature on the substitutability between other types of capital—especially human and physical capital (see, for example, Karabarbounis and Neiman 2014, 2018; Oberfield and Raval 2021).

Investing in natural capital

In 1817, David Ricardo, who developed the theory of land rent and comparative advantage, among other notable advances in economics, observed that nature's abundance was rarely rewarded because "where she is munificently beneficent she always works gratis" (Ricardo [1817] 1821).

Most natural capital is in the form of common property. Thus too often no price is paid for providing ecosystem services, no reward is given for maintaining natural capital, and no costs are incurred for actions that destroy natural capital. Most often, the costs of destruction and degradation are borne by entities other than those creating the losses. Improving air and water quality, maintaining habitat for species, and sequestering carbon to reduce climate impacts all generate benefits for society. However, a business or household that invests in nature typically receives little or no direct monetary return. Although the economy benefits from natural capital, no individual business or household has enough benefits, or control, to ensure its continued existence. The failure to adequately address climate change (IPCC 2014, 2018, 2021) and the failure to adequately manage marine fisheries are notable examples of such "tragedy of the commons" problems (Costello et al. 2010; World Bank 2017; World Bank and FAO 2009). Although many common property resources are well managed by the local communities that rely on them (Ostrom 1990; Ostrom et al. 1999), others are not (Brodie Rudolph et al. 2020). Meanwhile, greater challenges are encountered in managing large-scale regional or global common property resources, such as the global atmosphere that drives climate change (Dietz, Ostrom, and Stern 2003; Ostrom et al. 1999).

Misaligned incentives are often responsible for excessive levels of natural capital degradation, but problems of measurement also impede policies that could steer an economy toward a more sustainable development trajectory. One definition of sustainable development is nondeclining human well-being in which the prospects for future generations are no worse than those of the current generation (Arrow et al. 2004). Sustainable development in this sense does not necessarily require all natural capital to be maintained because some trade-offs between classes of capital assets may be beneficial. However, sustainable development does require that the bundle of assets bequeathed to future generations be capable of providing equal or greater benefits. The destruction and depreciation of natural capital (or any other type of capital) are acceptable, so long as the benefits gained from increases in other forms of capital outweigh the losses from the reduction in natural capital.

In principle, valuing the gains and losses in natural capital using a common (monetary) metric could determine whether such changes yield an overall increase in net benefit. However, this task has remained difficult to operationalize. Imperfect techniques for estimating shadow prices[3] exist, but they are computationally complex, typically cannot be verified empirically, and, in practice, are seldom used. Box 1.2 outlines the challenges in measuring sustainability.

BOX 1.2
Challenges in measuring sustainability

Moving toward a more sustainable society requires first defining *sustainability* and then developing techniques for measuring it. A central tenet of sustainability is maintenance of stocks of capital, including natural capital, to sustain future human well-being. The notion of strong sustainability is directed at conserving all forms of natural capital. The notion of weak sustainability is directed at maintaining a bundle of capital stocks capable of maintaining or increasing future well-being. The latter does not insist that all forms of capital be maintained. However, if natural capital is essential and irreplaceable in the sense that its loss would necessarily entail a decline in human well-being, then it would require conserving such essential and irreplaceable natural capital. The unique characteristics of some benefits derived from ecosystems make natural capital only imperfectly substitutable. Any damage to the stock of natural capital could permanently reduce, with long-lived effects, the flow of benefits from nature.

Continued

BOX 1.2
Continued

Because of the prominence of conservation of natural capital stocks in notions of sustainability, a straightforward approach to measuring sustainability would seem to be directly measuring natural capital to determine whether various stocks are increasing or decreasing. However, this approach has several drawbacks:

- *Measurement of capital.* Some approaches to measuring natural capital simply track the areas of forest, wetlands, and other types of land units. Although this is an important component of measuring natural capital, it leaves out many factors important in determining the flow of ecosystem services provided by natural capital. For example, a forest area broken up into small, isolated parcels may provide much less effective habitat for biodiversity than the same amount of forest area that consists of one large, intact forest parcel. Commonly in nature the whole is greater than the sum of its parts.
- *Valuing capital.* Focusing only on biophysical measurement obscures links to value. The value of natural capital is determined by the present value of the flow of benefits it generates, both now and in the future, as well as its nonuse and intrinsic values. However, assessing future values requires understanding how the ecosystem service will be valued in the future, which depends on future preferences and technology that at present are not knowable with any certainty.
- *Aggregating capital.* Without some way of aggregating or comparing different forms of natural capital, an analysis will produce only a long list of natural capital assets, typically with some types increasing and other types decreasing. Determining whether there is a net gain or loss requires understanding whether different types of capital are reasonable substitutes for each other. It is inappropriate to assume as a default that different forms of capital can replace each other at all, or at no or low cost. It is equally inappropriate to assume that there is never any substitutability.

To address some of these difficulties, economists have developed the notion of inclusive and comprehensive wealth (Arrow et al. 2004, 2012; Hamilton and Clemens 1999; Polasky et al. 2015). The challenge of trying to measure inclusive wealth has been summarized by Sen, Fitoussi, and Stiglitz (2010, 98–99):

[I]f we want to accomplish this [inclusive wealth], we need to convert all the stocks of resources passed on to future generations into a common metric, be it monetary or not . . . [but] such a goal seems overly ambitious. The aggregation of heterogeneous items seems possible up to a point for physical and human capital or some natural resources that are traded on markets. But the task appears much more complicated for most natural assets, due to the lack of relevant market prices and to the many uncertainties concerning the way these natural assets will interact with other dimensions of sustainability in the future.

Sen, Fitoussi, and Stiglitz (2010) propose a novel approach that uses market prices where they exist to aggregate some forms of capital into a summary measure of monetary value, while directly measuring other forms of capital in nonmonetary terms. This approach steers between the difficulty of trying to come up with a single aggregate measure, as in inclusive wealth, and the difficulty of having an uninformative array of unaggregated measures, as with pure biophysical measurement. The efficiency frontier approach developed in the next section is an example of such a hybrid approach.

A result of these challenges is that the apparent trade-offs between the environment and development often reflect incomplete measurement, in which the unmonetized services of natural capital are ignored. A partial accounting of the benefits will send the wrong policy signals when the unmeasured assets (say, watershed services from a forest) are in decline, while the measured services (say, manufacturing output) are increasing and used as the signal of economic progress. The consequence will be more environmental damage than is necessary or economically warranted, even in terms of a strict benefit-cost calculation.

Because the hidden contributions of natural capital are typically undervalued by society and ignored by policy makers, the result may be systematic policy biases. A full accounting of contributions, including those of the nonmarket ecosystem services, can sometimes reveal that conserving, rather than destroying, natural capital is the better strategy (Balmford et al. 2002; Nelson et al. 2009). The implication of this widespread undervaluing of natural capital is that there is substantial room for efficiency gains. Establishment of property rights and pricing of nature's benefits can be an effective approach to maintaining and restoring natural capital (Kinzig et al. 2011). For example, the only categories of nature's benefits that have increased over the past 50 years are the material benefits priced and sold in markets, such as agricultural commodities (IPBES 2019). Policies extend the categories of nature's benefits for which there is a monetary incentive to preserve natural capital, such as pollution pricing and payment for ecosystem services (Engel, Pagiola, and Wunder 2008; Pagiola 2008). Nevertheless, such policies can be difficult to enforce, and they are often insufficient in scope to capture the full benefits of natural capital.

Although it is often assumed that economic growth necessarily entails environmental degradation, at least in some circumstances this may be a false trade-off. A foundational principle in economics is that market failures (such as uncorrected externalities) generate deadweight losses and thus create scope for allocative efficiency gains through corrective policies. In such cases, there are better development paths that maintain natural capital, promote human health and net wealth—and may reduce inequality (Copeland and Taylor 2004; Lakner et al. 2020; Van Der Ploeg and Withagen 2013).

An efficiency frontier approach

This report describes an alternative approach to assessing whether countries are using their natural capital in ways that deliver maximum sustainable benefits. The measure of efficiency of sustainable output described here departs from both the simple biophysical measures and the "inclusive wealth" approach discussed earlier. In recognition of the structural failures that distort the way in which natural capital is allocated and used, this approach measures the *efficiency gap*. This gap is defined as the difference between the economic and environmental outputs currently produced in a country and the maximum amounts that could be *sustainably* produced if resources were allocated and used efficiently.

A sophisticated suite of models, combined with new data collected for this analysis, is used to estimate the maximum potential sustainable economic outputs and ecosystem services for 147 countries. This estimation is made possible by the latest developments in integrated ecological-economic modeling, computational techniques, and remote sensing observations.

The outcome of this new approach yields the construct of a *resource efficiency frontier*. The resource efficiency frontier describes the maximum sustainable outputs (economic and environmental) that can be produced with given endowments. Thus a country that is inside the resource efficiency frontier will gain by moving toward the frontier. This progress can be achieved by allocating resources more efficiently across different uses, or by using existing resources more efficiently, or by both strategies. An example is providing farmers with water for irrigation. Irrigation supplies are typically provided at no cost or at a nominal fee. Water is therefore often used wastefully and not allocated to its most productive uses. Improving both the efficiency of water use and its allocation toward more productive sectors implies that output can be increased without further consumption of water. Another example is the use of land, which can be reallocated between different uses such as crop production, grazing, or forestry (extensive margin), or more efficient methods of growing crops can be used on existing cropland to increase yields (intensive margin). However, once a country has reached the resource efficiency frontier, it is not possible to produce more of one output without producing less of another.

Figure 1.1 illustrates the approach by showing an efficiency (or production possibility) frontier for a country in Africa. The frontier (shown in blue) indicates the maximum sustainable amount of income (in US dollars, measured on the horizontal axis) and environmental outcome (carbon storage and sequestration,[4] measured on the vertical axis) that can be obtained through the efficient allocation of land and other inputs across agricultural crop production, grazing, managed forestry, and conservation areas. Along the frontier, more income involves less carbon sequestration—a trade-off. Point A, in the middle, shows the current sustainable level of income and carbon storage. The sustainable current scenario mirrors the real world, but it penalizes countries harvesting resources in an unsustainable way by reducing the value on the horizontal axis to only the value of production that is sustainably generated. Unsustainable ways include unsustainable forest extraction, as well as water—both surface and groundwater—that is extracted beyond renewable levels. In other words, the sustainable current scenario represents a sustainable steady-state version of the present day.

At point A, the country is sustainably producing US$174 million in net production from crops, grazing, and forestry, and it is storing 3.6 billion metric tons of carbon dioxide equivalent (CO_2eq). With better policies, this country

FIGURE 1.1

Graphical illustration of a production possibility frontier

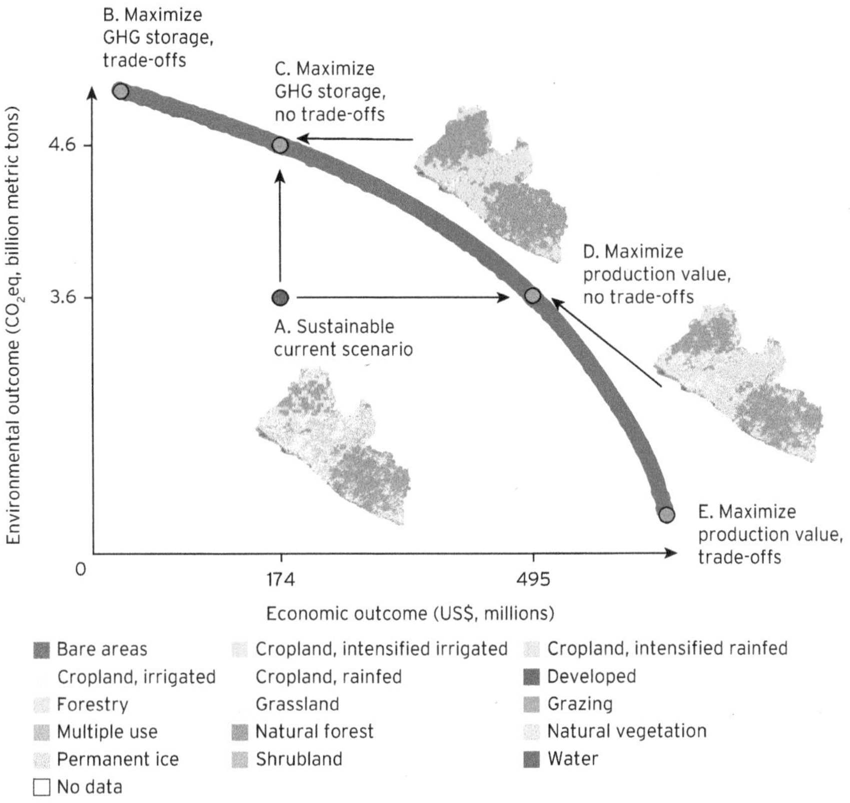

Source: World Bank.

Note: Figure shows for a country in Africa the maximum feasible combinations of the value of market returns (horizontal axis) and environmental outcomes (vertical axis). Land uses include agricultural crop production, grazing, managed forests, and conserved natural areas. Urban land inside an urban growth boundary is excluded from the analysis. Points B through E rest on the efficiency frontier, and the associated maps show the land use patterns that achieve points C and D on the efficiency frontier. Point A is the outcome of the existing land use pattern, which is inefficient because it lies inside the efficiency frontier. Point C is the maximum possible increase in the environmental outcome with no decline in the economic income. Point D is the maximum possible increase in the economic outcome with no decrease in the environmental outcome. CO_2eq = carbon dioxide equivalent; GHG = greenhouse gas.

can improve both of these metrics, with moves to anywhere along the efficiency frontier, represented by the blue line. By choosing to focus on improving GHG storage, the country can shift directly upward on the graph to point C, resulting in an additional 1 billion metric tons of CO_2eq storage with no change in economic production. This figure represents over 83 years of business-as-usual emissions from this country's 2030 nationally declared commitment level. Likewise, by choosing to focus on economic production, the country can shift directly to the right to point D. Here, the net value of economic production increases to US$495 million, a 180 percent increase in net economic production with no environmental trade-offs relative to the current situation. Any point on the blue line between points C and D are also possible, where increases in both economic and environmental outcomes occur simultaneously. Areas on the blue line outside of points B and C are also feasible, but result in trade-offs in which one outcome is improved at the expense of the other outcome. However, as one moves toward the extremes of the frontier, especially the bottom right where economic production is maximized, the risks of crossing tipping points, where ecological breakdown is possible, increase significantly. In this case, the frontier may actually curve inward as key ecosystem services such as pest control, pollination, soil management, and water filtration and storage are lost, making lands less fertile and reducing net economic gains. Thus short-sighted policies that support large-scale transformation of landscapes for unsustainable monetary gains risk both ecosystem and economic collapse and should be avoided.

All points along the efficiency frontier in figure 1.1 are Pareto efficient. Pareto efficiency implies that it is not possible to increase one output without decreasing another output—that is, trade-offs are inevitable. Choosing which efficient outcome is preferred involves a value judgment about the relative weights (values) to put on different benefits.

However, all inefficient outcomes (points inside the efficiency frontier) are inferior to some point on the efficient frontier because at least some benefits can be improved without lowering any other benefit. The potential efficiency gain can be measured by the distance to the efficiency frontier. The measure of efficiency gain summarizes the potential gains (win-win solutions) that can be obtained relative to a specific starting point.

The example in figure 1.1 shows it is possible for the country depicted to achieve both higher levels of carbon storage and higher values of marketed commodities relative to what is currently achieved (point A). Such win-win outcomes, or so-called Pareto improvements, improve at least one outcome without simultaneously worsening any others. In general, many outcomes will be efficient—Pareto improvements in this sense. In figure 1.1, a shift from point A to points C, D, or any point in between these two would be considered a Pareto improvement because both economic and carbon benefits increase. Points on the frontier to the right of point D, such as point E, would not be considered a Pareto improvement because, although economic benefits increase significantly, they come at the cost of less carbon storage. Similarly, points to the left of point C, such as point B, would not be considered Pareto improvements because they would lead to declines in economic benefits. Thus Pareto improvements imply net benefits in one or more attributes without a net loss in any other attribute—in most cases, resulting in a win-win scenario or, at worst, a win-neutral one.

Gains in both carbon storage and market commodity values are achieved by changing the pattern of land use as indicated by the maps along the efficiency frontier. These maps show the land use and land management patterns that achieve various efficient outcomes and can be contrasted with the map of the current landscape at A. This example illustrates that the current land use patterns (point A) do not maximize the full range of potential outputs that could be generated. Thus there is a gap between the actual and potential outputs. Reasons for such gaps vary, but they include factors such as policy choices, market failures, frictions, and informational constraints.

The curve of the efficiency frontier also provides information on the magnitude of trade-offs between one objective and another. The curve indicates that, across some areas of the frontier, increasing one type of benefit may impose large costs on other benefits. For example, moves from point C to point B impose large monetary losses for modest carbon storage gains; moves from point D to point E impose the opposite—large carbon losses for modest economic gains.

This exercise provides a set of statistics pivotal to indicating the broad scope for sustainable improvements. The indicators measure (1) whether there are gaps in the efficiency with which natural capital is currently being used; (2) how these gaps may be closed; and (3) the trade-offs across desired outputs that arise once all efficiencies are exhausted. Highlighting the existence of such opportunities will be useful to policy makers, even when there is resistance to change.

The efficiency approach developed in this study can be used for virtually any natural capital asset for which data and reliable models describing ecosystem functioning are available. The first part of the report presents results for land-based efficiency indicators (for crop production, grazing, timber), greenhouse gases, and biodiversity. The second part considers the impact of air quality measured through $PM_{2.5}$ (particulate matter that is 2.5 microns or less in diameter) on human health. Of course, many other ecosystem services provided by land-based natural resources and a bewildering array of other pollutants are harmful to human health. This study focuses on the more critical services for which there are data, adequate scientific information, and models to estimate sustainable use and their economic consequences.

The approach used in this exercise is related to a prominent body of literature in macroeconomics that investigates differences in productivity[5] across and within countries (Adamopoulos et al. 2022; Hsieh and Klenow 2009; Restuccia, Yang, and Zhu 2008). A key insight of that literature is that much of the difference in living standards and total factor productivity arises because key inputs—especially capital and labor—are not allocated to their most productive uses. This study extends that approach and finds that the problem is even more pronounced when dealing with natural capital. Because natural capital is routinely underpriced due to market failures, two significant distortions emerge. First, being underpriced or provided free, natural capital is often used wastefully and inefficiently. Second, the "wrong" price also implies that these resources are seldom allocated in ways that maximize the value of the benefits they could produce. In other words, inefficiencies are also caused by the misallocation of scarce natural resources. The consequence is depletion and degradation far in excess of what would be deemed economically prudent. Box 1.3 summarizes in more detail some of the implications and causes of resource depletion.

This study is also related to a rapidly expanding literature pointing to the existence of large agricultural yield gaps between lower- and higher-income countries

---

BOX 1.3
Will the world run out of resources?

With rising populations and expanding economies, countries face legitimate fears that the demand for resources, especially for finite and nonrenewable ones (such as minerals), will outstrip supplies. It is therefore paradoxical that there is no known case of the world ever having exhausted an economically valuable nonrenewable natural resource (such as a mineral). Conversely, extinction, overharvesting, and exhaustion of common property renewable resources are a widespread problem. Indeed, ecologists assert that the world is in the midst of the sixth mass extinction. Meanwhile, carbon stored in terrestrial and marine systems is released to the atmosphere, leading to more intense climate change, and airsheds and watersheds are being routinely depleted, degraded, and polluted, resulting in elevated levels of premature mortality, morbidity, and stillbirths among affected populations.

The reasons for this paradox are well known and widely documented. Because they are privately owned and marketed, the demand and extraction of minerals and subsoil assets are guided by prices. When prices rise to signal scarcity, consumption of the commodity declines and investment in exploration and the search for substitutes rises, all of which lower depletion rates.

No such signals limit and guide the use of common property renewable resources, even when there may be growth-constraining or life-threatening impacts. A combination of factors often associated with open access, lack of property rights, and absence of price signals makes renewable resources especially vulnerable to overuse and depletion.

Although imperfect property rights can lead to resource depletion, it would be misleading to assume that privatization is the policy panacea that will ensure sustainability. A significant literature explains why establishing property rights cannot completely and solely resolve problems of overextraction. If, for example, a natural resource grows at a slow rate (such as old-growth forests or a population of whales), it would pay for a private investor to liquidate that resource and invest the proceeds in a higher-yielding asset. Thus extirpation becomes the more profitable strategy (Clark 1973). Incentives to invest in natural capital will also be missing when there are spatial externalities such as when environmental benefits are shared or accrue to others. For example, that old-growth forest may provide benefits to downstream residents in the form of flood protection and clean drinking water. But these benefits will not be considered by the owner of the forest, and the forest will therefore be undervalued by that owner. Thus it is no surprise that biodiversity is found in greater abundance on public than on private lands (Vucetich 2021).

Finally, although this study focuses on efficiency, the efficient use of a renewable resource does not ensure that it is used sustainably. For example, fish stocks can be harvested with great efficiency using highly sophisticated technologies until rendered extinct. Sustainability requires effective management and the appropriate incentives to manage for the long run.

(Lobell, Cassman, and Field 2009; Mueller et al. 2012). The richest nations have increased their agricultural production by increasing yields. By contrast, the poorer nations have mainly met the increased food demands of their rapidly growing and increasingly wealthy populations by expanding their cropland, not by increasing yields, even where actual farm output is far below potential output (Polasky et al. 2022). The projected effect of the severity of such expansion on habitat area can lead to widespread declines in biodiversity (Williams et al. 2021), loss of carbon sequestration potential, and increases in greenhouse gas emissions (Folberth et al. 2020). This report looks at some of the implications of these perverse trends, which, if left unchecked, would place the United Nations' Sustainable Development Goals and the Paris Agreement targets out of reach.

This report extends the suite of related research on the economics of sustainability conducted at the World Bank. An earlier example of bringing sustainability into the policy dialogue was the *Inclusive Green Growth* report (World Bank 2012). More recently the World Bank's comprehensive wealth estimates under the Changing Wealth of Nations initiative demonstrate that natural capital is in decline (World Bank 2021b). The Economics of Nature program illuminates the implications of the decline in ecosystem services for economic growth using a computable general equilibrium model (Johnson et al. 2021). The Repurposing Agricultural Policies and Support program focuses on the consequences of perverse subsidies in agriculture and provides guidance to countries seeking to reform agricultural support in ways that simultaneously enhance productivity and sustainability (Gautam et al. 2022). Finally, this report identifies the scope for improving economic productivity and environmental services through improvements in efficiency and allocation that do not call for trade-offs. This is especially significant in some of the poorest developing countries that host a vast amount of the world's tropical forests providing vital global benefits through biodiversity and GHG sequestration services. It is also of relevance to countries at other levels of development that can both increase their contribution to global environmental services as well as grow their economies through better use of their natural endowments.

The remainder of this report is organized as follows. Chapter 2 presents the methodology and data underlying the analysis. It describes the novelty of the resource efficiency approach, as well as the new cutting-edge data that make such an analysis possible. Chapter 3 describes the results of the land model. In doing so, it presents several metrics to measure how efficient each country is in using its land in terms of economic productivity, carbon sequestration, and supporting biodiversity. It also presents global estimates of what benefits could be achieved if countries were to move toward their efficiency frontiers. Chapter 4 presents a range of policy solutions that will be needed to help countries achieve their efficiency potentials. Instead of a one-size-fits-all approach, these solutions are tailored to the specific challenges faced by countries. Chapter 5 then applies the efficiency frontier approach to air pollution and discusses the scope to improve health outcomes and save lives through efficiency gains with appropriate policies. Chapter 6 is composed of several country spotlights that demonstrate how the results of this study can be used by countries in making policy recommendations for utilizing natural capital more efficiently. The concluding chapter 7 briefly details the headwinds to change, some caveats, and recommendations for future work. The online technical appendix[6] then provides a more in-depth look at the data and modeling.

Notes

1. Quoted in Sheppard, R. Z. "Nature: Splendor in the Grass," *Time*, September 3, 1990, https://content.time.com/time/subscriber/article/0,33009,971049,00.html.

2. In the sparse available literature, there are as many instances of complementarity between natural and other forms of capital as there are examples of substitutability (Cohen, Hepburn, and Teytelboym 2019; Drupp 2018; Fitter 2013; Markandya and Pedroso-Galinato 2007; Rouhi Rad et al. 2021).

3. A shadow price is a monetary value assigned to currently unknowable or difficult-to-calculate costs in the absence of correct market prices. Such prices are used to estimate the value of inputs or outputs when markets are limited or nonexistent.

4. The term *carbon storage and sequestration* refers to the amount of carbon stored in land, mostly in vegetation and soils. The vertical axis will also capture changes in emissions from livestock. All greenhouse gases are converted to CO_2 equivalents.

5. In this report, *productivity* refers to producing more or the same amount of any good or service under consideration with the same or fewer inputs. It is, therefore, synonymous with the standard definitions of *efficiency* used in economics.

6. The online technical appendix (appendix B) is available with the text of this book in the World Bank's Online Knowledge Repository, https://openknowledge.worldbank.org/handle/10986/39453.

References

Adamopoulos, T., L. Brandt, C. Chen, D. Restuccia, and X. Wei. 2022. "Land Security and Mobility Frictions." NBER Working Paper 29666. National Bureau of Economic Research, Cambridge, MA.

Arrow, K., P. Dasgupta, L. Goulder, G. Daily, P. Ehrlich, G. Heal, S. Levin, et al. 2004. "Are We Consuming Too Much?" *Journal of Economic Perspectives* 18: 147–72. https://doi.org/10.1257/0895330042162377.

Arrow, K., P. Dasgupta, L. H. Goulder, K. J. Mumford, and K. Oleson. 2012. "Sustainability and the Measurement of Wealth." *Environment and Development Economics* 17: 31–53. https://doi.org/10.3386/w16599.

Ashendorff, A., M. A. Principe, A. Seely, J. LaDuca, L. Beckhardt, W. Faber, and J. Mantus. 1997. "Watershed Protection for New York City's Supply." *Journal of American Water Works Association* 89 (3): 75–88. https://doi.org/10.1002/j.1551-8833.1997.tb08195.x.

Bai, Z., D. L. Dent, L. Olsson, and M. E. Schaepman. 2008. "Proxy Global Assessment of Land Degradation." *Soil Use and Management* 24 (3): 223–34. https://doi.org/10.1111/j.1475-2743.2008.00169.x.

Balmford, A., A. Bruner, P. Cooper, R. Costanza, S. Farber, R. E. Green, M. Jenkins, et al. 2002. "Economic Reasons for Conserving Wild Nature." *Science* 297: 950–53. https://doi .org/10.1126/science.1073947.

Barbier, E. B., and J. P. Hochard. 2016. "Does Land Degradation Increase Poverty in Developing Countries?" *PLoS ONE* 11 (5): 13–15. https://doi.org/10.1371%2Fjournal .pone.0152973.

Bastien-Olvera, B. A., and F. C. Moore. Forthcoming. "Climate Impacts on Natural Capital: Consequences for the Social Cost of Carbon." *Annual Review of Resource Economics* 14: 515–32. https://doi.org/10.1146/annurev-resource-111820-020204.

Brauman, K. A., L. A. Garibaldi, S. Polasky, Y. Aumeeruddy-Thomas, P. H. S. Brancalion, F. DeClerck, U. Jacob, et al. 2020. "Global Trends in Nature's Contributions to People." *Proceedings of the National Academy of Sciences* 117 (51): 32799–805. https://doi.org/10.1073 /pnas.2010473117.

Brodie Rudolph, T., M. Ruckelshaus, M. Swilling, E. Allison, H. Osterblom, S. Gelcich, and P. Mbatha. 2020. "A Transition to Sustainable Ocean Governance." *Nature Communications* 11: 3600. https://doi.org/10.1038/s41467-020-17410-2.

Chichilnisky, G., and G. Heal. 1998. "Economic Returns from the Biosphere." *Nature* 391: 629–30. https://doi.org/10.1038/35481.

Clark, C. W. 1973. "Profit Maximization and the Extinction of Animal Species." *Journal of Political Economy* 81 (4): 950–61. https://www.jstor.org/stable/1831136.

Cohen, F., C. J. Hepburn, and A. Teytelboym. 2019. "Is Natural Capital Really Substitutable?" *Annual Review of Environment and Resources* 44: 425–48. https://doi.org/10.1146 /annurev-environ-101718-033055.

Copeland, S., and S. Taylor. 2004. "Trade, Growth, and the Environment." *Journal of Economic Literature* 42 (1): 7–71. https://www.jstor.org/stable/3217036.

Costello, C., J. Lynham, S. E. Lester, and S. D. Gaines. 2010. "Economic Incentives and Global Fisheries Sustainability." *Annual Review of Resource Economics* (2): 299–318. https://doi .org/10.1146/annurev.resource.012809.103923.

Damania, R., S. Desbureaux, A. S. Rodella, J. Russ, and E. Zaveri. 2019. *Quality Unknown: The Invisible Water Crisis.* Washington, DC: World Bank.

Díaz, S., J. Settele, E. S. Brondízio, H. T. Ngo, J. Agard, A. Arneth, P. Balvanera, et al. 2019. "Pervasive Human-Driven Decline of Life on Earth Points to the Need for Transformative Change." *Science* 366: eaax3100. https://doi.org/10.1126/science.aax3100.

Dietz, T., E. Ostrom, and P. C. Stern. 2003. "The Struggle to Govern the Commons." *Science* 302: 1907–12. https://doi.org/10.1126/science.1091015.

Dobson, A., S. L. Pimm, L. Hannah, L. Kaufman, J. A. Ahumada, A. W. Ando, A. Bernstein, et al. 2020. "Ecology and Economics for Pandemic Prevention." *Science* 369: 379–81. https:// doi.org/10.1126/science.abc3189.

Drupp, M. A. 2018. "Limits to Substitution between Ecosystem Services and Manufactured Goods and Implications for Social Discounting." *Environmental and Resource Economics* 69: 135–218. https://doi.org/10.1007/s10640-016-0068-5.

Drupp, M. A., and M. C. Hänsel. 2021. "Relative Prices and Climate Policy: How the Scarcity of Nonmarket Goods Drives Policy Evaluation." *American Economic Journal: Economic Policy* 13 (1): 168–201. https://doi.org/10.1257/pol.20180760.

Engel, S., S. Pagiola, and S. Wunder. 2008. "Designing Payments for Environmental Services in Theory and Practice: An Overview of the Issues." *Ecological Economics* 65 (4): 663–74. https://doi.org/10.1016/j.ecolecon.2008.03.011.

Fitter, A. H. 2013. "Are Ecosystem Services Replaceable by Technology?" *Environmental and Resource Economics* 55: 513–24. https://doi.org/10.1007/s10640-013-9676-5.

Folberth, C., N. Khabarov, J. Balkovič, R. Skalský, P. Visconti, P. Ciais, I. A. Janssens, et al. 2020. "The Global Cropland-Sparing Potential of High-Yield Farming." *Nature Sustainability* 3 (4): 281–89. https://doi.org/10.1038/s41893-020-0505-x.

Gautam, M., D. Laborde, A. Mamun, W. Martin, V. Pineiro, and R. Vos. 2022. *Repurposing Agricultural Policies and Support: Options to Transform Agriculture and Food Systems to Better Serve the Health of People, Economies, and the Planet.* Washington, DC: World Bank. https://openknowledge.worldbank.org/handle/10986/36875.

Hamilton, K., and M. Clemens. 1999. "Genuine Saving Rates in Developing Countries." *World Bank Economic Review* 13: 333–56. https://doi.org/10.1093/wber/13.2.333.

Hsieh, C. T., and P. J. Klenow. 2009. "Misallocation and Manufacturing TFP in China and India." *Quarterly Journal of Economics* 124 (4): 1403–48. https://doi.org/10.1162/qjec.2009.124.4.1403.

IPBES (Intergovernmental Science-Policy Platform on Biodiversity and Ecosystem Services). 2019. "Summary for Policymakers of the Global Assessment Report on Biodiversity and Ecosystem Services of the Intergovernmental Science-Policy Platform on Biodiversity and Ecosystem Services." IPBES Secretariat, Bonn, Germany.

IPCC (Intergovernmental Panel on Climate Change). 2014. *Climate Change 2014: Synthesis Report. Contribution of Working Groups I, II and III to the Fifth Assessment Report of the Intergovernmental Panel on Climate Change.* Geneva, Switzerland: IPCC.

IPCC (Intergovernmental Panel on Climate Change). 2018. *Global Warming of 1.5°C: An IPCC Special Report on the Impacts of Global Warming of 1.5°C above Pre-Industrial Levels and Related Global Greenhouse Gas Emissions Pathways, in the Context of Strengthening the Global Response to the Threat of Climate Change.* Geneva, Switzerland: IPCC.

IPCC (Intergovernmental Panel on Climate Change). 2021. "Summary for Policymakers." In *Climate Change 2021: The Physical Science Basis. Contribution of Working Group I to the Sixth Assessment Report of the Intergovernmental Panel on Climate Change,* edited by V. Masson Delmotte, P. Zhai, A. Pirani, S. L. Connors, C. Péan, S. Berger, N. Caud, et al. Cambridge, UK: Cambridge University Press. https://www.ipcc.ch/report/ar6/wg1/.

Johnson, J. A., G. Ruta, U. Baldos, R. Cervigni, S. Chonabayashi, E. Corong, O. Gavryliuk, et al. 2021. *The Economic Case for Nature: A Global Earth-Economy Model to Assess Development Policy Pathways.* Washington, DC: World Bank. https://openknowledge.worldbank.org/handle/10986/35882.

Karabarbounis, L., and B. Neiman. 2014. "The Global Decline of the Labor Share." *Quarterly Journal of Economics* 129 (1): 61–103. https://doi.org/10.3386/w19136.

Karabarbounis, L., and B. Neiman. 2018. "Accounting for Factorless Income." NBER Working Paper 24404, National Bureau of Economic Research, Cambridge, MA. https://www.nber.org/papers/w24404.

Kinzig, A. P., C. Perrings, S. Polasky, V. K. Smith, D. Tilman, and B. L. Turner. 2011. "Paying for Ecosystem Services: Promise and Peril." *Science* 334 (6056): 603–4. https://doi.org/10.1126/science.1210297.

Lakner, C., D. G. Mahler, M. Negre, and E. B. Prydz. 2020. "How Much Does Reducing Inequality Matter for Global Poverty?" Global Poverty Monitoring Technical Note No. 13, World Bank, Washington, DC.

Landrigan, P. J., R. Fuller, N. J. Acosta, O. Adeyi, R. Arnold, A. B. Baldé, R. Bertollini, et al. 2018. "The Lancet Commission on Pollution and Health." *Lancet* 391 (10119): 462–512. https://doi.org/10.1016/S0140-6736(17)32345-0.

Lenton, T. M., H. Held, E. Kriegler, J. W. Hall, W. Lucht, S. Rahmstorf, and H. J. Schellnhuber. 2008. "Tipping Elements in the Earth's Climate System." *Proceedings of the National Academy of Sciences* 105 (6): 1786–93. https://doi.org/10.1073/pnas.0705414105.

Lenton, T. M., J. Rockström, O. Gaffney, S. Rahmstorf, K. Richardson, W. Steffen, and H. J. Schellnhuber. 2019. "Climate Tipping Points: Too Risky to Bet Against." *Nature* 575 (7784): 592–95. https://doi.org/10.1038/d41586-019-03595-0.

Lobell, D. B., K. G. Cassman, and C. B. Field. 2009. "Crop Yield Gaps: Their Importance, Magnitudes, and Causes." *Annual Review of Environment and Resources* 34: 179–204. https://doi.org/10.1146/annurev.environ.041008.093740.

Lovejoy, T. E., and C. Nobre. 2019. "Amazon Tipping Point: Last Chance for Action." *Science Advances* 5 (12): 4–6. https://doi.org/10.1126/sciadv.aba2949.

Markandya, A., and S. Pedroso-Galinato. 2007. "How Substitutable Is Natural Capital?" *Environmental and Resource Economics* 37: 297–312. https://doi.org/10.1007/s10640-007-9117-4.

Moore, J. C. 2018. "Predicting Tipping Points in Complex Environmental Systems." *Proceedings of the National Academy of Sciences* 115 (4): 635–36. https://doi.org/10.1073/pnas.1721206115.

Mueller, N. D., J. S. Gerber, M. Johnston, D. K. Ray, N. Ramankutty, and J. A. Foley. 2012. "Closing Yield Gaps through Nutrient and Water Management." *Nature* 490 (7419): 254–57. https://doi.org/10.1038/nature11420.

Nelson, E., G. Mendoza, J. Regetz, S. Polasky, H. Tallis, D. R. Cameron, K. M. A. Chan, et al. 2009. "Modeling Multiple Ecosystem Services, Biodiversity Conservation, Commodity Production, and Tradeoffs at Landscape Scales." *Frontiers in Ecology and the Environment* 7 (1): 4–11. https://doi.org/10.1890/080023.

Nobre, C. A., and L. D. S. Borma. 2009. "'Tipping Points' for the Amazon Forest." *Current Opinion in Environmental Sustainability* 1 (1): 28–36. https://doi.org/10.1016/j.cosust.2009.07.003.

Oberfield, E., and D. Raval. 2021. "Micro Data and Macro Technology." *Econometrica* 89 (2): 703–22. https://doi.org/10.3982/ECTA12807.

Ostrom, E. 1990. *Governing the Commons: The Evolution of Institutions for Collective Action.* Cambridge, UK: Cambridge University Press.

Ostrom, E., J. Burger, C. B. Field, R. B. Norgaard, and D. Policansky. 1999. "Revisiting the Commons: Local Lessons and Global Challenges." *Science* 284: 278–82. https://doi.org/10.1126/science.284.5412.278.

Pagiola, S. 2008. "Payments for Environmental Services in Costa Rica." *Ecological Economics* 65 (4): 712–24. https://doi.org/10.1016/j.ecolecon.2007.07.033.

Polasky, S., B. Bryant, P. Hawthorne, J. Johnson, B. Keeler, and D. Pennington. 2015. "Inclusive Wealth as a Metric of Sustainable Development." *Annual Review of Environment and Resources* 40: 6.1–6.22. https://doi.org/10.1146/annurev-environ-101813-013253.

Polasky, S., E. Nelson, D. Tilman, J. Gerber, J. A. Johnson, F. Isbell, J. Hill, and C. Packer. 2022. "Reversing the Great Degradation of Nature." Unpublished manuscript, University of Minnesota, St. Paul.

Raudsepp-Hearne, C., G. D. Peterson, M. Tengö, E. M. Bennett, T. Holland, K. Benessaiah, G. K. MacDonald, et al. 2010. "Untangling the Environmentalist's Paradox: Why Is Human Well-Being Increasing as Ecosystem Services Degrade?" *Bioscience* 60: 576–89. https://doi.org/10.1525/bio.2010.60.8.4.

Restuccia, D., D. T. Yang, and X. Zhu. 2008. "Agriculture and Aggregate Productivity: A Quantitative Cross-Country Analysis." *Journal of Monetary Economics* 55 (2): 234–50. https://doi.org/10.1016/j.jmoneco.2007.11.006.

Ricardo, D. 1817 (1821). *On the Principles of Political Economy and Taxation.* 3d ed. London: John Murray. http://la.utexas.edu/users/hcleaver/368/368RicardoPrinCh2Renttable.pdf.

Rockström, J., W. Steffen, K. Noone, Å. Persson, F. S. Chapin III, E. F. Lambin, T. M. Lenton, et al. 2009. "A Safe Operating Space for Humanity." *Nature* 461 (7263): 472–75. https://doi.org/10.1038/461472a.

Rouhi Rad, M., W. Adamowicz, A. Entem, E. P. Fenichel, and P. Lloyd-Smith. 2021. "Complementarity (Not Substitution) between Natural and Produced Capital: Evidence from the Panama Canal Expansion." *Journal of the Association of Environmental and Resource Economists* 8 (6). https://doi.org/10.1086/714675.

Scheffer, M., S. Carpenter, J. A. Foley, C. Folke, and B. Walker. 2001. "Catastrophic Shifts in Ecosystems." *Nature* 413 (6856): 591–96. https://doi.org/10.1038/35098000.

Sen, A., J. P. Fitoussi, and J. Stiglitz. 2010. *Mismeasuring Our Lives: Why GDP Doesn't Add Up.* The New Press.

Steffen, W., K. Richardson, J. Rockström, S. E. Cornell, I. Fetzer, E. M. Bennett, R. Biggs, et al. 2015. "Planetary Boundaries: Guiding Human Development on a Changing Planet." *Science* 347 (6223). https://doi.org/10.1126/science.1259855.

UNEP (United Nations Environment Programme). 2021. *Making Peace with Nature: A Scientific Blueprint to Tackle the Climate, Biodiversity and Pollution Emergencies.* Nairobi, Kenya: UNEP.

Van Der Ploeg, R., and C. Withagen. 2013. "Green Growth, Green Paradox and the Global Economic Crisis." *Environmental Innovation and Societal Transitions* 6: 116–19. https://doi.org/10.1016/j.eist.2012.11.003.

Vucetich, J. A. 2021. *Restoring the Balance: What Wolves Tell Us about Our Relationship with Nature.* Baltimore, MD: Johns Hopkins University Press.

Williams, D. R., M. Clark, G. M. Buchanan, G. F. Ficetola, C. Rondinini, and D. Tilman. 2021. "Proactive Conservation to Prevent Habitat Losses to Agricultural Expansion." *Nature Sustainability* 4 (4): 314–22. https://doi.org/10.1038/s41893-020-00656-5.

Woodward, R. T., and Y.-S. Wui. 2001. "The Economic Value of Wetland Services: A Meta-Analysis." *Ecological Economics* 37: 257–70. https://doi.org/10.1016/S0921-8009(00)00276-7.

Woolhouse, M., F. Scott, Z. Hudson, R. Howey, and M. Chase-Topping. 2012. "Human Viruses: Discovery and Emergence." *Philosophical Transactions of the Royal Society* B 367: 2864–71. https://doi.org/10.1098%2Frstb.2011.0354.

World Bank. 2012. *Inclusive Green Growth: The Pathway to Sustainable Development.* Washington, DC: World Bank. https://openknowledge.worldbank.org/handle/10986/6058.

World Bank. 2017. *The Sunken Billions Revisited: Progress and Challenges in Global Marine Fisheries.* Washington, DC: World Bank.

World Bank. 2021a. *Green, Resilient and Inclusive Development.* Washington, DC: World Bank. https://openknowledge.worldbank.org/handle/10986/36322.

World Bank. 2021b. *The Changing Wealth of Nations 2021: Managing Assets for the Future.* Washington, DC: World Bank. https://openknowledge.worldbank.org/handle/10986/36400.

World Bank and FAO (Food and Agriculture Organization). 2009. *The Sunken Billions: The Economic Justification for Fisheries Reform.* Washington, DC: World Bank.

Zedler, J., and S. Kercher. 2005. "Wetland Resources: Status, Trends, Ecosystem Services, and Restorability." *Annual Review of Environment and Resources* 30: 39–74. https://doi.org/10.1146/annurev.energy.30.050504.144248.

CHAPTER 2

Identifying a Sustainable Resource Efficiency Frontier: An Overview of the Approach

Essentially all models are wrong, but some are useful.
George E. P. Box, British statistician[1]

Key messages

- This chapter is a nontechnical overview of the data and techniques used to develop sustainable resource efficiency frontiers.

- This process requires bridging two disciplines—ecology and economics. Understanding how natural resources and earth systems generate life-supporting services is a central concern in ecology. The efficient allocation of natural resources is a central concern in economics.

- Insights from both disciplines were used to construct sustainable resource efficiency frontiers. New data were applied to state-of-the-art models to describe biophysical processes. This information was then fed into economic models that quantify impacts on land-based production systems.

- Comparing potential outputs on the efficiency frontier with actual outputs produced in a country provides an indication of the magnitude of inefficiencies (that is, feasible Pareto improvements), allows identification of trade-offs, and can inform the broad contours of policies aimed at enhancing sustainability and efficiency.

Introduction

This chapter describes the approaches applied to derive an efficiency frontier, which indicates the range of marketed and environmental outputs that could be produced if resources are used and allocated efficiently. The frontier is employed to derive various measures of performance that describe how well a country is using its land-based endowments, the opportunities available for improvements, and the trade-offs that may emerge. The chapter summarizes the data and methods used to measure the current economic payoffs from crops, grazing, and timber, and it describes the environmental benefits in terms of greenhouse gas (GHG) sequestration and biodiversity. The current performance across these metrics is compared with the maximum feasible sustainable outputs to derive estimates of output gaps for economic activities and environmental services. A variety of measures are derived, including those that identify the shortest path to the efficiency frontier, the shortest path to maximizing economic returns without lowering environmental benefits, and the shortest path to maximizing environmental outputs without loss of economic benefits. Chapter 3 then applies the approach to 147 countries and finds considerable variability of performance across countries. Readers who prefer to skip these technical details can move directly to chapter 3, which summarizes the key results.

Modeling land use efficiency: A summary of the methodology

This study models and maps how land use and land management influence economic outputs, natural capital, and the resulting ecosystem processes that provide people with flows of ecosystem benefits ("ecosystem services"). State-of-the-art models are employed to use changes in landscape to estimate changes in biophysical processes (Chaplin-Kramer et al. 2019; Favero, Daigneault, and Sohngen 2020; Mueller et al. 2012). These changes are then linked with social and economic information to quantify the effects on revenue of land production systems (agricultural crops, grazing, and forestry), and nonmarket environmental metrics, including GHG emissions and biodiversity. Innovative science taking advantage of new technologies and data sources contributed information about biodiversity, ecosystems, and their economic and health impacts, offering a standard method for evaluating the consequences of changes in landscape. This study uses standardized methods and data to evaluate economic and environmental outputs for countries worldwide and to show the maximum sustainable feasible combinations of multiple outputs. To the authors' knowledge, such an exercise has not been attempted at such a fine scale of geographic spatial resolution or at this scope, covering the critical natural resources—land, water, air, and biodiversity.

The analysis relies on spatially explicit data at a fine-scale resolution (300 × 300 meter pixels) with global coverage, which can be displayed in maps (map 2.1). These maps show the world as it stands today in terms of land use, agricultural productivity, carbon sequestration, and biodiversity capacity. As for a sense of the size of these pixels, nearly 8.4 billion pixels span the world, or 1.85 billion pixels once water and the permanent ice cover are excluded. For a sense of the number of pixels at a national level, Vietnam contains 14.1 million pixels. Each nonwater pixel assumes one of five types of land use: natural habitat, cultivated, grazing, forestry, or urban. Land designated as natural habitat is

MAP 2.1
Current land use and potential land use, globally

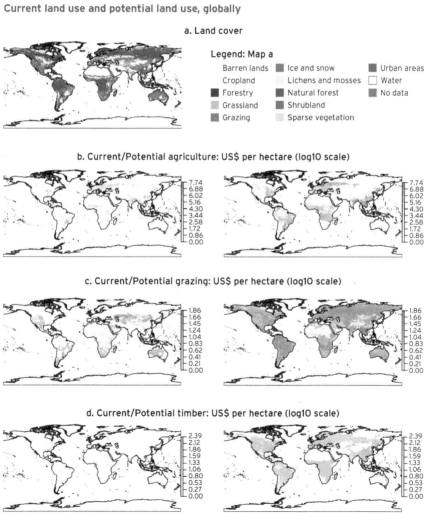

a. Land cover

Legend: Map a

Barren lands	Ice and snow	Urban areas
Cropland	Lichens and mosses	Water
Forestry	Natural forest	No data
Grassland	Shrubland	
Grazing	Sparse vegetation	

b. Current/Potential agriculture: US$ per hectare (log10 scale)

7.74
6.88
6.02
5.16
4.30
3.44
2.58
1.72
0.86
0.00

c. Current/Potential grazing: US$ per hectare (log10 scale)

1.86
1.66
1.45
1.24
1.04
0.83
0.62
0.41
0.21
0.00

d. Current/Potential timber: US$ per hectare (log10 scale)

2.39
2.12
1.86
1.59
1.33
1.06
0.80
0.53
0.27
0.00

Continued

MAP 2.1
Continued

e. Current/Potential carbon: Tonnes of carbon per hectare

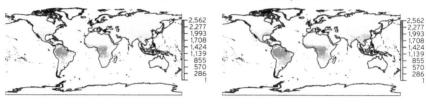

f. Current/Potential species richness: Number of vertebrate species per pixel

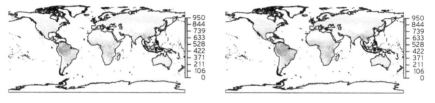

g. Current/Potential T/E richness: Number of threatened
and endangered vertebrate species per pixel

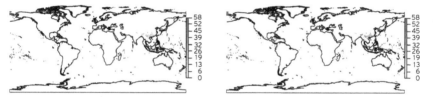

Source: World Bank.
Note: The sets of maps show the input data (left) and maximized data (right) for agriculture (crops), grazing, timber, carbon, species richness, and threatened and endangered species.

designated as forest, grassland, shrubland, wetland, or barren, and within these classes are further distinctions for types of forest or other systems for which there are important differences in biodiversity, carbon storage, or other ecosystem functions. The designations are based on the ecological potential for that pixel. Cultivated land is further subdivided into one of the 10 alternative management practices. These practices consist of (1) five management alternatives under expanded or altered cropland area (current management and four intensified management alternatives with combinations of sustainable irrigated versus rainfed and adoption versus nonadoption of best management practices such as buffer strips along streams) and (2) the same five management practices with current cropland area. These 10 agricultural management options, together with grazing, forestry, natural habitat, and urban areas, generate a total of 14 possible land use and land management alternatives. Additional detailed descriptions appear in the online technical appendix.[2]

The analysis combines a map that specifies the land use and land management for each pixel with biophysical and economic models (as described in section A of the online technical appendix) to quantify three key economic and environmental dimensions:

1. *Net production value of marketed outputs* for crops, grazing, and forestry, measured in monetary terms

2. *Net greenhouse gas sequestered,* including changes in carbon storage due to land use changes, as well as methane emissions from livestock production

3. *Biodiversity,* including measures of potential species richness, threatened and endangered species, endemic species, rare ecoregions, key biodiversity areas, and forest intactness.

The outcomes of these key dimensions of land cover and land use are then aggregated across all pixels within a country to provide country-level figures for each of these three key outputs.

The first map evaluated for each country is based on its current land use and land management, with one exception: unsustainable use is not allowed. For example, crop irrigation is not allowed in areas where such irrigation involves mining groundwater or consuming surface water beyond sustainable levels. Thus, although water use is not an explicit output of the model, it is used as a constraint to ensure that water is used sustainably. Similarly, harvesting of timber in excess of regrowth is also not allowed. This exercise establishes the current level of sustainable performance on each of the three key dimensions.

After determining the current sustainable outcomes across the three dimensions, an optimization analysis is employed to identify the land use and land management patterns that maximize a weighted sum of the outcomes. Varying the weights on the different objectives generates an efficiency frontier that shows all Pareto-efficient land use and land management patterns. Pareto efficiency describes a situation in which resources are allocated and used in ways that generate the maximum level of efficiency. Once on the Pareto efficiency frontier, no change is feasible without a trade-off that reduces some output in order to increase another output. The exercise applies weights to income generation, greenhouse gas mitigation, and biodiversity, and the optimization algorithm searches all feasible land use and land management alternatives for each pixel and chooses the option that maximizes the weighted objective measure. Although this exercise is restricted to these three objectives, there is no theoretical limit on the number of objectives that can be examined.

Transitions between land uses typically involve an upfront investment cost. For example, converting land from natural vegetation to cropland entails costs for clearing the land and planting crops. Restoring agricultural cropland to natural habitat typically requires replanting and other restoration costs. In areas without established irrigation, transitioning to irrigated agriculture requires an investment in the installation of irrigation infrastructure. These costs are included in the analysis outlined in section B.4 of the online technical appendix. The capital costs of irrigation are taken from the International Water Management Institute, but no data are available on irrigation operating costs. Similarly, no account is taken of the costs of managing natural habitats because of lack of suitable data and the wide variation within and across countries.

The analysis imposes several constraints on what are considered feasible alternative land use and land management alternatives in a pixel. One such constraint—that urban pixels remain unchanged—is employed because of the unrealistic and costly nature of moving entire cities and resettling populations. In another constraint, protected areas remain natural habitats and are not converted to human-dominated uses, recognizing the need for conserving the remaining natural habitats for both environmental and economic reasons and the political intention to do so within protected areas. Constraints are imposed as well on where agriculture is viable, such as not allowing crop production on steep slopes. Finally, sustainability constraints, as described earlier, are applied to the current landscape. For example, rainfed and irrigated cropland is allowed only where the water balance supports such production. Furthermore, irrigation—both from groundwater and surface water—is not allowed when such irrigation is unsustainable and requires the extraction of nonrenewable water (see section B.2 of the online technical appendix for details on constraints).

The sustainability constraints on both the current landscape and the Pareto solutions along the efficiency frontier are imposed to offer fair comparisons of current country performance and to rule out artificially inflating productivity in the short term by following unsustainable strategies that will harm future productive capacity. In summary, the focus is on *steady-state outcomes*, which is appropriate in view of the objective of assessing sustainable efficiency.

Measuring productivity through efficiency frontiers

A problem that economists face when trying to account for benefits or costs when goods and services are not marketed is measuring the benefits or costs using a common metric. Several imperfect methods have been developed for assigning monetary values to nonmarketed goods to enable comparison using a uniform metric. However, as highlighted in box 1.2 and box 2.1, none of the methods is fully accurate or entirely satisfactory. For example, the term *biodiversity* encompasses an entire spectrum of flora and fauna, some of which provide easily identifiable ecosystem services for human consumption (such as the pollination provided by bees). Implicit prices can be inferred for these services and many more that are not readily monetized. If monetization, or any other common denominator, cannot be found, one is often left with an apples to oranges comparison. For example, how many fewer cases of cholera or malaria or increases in crop production are needed to offset the destruction of a natural habitat and the potential extinction of a species? Any answer to such a question

BOX 2.1
Monetizing the unmonetized benefits

Is it possible to estimate prices for public goods and services that are not traded in markets? A common example may be a village deciding between an investment in a piped-water system for households and an irrigation system for agricultural production. On the one hand, the piped-water system would save residents time because they would no longer need to fetch water from a well, and it would improve the quality of water that households drink, reducing morbidity. On the other hand, the irrigation system can increase crop yields and thus household incomes. If investment in only one of these two areas is possible, on what basis should a decision be made? In other words, how can one compare the time savings and reduced morbidity from the water supply project with the higher agricultural yields from the irrigation project?

The existing methods for assigning monetary values are imprecise (see box 1.2). One might try to convert the expected benefits to a single measure for an apples to apples comparison. In this case, that single measure might be income. The reduced time spent fetching water can be "monetized" by estimating the value of time, perhaps through a wage rate. If the village's residents were not spending their time fetching water, they could be doing other productive activities that would earn them a wage, and thus one can put a monetary value on that time. Similarly, reduced morbidity means fewer missed days at work due to illness, which can also be monetized through a wage rate. If one were to add up the monetized time savings and the monetized morbidity impacts, then a direct comparison could be made with the financial benefits of irrigation.

More generally, if the unmarketed good or service is linked in any way (either as a substitute or as a complement) to a good or service traded in markets, then it may be possible to use the price of the traded good to infer values for the untraded good–the hedonic price technique. Alternatively, a large literature has developed that seeks to elicit values by asking people their willingness to pay for a new service or their willingness to accept money for the loss of a hypothetical service–the contingent valuation method. · Prices can also be derived using a variety of simulation techniques.

It is widely acknowledged that these methods are imperfect for several reasons. In the village example, residents of the village may value not getting sick at more than just their wage rate. Illness involves not just missing a day of work, but also possibly considerable suffering, possibly infecting loved ones, and possibly death. How does one put a fair price on these outcomes? Another problem is that because the benefits are not traded in markets, there is no way to empirically verify the accuracy of the estimated prices against the true shadow values that are unobserved. The experimental literature suggests the need for caution in using these approaches.

would be highly sensitive to the techniques used to assign values and would be controversial for several reasons, including ethical considerations that could be pivotal to many.

For these reasons, instead of trying to monetize all benefits from nature, this exercise is based on an *efficiency frontier* approach. This approach involves measuring the maximum combinations of various benefits that result from use of a given allocation of resources. The efficiency frontier provides an estimate of how the range and magnitude of outputs vary as the allocation of inputs is changed. For example, converting more forested land to crop production typically increases agricultural income, but it reduces other outputs such as biodiversity, carbon sequestration, and water quality. Each of the benefits is measured using a metric that makes the most sense for decision-making, such as lives saved for health benefits, tons of carbon sequestered for climate benefits, and monetary values for benefits with market values.

A stylized version of an efficiency frontier is shown in figure 2.1. The country depicted is currently producing at the large green dot, which sits inside the frontier, represented by the dark blue curve. Through more efficient allocation or use of resources, it is possible to produce at either the dark blue dot—where the level of environmental services is held constant, but the marketable good increases—or at the yellow dot—where the environmental services indicator increases, but the marketable good is held constant—or at any other point along the dark blue curve. As long as the country does *not* reach the frontier, it is possible to improve production in either or both outputs without any trade-offs.

FIGURE 2.1
Example of efficiency frontier

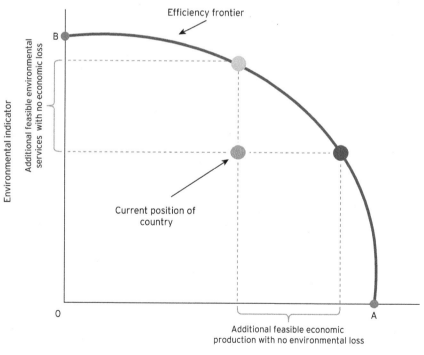

Source: World Bank.
Note: The country in this stylized depiction is producing at the large green dot, which sits inside the frontier, represented by the dark blue curve. Through more efficient allocation or use of resources, it is possible to produce at either the dark blue dot—where the level of environmental services is held constant, but the marketable good increases—or at the yellow dot—where the environmental services indicator increases, but the marketable good is held constant—or at any other point along the curve.

However, once the country improves efficiency enough to reach the frontier, any increase in either output will require a reduction in the other.[3]

In summary, a move toward the frontier can be achieved by improving efficiency and thus can produce more of one or all outputs. Such a move entails weak normative judgments. Conversely, moves along the frontier require giving up one good for more of another. Such trade-offs among objectives involve stronger value judgments.

A distinct advantage of the efficiency frontier approach is that it does not require measuring outputs using the same metric (such as monetary), and it does not impose value judgments on the relative desirability of various objectives (for example, biodiversity versus human health versus monetary returns). This feature is useful because there is not, in general, unanimity of views on the relative importance of different objectives. The only value judgment in the efficiency frontier analysis is whether achieving more of a desirable objective is better than achieving less with the same resources. In general, most would agree that if a country can do better on at least some dimensions without a net loss in others, it has improved its performance.

This approach can be extended beyond just two outputs by adding dimensions to the graph. A z-axis perpendicular to the page or screen could measure biodiversity conservation. Although anything more than two dimensions is difficult to illustrate graphically, any number of dimensions can be added and used to mathematically calculate a country's efficiency frontier. The analysis in this chapter highlights the efficiency gains that improve on three distinct outputs: biodiversity, climate (greenhouse gas storage and emissions), and conventional economic objectives (that is, solutions that are win-win-win), as well as the trade-off options. Although these three outputs are among the most important services provided by natural capital, they represent only a subset of those benefits. Future work may make it possible to explore additional dimensions of sustainability that are currently limited by data and science. Indeed, annex 2A explores the impact of including water quality in the factors considered in the analysis.

For each country, efficiency scores are computed for three outputs related to natural capital: economic output, greenhouse gas storage and emissions, and biodiversity supported. The values of crop agriculture, forestry, and grazing are aggregated into a single monetary metric of economic output because these are conventional marketed commodities, whereas separate measures are included for two important nonmarket environmental outputs: biodiversity and greenhouse gas storage and emissions. For each country, current performance is assessed relative to the maximum feasible levels of each of these outputs. Current performance for each country is also assessed in terms of how efficient it is in achieving multiple outcomes and to what extent the country could improve outcomes in multiple dimensions simultaneously using the landscape efficiency score, an overall summary metric that maps the shortest distance to the frontier.

BOX 2.2
Calculating the landscape efficiency score, nonmarket environmental score, and production value score

The landscape efficiency score, the nonmarket environmental score, and the production value score are illustrated in figure B2.2.1 for two dimensions: a single nonmarket environmental outcome on the vertical axis and the sum of production values (agricultural crop production, grazing, and forestry) on the horizontal axis. The current landscape score for these two outcome dimensions is shown as point Z. The efficiency frontier shows the maximum possible combinations of the nonmarket environmental outcome and production value that accrue from allocation and management decisions. The efficiency frontier is found using optimization methods (see section B.5 of the online technical appendix).[a] The current performance of the country depicted in figure B2.2.1 lies well inside the efficiency frontier at Z, indicating that improvements in both nonmarket environmental and production value dimensions are possible. The Euclidean distance between the coordinates of the *current outcome* (what has been achieved) and the coordinates of the closest point on the *efficiency frontier* (what could be achieved) is shown as α in figure B2.2.1. A country can move closer to the frontier either by changes in the intensive margin, such as increasing crop yields through adoption of better agricultural practices, or by changes in the extensive margin, such as moving land to uses that generate higher combinations of nonmarket environmental outcomes and monetary value. The yellow area in figure B2.2.1 represents the possible Pareto improvements (the win-wins) in which the outcome in both dimensions—nonmarket environmental outcomes and monetary values—could be improved.

One can also measure how much gain in both nonmarket environmental and production values has been achieved by measuring the Euclidian distance from the *minimum* possible

FIGURE B2.2.1
Performance metrics used in calculating an efficiency frontier score

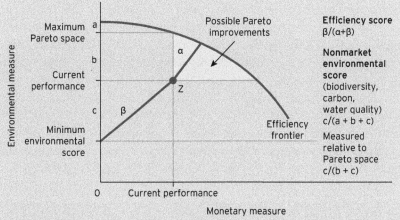

Source: World Bank.
Note: The upper curve shows the efficiency frontier, in which the maximum possible performance for the environmental measure is obtained for a given level of the monetary measure and vice versa. The shaded area is the Pareto space in which it is possible to improve both the environmental measure and the monetary measure relative to the current level of performance without sacrifice in the other measure.

Continued

BOX 2.2
Continued

scores to the scores for the *current* landscape, shown as β in figure B2.2.1. The minimum scores may be 0, as for the production values, or positive as shown for the nonmarket environmental scores. A minimum score that is not 0 occurs when some value is remaining even for the worst possible land use pattern. For example, some remnants of biodiversity remain even when the landscape is totally transformed to human-dominated uses. These are species that do not become extinct regardless of the land use pattern, but their conservation receives no credit in the analysis. Instead, it nets them out by setting the minimum value for biodiversity above 0.

The landscape efficiency score is defined as the ratio of the gains achieved by the current landscape, compared with the potential gains achieved by moving to the efficiency frontier. In the simple two-dimensional graph in figure B2.2.1, the landscape efficiency score is defined as $\beta/(\alpha + \beta)$.[b]

If current performance is close to the efficiency frontier, the landscape efficiency score will be close to 1 (because α will be close to 0). As the distance to the efficiency frontier increases (that is, α grows and β shrinks), the landscape efficiency score will fall. The size of β is equally as important as the size of α in determining the landscape efficiency score. The fact that the length of β is partially determined by the minimum environmental outcome has important implications for the landscape efficiency score. It implies that countries having high minimum environmental productivity relative to their maximum environmental productivity will tend to perform better on this metric. The implications of this factor are discussed in chapter 3.

The landscape efficiency score can be generalized to more than two goods. With n dimensions, it is defined as

$$
L \frac{\sqrt{\sum_{i=1}^{N}\left(x_i^c - x_i^{Min}\right)^2}}{\sqrt{\sum_{i=1}^{N}\left(x_i^c - x_i^{Min}\right)^2} + \sqrt{\sum_{i=1}^{N}\left(x_i^{EF} - x_i^c\right)^2}},
$$

where x_i^c is the score for the current landscape for output i; x_i^{Min} is the minimum possible score for output i; and x_i^{EF} is the score on the nearest point on the efficiency frontier for output i, $i = 1, 2, ..., N$.

The landscape efficiency score is not a strict average of the dimension-specific scores. Indeed, a country can perform very poorly on two dimensions, but if it scores very well on the third, that can partly compensate for the poor performance in the other categories and place the country in a higher position than would otherwise occur. In figure B2.2.1, a point near the top of the graph can be near the frontier in the vertical axis direction, but far from the frontier in the horizontal axis direction. Accordingly, the overall frontier efficiency score will be high because there will be a short distance to the frontier.

Another relevant statistic measures how well a country is doing in achieving the best possible outcome in a single dimension, irrespective of whether any trade-offs are involved. For a single dimension such as biodiversity, the nonmarket environmental score is defined as the distance from the current position to the maximum feasible output, or $c/(a + b + c)$. The maximum feasible level of one output may require large sacrifices in other outputs.

An alternative performance measure compares current performance in one dimension relative to that achieved *without* sacrifice in any another dimension. In this Pareto improvement, one output can be increased without sacrificing another outcome.

Individual subindexes across the three components (one economic and two environmental) are also reported. Box 2.2 describes how these scores are calculated in a two-dimensional and n (>2) dimensional space.

Impacts not considered: Shifts in the efficiency frontier

All models are simplifications of a more complex reality, but they are useful for generating insight by focusing on system elements that matter while holding other factors constant. The efficiency frontiers developed in this study are directed at critical economic and ecosystem service benefits for which there are globally available data and a sufficient scientific understanding for quantitative simulations. This exercise looks at the potential gains from alternative policy and management choices analyzed under current conditions and does not include analysis that involves changes in other variables that may occur through time and are not readily knowable. Because the simultaneous consideration of all other relevant factors is beyond computational bounds, it is important to assess how key results may shift when there are changes in factors not explicitly included or varied in the models.[4] This section investigates some of the more important changes that may warrant consideration and describes how these would modify the results and qualify the conclusions.

Transboundary considerations. Biodiversity, ecosystems, and environmental impacts rarely map neatly into jurisdictional boundaries. Species migrate, some 60 percent of the world's rivers flow across international boundaries (UNEP 2016), and about 400,000 premature deaths each year are due to cross-boundary $PM_{2.5}$ (particulate matter that is 2.5 microns or less in diameter) pollution (Zhang et al. 2017). Thus decisions in one country can have spillover effects in

FIGURE 2.2
Shifts in the resource efficiency frontier

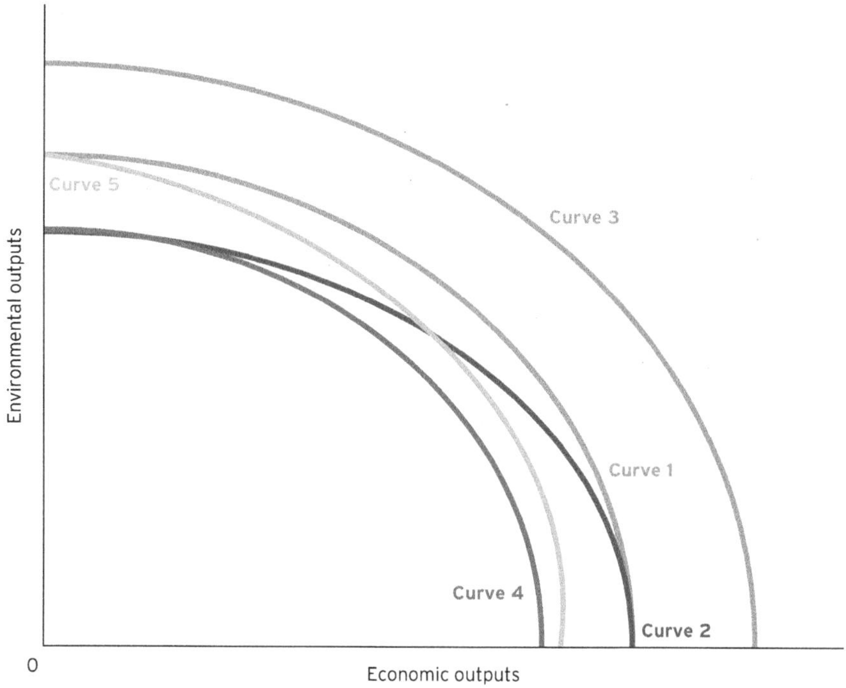

Source: World Bank.

other countries. When upstream or upwind countries take actions that worsen environmental conditions downstream or downwind, the efficiency frontier will tend to shift downward because it will no longer be feasible to attain the same high environmental outcomes (a shift from curve 1 to curve 2 in figure 2.2). Shared natural resources are best governed as an integrated whole. Planning across entire ecoregions, river basins, or airsheds yields greater flexibility in determining how total benefits can best be realized and risks reduced. But such cooperation has often proven to be challenging.

Technological advances. Throughout much of human history, technological change has transformed economies, enabling significant increases in productivity and economic growth. In this analysis, however, efficiency frontiers were derived assuming the current level of technology. Advances in technology would shift the efficiency frontiers outward by enabling greater production of both economic and environmental services with the same level of resources. Irrespective of whether the new technology is geared toward increasing economic outputs (such as improvements in digital technology) or environmental outputs (such as an improved pollution abatement technology), it would enable increases in outputs across all goods in most circumstances. Thus technology changes entail a shift, such as from curve 1 to curve 3 in figure 2.2.

Climate change and shocks. Ongoing climate change will also affect the provision of economic and ecosystem service benefits. Climate change often has a negative impact on outputs, such as depressing agricultural yields in many parts of the world (Zhao et al. 2017). Climate change may also negatively affect biodiversity and ecosystem services. For negative impacts, the efficiency frontier would shift inward such as from curve 1 to curve 4 in figure 2.2. However, climate could increase productivity in some areas, such as agricultural productivity in far northern or southern latitudes. Likewise, climate shocks such as drought, floods, and other natural disasters could redefine the economic and ecological equilibrium and change what is feasible from an efficiency standpoint. In these cases, a recalculation of the frontier may be necessary because the underlying ecological relationships may change.

Water quality. Many of the movements toward the efficiency frontier, especially movements to the right that increase the value of production, involve agricultural intensification, which reduces water quality—even when it can be done in ways that do not worsen biodiversity and carbon scores. Requiring these shifts to not worsen water quality in the Pareto calculation will generally rule out many points on the current Pareto frontier and will shift the Pareto curve inward from the right. This shift (curve 5 in figure 2.2) is most pronounced for moves toward increasing production value, which tend to involve more intensification without the ameliorating effects of returning land to natural habitat (see annex 2A for a more detailed discussion of how water quality affects the main results of this exercise).

Tipping points. Crossing tipping points can cause dramatic (nonlinear) and potentially irreversible environmental changes with a potentially large disruption in the flow of benefits from environmental assets (Scheffer et al. 2001). Tipping points may be breached on a global scale, such as when global temperatures cross critical thresholds, or on a local scale, such as when local environmental degradation causes a freshwater lake to fill with algae (Scheffer and Carpenter 2003). The risks of crossing tipping points may increase as countries move beyond the Pareto (no trade-off) space and increase economic outputs by depleting their natural assets. Economies reliant on environmentally sensitive sectors such as agriculture, fisheries, or forestry are at particular risk when the growth of these sectors depletes the very natural resource base on which they depend. Although the models used here are unable to capture where tipping points may be crossed, the potentially significant risks posed suggest the need for considerable caution in moving beyond the Pareto space. In terms of the efficiency frontiers, the existence of tipping points implies that there are fewer possibilities for expanding economic production beyond the Pareto space—the greater the depletion of natural assets the greater the risks. In terms of the resource efficiency frontier, once a tipping point is crossed, no further production is possible, implying a truncation.

Other forms of capital. The models in this analysis include services from natural capital as well as complementary forms of physical capital such as irrigation systems and farm and forestry machinery. In addition, they implicitly assume that sufficient human capital is available to manage crop, livestock, and forestry production, as well as to transition land use and management to frontier systems. If these assumptions do not hold, then the frontier is likely to bend in on the horizontal side, reducing the maximum attainable production value on the extreme end of the horizontal axis. Nevertheless, because of the large rural populations in most lower-income countries and the declining farm sizes in regions such as Sub-Saharan Africa and South Asia (Jayne, Chamberlin, and Headey 2014), it is unlikely that labor or human capital will be a binding constraint throughout the developing world.

Other damages. Many other ecosystem changes, ecosystem services, and pollutants are not included in the model largely because of the paucity of data or insufficient information on impacts. If there are adverse impacts on either economic potential or environmental services from whatever source (whether natural disasters, a different pollutant or environmental pressure, or unaccounted economic changes and shocks), opportunities for growth shrink and result in a contraction of the efficiency frontier. Likewise, if the costs of transitioning between land uses or maintaining a particular land use are not in the model, these will pivot the efficiency frontier inward, and the opposite would hold if these costs were inflated in the derivation of efficiency frontiers.

Building on the description here of the methodology used to estimate the efficiency frontier and the caveats that apply, chapter 3 investigates efficiency gaps, the scope for improvement, and where trade-offs emerge. A taxonomy based on the location of countries on or within their frontiers provides broad guidance on the policy directions needed to reach the frontier. Some countries, based on their performance and endowments, have large scope to improve land-based economic productivity; others have opportunities to improve the provision of environmental services; and still others on or near their frontier may face steep trade-offs.

Annex 2A: Water quality and the resource efficiency frontiers

The efficiency frontiers reported here are the maximal combinations of GHG reductions, biodiversity, and net monetary returns for agricultural crop production, grazing, and forestry. The land use and land cover solutions on the efficiency frontiers have also been run through the water model to determine how drinking water quality changes for various points on the efficiency frontier when compared with the current landscape. These results do not optimize for water quality but rather evaluate the change in water quality for the results that optimize for GHG reductions, biodiversity, and net monetary returns.

Some points on the efficiency frontiers show an improvement in water quality relative to the current landscape. These solutions are win-win-win-win in that they result in better outcomes for biodiversity, greenhouse gases, net returns from production, and water quality improvements. For a small subset of countries, all European except Bangladesh, movements to the Pareto frontier also show improvements in water quality. These countries have much land in agricultural crop production, and movements to the frontier involve increasing natural habitat. Reducing the amount of land in crop production and increasing the amount of land in natural vegetation will tend to reduce nutrient loads and improve water quality.

However, for the vast majority of countries at least some points on the efficiency frontier show a decline in water quality relative to the current landscape. Increasing cropland area (extensification) or inputs to achieve higher yields (intensification) will tend to increase nutrient loads and decrease water quality. Many of the solutions on the efficiency frontier involve some degree of extensification and intensification, with the result that water quality is reduced, compared with the current sustainable landscape. Therefore, requiring that water quality does not worsen in the Pareto calculations will generally rule out some solutions on the current Pareto frontier, thereby shifting the Pareto curve inward to some degree for most countries. This inward shift is most pronounced on moves that increase the net production value, which tend to involve more extensification and intensification without the ameliorating effects for water quality of putting land back into natural habitat. The reductions in Pareto space arising from requiring water quality improvements tend to be more pronounced in lower-income countries that currently score well on biodiversity and carbon but low on production value.

For about two-thirds of all countries, the entire Pareto frontier optimized for biodiversity, GHG reductions, and net production value shows a decrease in water quality relative to the current landscape. This occurs in many countries that currently have very low levels of nutrient pollution from agriculture or grazing, and where moves to intensify agriculture result in a net increase in nutrient pollution. This worsening of water quality occurs even when keeping net production value constant and increasing biodiversity and GHG sequestration scores, which typically involves increases in natural habitat. The increased intensification required to maintain a constant net production value is what results in lower water quality scores.

Because water quality is not being optimized, it is not altogether surprising that many of the solutions do not result in water quality improvements. Explicitly maximizing for water quality improvements would expand the set of win-win-win-win solutions. Such solutions would tend to emphasize restoration of native habitats along streams and rivers and other measures targeted to water quality improvements. Such solutions would not increase biodiversity, GHG reductions, and net production values as much as is possible while ignoring water quality, but would show that there remains considerable scope for improved outcomes even with the additional constraints of improving water quality.

Annex 2B: Aggregation and the "headline" landscape efficiency score

As shown in box 2.2, information in an efficiency index can be aggregated in several ways to produce a single summary headline metric, such as gross domestic product for the economic accounts, or gross ecosystem production to summarize the value of ecosystem services, or the World Bank's Human Capital Index. Ideally, the single summary metric would capture the wealth of information about natural capital. Currently, however, no single metric is able to capture the full range of information, but what follows describes several options.

Landscape efficiency score

The landscape efficiency score is defined as the Euclidean distance between the vector of scores for the current landscape and the vector of minimum scores, divided by the Euclidean distance between the vector of scores for the current landscape and the vector of minimum scores plus the Euclidian distance between the vector of scores for the current landscape and the vector of scores for the nearest point on the efficiency frontier to the current landscape. It then follows that

$$\text{landscape efficiency score} = \frac{\sqrt{\sum_{i=1}^{N}\left(x_i^C - x_i^{Min}\right)^2}}{\sqrt{\sum_{i=1}^{N}\left(x_i^C - x_i^{Min}\right)^2} + \sqrt{\sum_{i=1}^{N}\left(x_i^{EF} - x_i^C\right)^2}}, \qquad (2B.1)$$

where x_i^C is the score for the current landscape for output i; x_i^{Min} is the minimum possible score for output i; and x_i^{EF} is the score on the nearest point on the efficiency frontier for output i, $i = 1, 2, …, N$.

In simple terms, the landscape efficiency score measures the proportion of potential gains realized by current land use and land management. This measure equals 1 for a point on the efficiency frontier and drops to 0 as scores fall to the minimum possible. The mean score is 0.86 (range, 0.996–0.61).

Strengths. The landscape efficiency score is a good summary measure of the efficiency of the sustainable use of natural capital by a country. It captures how close to or far from the efficiency frontier a country is as a percentage of the total possible gains. It considers all dimensions and is not tied to a score in any particular dimension. Adding more dimensions will lead to higher scores because, if all else remains equal, each new dimension adds a positive real number (<1) to the old score. In addition, if a greater number of dimensions leads to a greater probability of a very high score in some dimension, then the landscape efficiency scores will tend to increase with the number of dimensions.

Weaknesses. The landscape efficiency score tends to focus on the best dimensional score and give little weight to poor performance in other dimensions.

Because an objective of this exercise is to determine where opportunities lie, this focus may inadvertently lead to neglecting cases where improvements can occur.

Pareto geometric mean

The Pareto geometric mean is defined as the geometric mean of the Pareto scores across all the dimensions, where the Pareto score in each dimension is measured as the proportion of the maximum possible gains in the Pareto space obtained by the current landscape. It then follows that

$$\text{Pareto geometric mean} = \sqrt[N]{\prod_{i=1}^{N}\left(\frac{x_i^C - x_i^{Min}}{\left(x_i^{PMax} - x_i^{Min}\right)}\right)}, \quad (2B.2)$$

where x_i^C is the score for the current landscape for output i; x_i^{Min} is the minimum possible score for output i; and x_i^{PMax} is the maximum score for output i constrained to the Pareto space relative to the current landscape, $i = 1, 2, ..., N$.

The average score for the Pareto geometric mean in 0.69 (range, 0.99–0.41).

Strengths. The Pareto geometric mean restricts attention to the Pareto space, thereby capturing some of the notions of efficiency. This geometric mean uses each dimensional score and penalizes countries doing poorly in any single dimension. A high score is given only to those countries doing well in all dimensions relative to what is jointly possible. A geometric mean also has the advantage of ensuring that if a country obtains 0 in any one dimension, then the overall score becomes 0. This approach embodies the notion that both environmental and economic services are necessary.

Weaknesses. The Pareto geometric mean emphasizes the weakest dimension. A country can be relatively efficient in the sense of being close to the efficiency frontier but still score low on the Pareto geometric mean. This outcome occurs for countries that are largely pristine but with untapped economic potential or those that are highly productive but with an ability to improve their environmental outcomes.

Geometric mean

This option is defined as the geometric mean scores relative to the maximum possible scores across all the dimensions. The difference between this measure and the Pareto geometric mean is that this measure compares the current landscape with the maximum possible score instead of restricting the comparison to be within the Pareto space relative to the current landscape—that is,

$$\text{geometric mean} = \sqrt[N]{\prod_{i=1}^{N}\left(\frac{x_i^C - x_i^{Min}}{\left(x_i^{Max} - x_i^{Min}\right)}\right)}, \quad (2B.3)$$

where x_i^C is the score for the current landscape for output i; x_i^{Min} is the minimum possible score for output i; and x_i^{Max} is the maximum score for output i, $i = 1$, 2, ..., N.

The average score for the Pareto geometric mean is 0.53 (range, 0.75–0.23).

Strengths. The geometric mean shares many of the same strengths as the Pareto geometric mean.

Weaknesses. The geometric mean shares many of the same weaknesses as the Pareto geometric mean. In addition, a country can score poorly on the geometric mean if there are large unavoidable trade-offs among different scores.

Pareto arithmetic mean

The Pareto arithmetic mean is defined as the arithmetic mean of the Pareto scores across all the dimensions, where the Pareto score in each dimension is measured as the proportion of the maximum possible gains in the Pareto space obtained by the current landscape, or

$$\text{Pareto arithmetic mean} = \frac{1}{N} \sum_{i=1}^{N} \left(\frac{x_i^C - x_i^{Min}}{\left(x_i^{PMax} - x_i^{Min} \right)} \right). \tag{2B.4}$$

The average score for the Pareto arithmetic mean is 0.72 (range, 0.99–0.47).

Strengths. This mean restricts attention to the Pareto space, and so it still captures some of the notions of efficiency in the landscape efficiency score. Unlike the Pareto geometric mean, the arithmetic mean weights all dimensions equally, and thus it does not penalize a country excessively for doing poorly in one dimension.

Weaknesses. There is no clear reason for thinking that percentage changes in one dimension should be treated the same as percentage changes in another dimension. A country can be relatively efficient and still score low on the arithmetic mean, which will occur for countries that are largely pristine but with untapped economic potential, or are highly productive but with an ability to improve their environmental outcomes.

Arithmetic mean

The arithmetic mean is defined as the arithmetic mean of the scores across all the dimensions, relative to the maximum possible scores across all the dimensions:

$$\text{arithmetic mean} = \frac{1}{N} \sum_{i=1}^{N} \left(\frac{x_i^C - x_i^{Min}}{\left(x_i^{Max} - x_i^{Min} \right)} \right) \tag{2B.5}$$

The average score for the Pareto geometric mean is 0.58 (range, 0.76–0.35).

Strengths. The arithmetic mean shares many of the same strengths as the Pareto arithmetic mean.

Weaknesses. The arithmetic mean shares many of the same weaknesses as the Pareto arithmetic mean. In addition, a country can score poorly on the arithmetic mean if there are large unavoidable trade-offs among different scores (for example, a country can do well in terms of either market value or nonmarket environmental scores, but not both).

Other indicators

The individual dimension scores tell important stories in their own right. It is useful to report the share of potential gains, either relative to the Pareto space or the maximum possible scores, for the monetary returns (sum of agricultural crop production, grazing, and forestry), greenhouse gases (carbon dioxide and methane), and biodiversity (potential species richness, threatened and endangered species, endemic species, rare ecoregions, key biodiversity areas, and forest intactness). These scores are often as informative (or more informative) than the aggregate metrics. It can also be useful to sum up the environmental measures to look at an environmental geometric (arithmetic) mean.

Each index tell a rich but different story by emphasizing different elements. No measure captures all elements, and the choice of metric should be guided by the issue under consideration.

Notes

1. Cited in Box, G. E., and N. R. Draper. 1987. *Empirical Model-Building and Response Surfaces.* New York: John Wiley & Sons.

2. The online technical appendix (appendix B) is available with the text of this book in the World Bank's Online Knowledge Repository, https://openknowledge.worldbank.org /handle/10986/39453.

3. For countries on the frontier, the slope of the frontier curve defines the trade-offs between the two outputs. When a country is in the upper-left part of the frontier curve, the shallow slope implies that a small reduction in the environmental output can lead to a large increase in the economic output. As one moves to the right, the slope increases, implying that one gets a smaller increase in economic output for the same decrease in the environmental output. This is an example of the law of diminishing returns.

4. That is, moving from ceteris paribus (all else being equal) to mutatis mutanda (allowing for change and interactions).

References

Chaplin-Kramer, R., R. P. Sharp, C. Weil, E. M. Bennett, U. Pascual, K. K. Arkema, K. A. Brauman, et al. 2019. "Global Modeling of Nature's Contributions to People." *Science* 366 (6462): 255–8. https://doi.org/10.1126/science.aaw3372.

Favero, A., A. Daigneault, and B. Sohngen. 2020. "Forests: Carbon Sequestration, Biomass Energy, or Both?" *Science Advances* 6 (13): eaay6792. https://doi.org/10.1126/sciadv.aay6792.

Jayne, T. S., J. Chamberlin, and D. D. Headey. 2014. "Land Pressures, the Evolution of Farming Systems, and Development Strategies in Africa: A Synthesis." *Food Policy* 48: 1–17. https://doi.org/10.1016/j.foodpol.2014.05.014.

Mueller, N. D., J. S. Gerber, M. Johnston, D. K. Ray, N. Ramankutty, and J. A. Foley. 2012. "Closing Yield Gaps through Nutrient and Water Management." *Nature* 490 (7419): 254–7. https://doi.org/10.1038/nature11420.

Scheffer, M., and S. R. Carpenter. 2003. "Catastrophic Regime Shifts in Ecosystems: Linking Theory to Observation." *Trends in Ecology and Evolution* 8 (12): 648–56. https://doi.org/10.1016/j.tree.2003.09.002.

Scheffer, M., S. R. Carpenter, J. A. Foley, C. Folke, and B. Walker. 2001. "Catastrophic Shifts in Ecosystems." *Nature* 413: 591–6. https://doi.org/10.1038/35098000.

UNEP (United Nations Environment Programme). 2016. "Transboundary Waters Systems—Status and Trends: Crosscutting Analysis." Nairobi, Kenya: UNEP.

Zhang, Q., X. Jiang, D. Tong, S. J. Davis, H. Zhao, G. Geng, T. Feng, et al. 2017. "Transboundary Health Impacts of Transported Global Air Pollution and International Trade." *Nature* 543: 705–9 (2017). https://doi.org/10.1038/nature21712.

Zhao, C., B. Liu, S. Piao, X. Wang, D. B. Lobell, Y. Huang, M. Huang, et al. 2017. "Temperature Increase Reduces Global Yields of Major Crops in Four Independent Estimates." *PNAS* 114 (35): 9326–31. https://doi.org/10.1073/pnas.1701762114.

Envisioning a More Sustainable Future through a More Efficient Present

What we are doing to the forests of the world is but a mirror reflection of what we are doing to ourselves and to one another.
Chris Maser, U.S. social-environmental sustainability expert[1]

Key messages

- This chapter presents the results of the landscape efficiency analysis following the methodology presented in chapter 2.

- Overall, income status and region are found to be poor predictors of landscape efficiency. Instead, this study develops a typology of countries to categorize and explain why some countries perform better than others in terms of marketed production efficiency (agriculture, grazing, and forestry), and nonmarketed production efficiency (greenhouse gas storage and biodiversity).

- Through more efficient use of landscapes, an increase in greenhouse gas (GHG) storage of 85.6 billion metric tons of carbon dioxide equivalent (CO_2eq) can be achieved without reducing the economic production of the land or biodiversity. This quantity is equivalent to 1.7 years of global emissions.

- Alternatively, scenarios that increase the efficiency of landscapes can also result in an increase in production value of US$329 billion per year, while maintaining current biodiversity and GHG storage levels.

- These benefits derive partly from more efficient use of resources (intensification explains 55 percent of the gains), as well as through improved allocation of resources to their most productive uses.
- These results imply that there are significant opportunities to increase economic growth and meet growing food security challenges without further encroaching on the environment and ecosystem services.

Introduction

This chapter explores how land use and land management patterns contribute to income generation from crops, grazing, and timber, and two important nonmarketed environmental benefits: greenhouse gas (GHG) sequestration and the conservation of biodiversity. Specifically, it looks at whether and to what extent inefficiencies in the use and allocation of land-related resources reduce income, increase carbon emissions and pollution, and contribute to declining biodiversity, compared with what is feasible given a country's resources. The results demonstrate how the allocation of land-related resources across sectors and the productive capacity of land can be improved to meet economic and environmental goals in sustainable ways. Indeed, they reveal the degree to which land resources are being utilized to simultaneously attain these multiple goals, along with the trade-offs and synergies among the goals.

How efficiently does the world use its land-based natural endowments?

Several complementary statistics can help countries assess opportunities for gaining efficiency and identify where trade-offs emerge. This chapter begins by presenting a landscape efficiency score, which is a *summary statistic* identifying where a country currently stands in relation to the overall efficiency frontier. This statistic combines performance across three dimensions: (1) economic returns from agriculture, grazing, and forestry; (2) greenhouse gas storage; and (3) biodiversity. This composite indicator serves as the big picture—that is, the magnitude of potential gains jointly possible across the three components of net economic returns, GHG storage, and biodiversity. Although aggregate measures may serve as a useful summary, they are usually of limited policy relevance because performance is unlikely to be uniform across all of their components. Thus disaggregated measures of efficiency gaps are provided for each of the score's dimensions (net economic returns, GHG storage, and biodiversity) to examine performance at the dimension level. These measures help identify where there is scope for improvement to guide country-specific policies. Gaps between actual outputs and potential outputs emerge for familiar reasons such as under-investment; the inefficient use of natural endowments (such as water, forests, or land); and the use of land for other than its most productive potential. Once a country reaches its efficiency frontier, trade-offs necessarily emerge.

The results reveal a typology of countries:

- Countries experiencing significant efficiency gaps in economic performance, suggesting it is possible to produce more (marketed) output with the given set of inputs without using resources in unsustainable ways.

- Countries with a large scope to improve the provision of nonmarketed environ-mental services, often through the spatial reallocation of economic activities.

- Countries with large opportunities to improve efficiency in both the marketed and nonmarketed domains.

- Countries that are on or close to their efficiency frontiers where trade-offs are unavoidable and increasing one kind of output will entail sacrificing another.

Landscape efficiency scores

As described in chapter 2, landscape efficiency scores summarize how a country is performing relative to what is possible across two key environmental services (greenhouse gas mitigation and biodiversity) and marketed benefits (agricul-tural crop production, grazing, and forestry)—see box 2.2 in chapter 2 for the method of calculation and appendix A for the scores by country. The scores are to be used to compare each country's actual performance with its own potential performance and not with that of other countries. Cross-country comparisons may not be appropriate because of differences in endowments and circumstances. Some countries may be close to their efficiency frontier simply because they have few alternatives for land use, such as countries that are too dry or too cold for crop cultivation or forestry. Others may be close to their frontiers because they implement good policies. This chapter thus avoids such cross-country compar-isons beyond generalization about country clusters, focusing instead on how countries perform relative to their maximum potential.

The distribution of landscape efficiency scores across countries reveals in general very significant variation, with scores ranging from just over 60 percent to over 99 percent.[2] Figure 3.1 shows the distribution of scores by World Bank country income classification. Variation within country income groups dominates the variation across groups, implying that the aggregate levels of efficiency are not determined merely by development level. It may be, then, that alternative classification types are more useful for understanding the determinants of these scores than income classification.

FIGURE 3.1
Distribution of landscape efficiency scores, by country income group

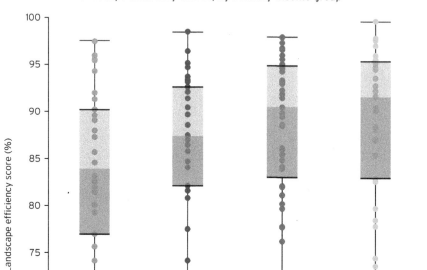

Source: World Bank.
Note: Circles represent individual country scores. The mean value across countries in each income group is indicated by the horizontal line that extends across the box. Inside the box, the upper, light blue portion is the second quartile (25th–50th percentile), and the lower, dark blue portion is the third quartile (50th–75th percentile). Outer lines are useful for identifying outliers.

The aggregate landscape efficiency score conceals much of the variation driving these scores. This factor is demonstrated in table 3.1, which breaks down the efficiency scores into their three components.[3] Specifically, these scores show how much better a country can perform in a single dimension, while holding performance in the other two dimensions constant—a Pareto improvement. For example, a 50 percent economic efficiency score (the green bars in figures in annex 3A) implies that through better policies and investments a country could conceivably double the net value of its output in terms of crops, grazing, and timber while holding greenhouse gas mitigation and biodiversity constant and not using resources such as water or land unsustainably. These results include the

TABLE 3.1

Landscape efficiency scores, by country income group

Country income group	(1) Mean economic efficiency within the Pareto space[a] (%)	(2) Mean carbon efficiency within the Pareto space (%)	(3) Mean biodiversity efficiency within the Pareto space (%)
Low income	47.5	74.2	77.6
Lower-middle income	51.7	78.9	81.0
Upper-middle income	55.1	83.0	84.9
High income	72.6	77.9	86.6

Source: World Bank.
Note: Numbers closer to 100 indicate higher levels of efficiency.
a. The Pareto space refers to outcomes where improvements in one of the key dimensions can be made without sacrifice in the other two dimensions.

key transition costs (see section B.4 of the online technical appendix for details). Typically, high-income countries perform significantly better on the economic components (crops, livestock, and timber) than middle-income and low-income countries (column 1 of table 3.1). The performance of low-income countries is weaker across all three efficiency measures, with the largest gap in the economic efficiency score. This result suggests that low-income countries, where agricultural yields systematically lag those of other income groups, can increase rural incomes without sacrificing natural capital, where natural endowments permit.

The geographic distribution of scores across the World Bank classification of regions is shown in figure 3.2. Once more, the mean landscape efficiency score exhibits limited variation *across* regions and much more variation *within* regions. Table 3.2 decomposes these aggregate scores into their subcomponents. Although there is much variation across regions, countries in the Middle East and North Africa and Europe and Central Asia tend to score better in economic efficiency than those in most other regions—with the caveat that these averages conceal large differences. South Asia performs, on average, relatively low in all three dimensions (reflected as well in the low average landscape efficiency score of 75.4 percent in figure 3.2), indicating a trend in countries that have a high population density, relatively low proportions of land as natural habitat, and relatively high yield gaps (the difference between actual and potential yields). With a large proportion of often marginal land converted to agriculture, these countries are far from the efficiency frontier in the production of environmental services, and with low yields they are also at a considerable distance from their maximum economic potential. Such observations give insights into the typology of countries discussed in the next section.

Maps 3.1 and 3.2 summarize some of the findings by displaying the distribution of country scores across the three key dimensions. Map 3.1 shows how well each country performs in terms of economic efficiency and carbon

FIGURE 3.2
Distribution of landscape efficiency scores, by region

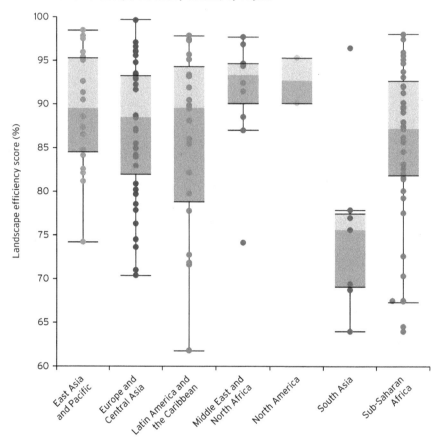

Source: World Bank.
Note: Circles represent individual country scores. The mean value across countries in each income group is indicated by the horizontal line that extends across the box. Inside the box, the upper, light blue portion is the second quartile (25th–50th percentile), and the lower, dark blue portion is the third quartile (50th–75th percentile). Outer lines are useful for identifying outliers.

sequestration efficiency. The scores on each dimension indicate the gains that could be made through improvements in efficiency without sacrificing any other output (the Pareto space). Map 3.2 shows economic efficiency and biodiversity efficiency scores, which summarize the extent of gains feasible in one dimension without lowering scores in any other dimension considered (the Pareto space). The maps again highlight that performance is not systematically related to either development level or region. Thus the next section identifies clusters of countries based on their performance rather than region or income level.

TABLE 3.2
Landscape efficiency scores, by region

Region	Mean economic efficiency within the Pareto space (%)	Mean carbon efficiency within the Pareto space (%)	Mean biodiversity efficiency within the Pareto space (%)
East Asia and Pacific	62.8	83.7	86.1
Europe and Central Asia	72.3	75.2	87.5
Latin America and the Caribbean	37.4	82.0	83.3
Middle East and North Africa	76.9	83.5	79.4
South Asia	53.0	60.2	79.2
Sub-Saharan Africa	46.7	79.8	78.2

Source: World Bank.
Note: Numbers closer to 100 indicate higher levels of efficiency.

MAP 3.1
Country performance across economic efficiency and carbon sequestration efficiency in Pareto spaces

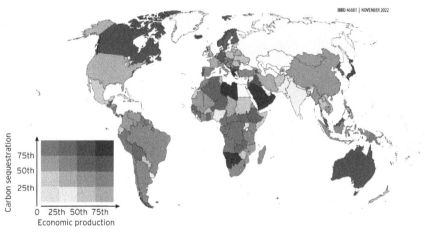

Source: World Bank.
Note: No data is available for the countries shaded in the palest gray.

In addition, the maps demonstrate that most countries have the scope to make significant improvements in one or several of the three dimensions investigated, while maintaining scores on the other dimensions. Although there is variation, the average of the minimum Pareto scores across countries is 54 percent, indicating that, on average, countries can almost double at least one dimension without reducing any other dimension. For most low-income countries, significant increases in net economic returns are possible without sacrificing environmental quality. In many high-income countries, substantial increases in greenhouse gas mitigation or biodiversity can be made without sacrificing net economic returns.

MAP 3.2
Country performance across economic efficiency and biodiversity efficiency in Pareto spaces

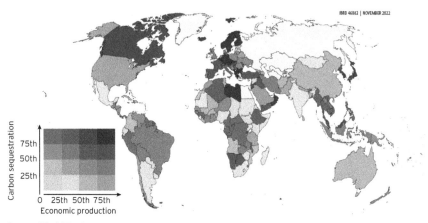

Source: World Bank.
Note: No data is available for the countries shaded in the palest gray.

A typology

If development level and region do little to explain the variation in landscape efficiency scores, what else might explain the differences across countries? The relationship is more complex. It implies that countries rich and poor alike have opportunities to improve the efficiency of landscapes with limited opportunity costs. This section describes a five-part typology of countries that determines how much scope countries have to improve their natural capital efficiency and economic and environmental outcomes. The five clusters are summarized in figure 3.3, which shows where efficiency improvements may emerge relative to each country's own efficiency frontier.

A. High-income, highly efficient countries

Group A in figure 3.3 is composed of high-income countries with highly efficient economies. These countries include most of the advanced economies in the European Union (EU) and the Organisation for Economic Co-operation and Development. They tend to be close to their maximum potential in terms of the economic indicators, despite not necessarily performing uniformly well on one or more of the environmental dimensions. For these countries, significant shifts to a more environmentally friendly landscape that mitigates more GHGs and preserves more biodiversity might require economic trade-offs. Nevertheless, some Pareto shifts (efficiency improvements) are still possible in many cases.

FIGURE 3.3
Typology of countries, by environmental indicator and production value

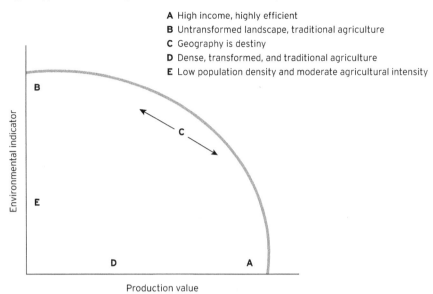

A High income, highly efficient
B Untransformed landscape, traditional agriculture
C Geography is destiny
D Dense, transformed, and traditional agriculture
E Low population density and moderate agricultural intensity

Source: World Bank.

Figure 3.4 demonstrates this result for one such high-income EU country, Sweden. It compares this country's economic efficiency (horizontal axis) with a composite environmental efficiency score that combines biodiversity and GHG sequestration (vertical axis). The graph clearly shows that the high efficiency score results from the country's economic production value being very close to its maximum possible score. By holding economic production constant, it is possible for the country to shift upward and increase environmental services. Nevertheless, shifts above this—such as shifts above a score of 0.6 in the normalized environmental score, which would put Sweden in the range of sequestering 3 billion metric tons of carbon dioxide equivalent (CO_2eq) or more—would require trade-offs (that is, moving left and upward toward the frontier) because the economic production value would have to decline.

B. Untransformed landscape, traditional agriculture

Perhaps the single best predictor of the landscape efficiency score of this group of countries is the percentage of land within a country that is natural habitat (that is, land that is not in cropland, grazing, forestry, or urban). Countries with more than two-thirds of their land in natural habitat almost uniformly have high landscape efficiency scores higher than 90 percent. These countries—which include many West African countries and some in

FIGURE 3.4
Efficiency frontier of a high-income country realizing most of its potential economic gains: Sweden

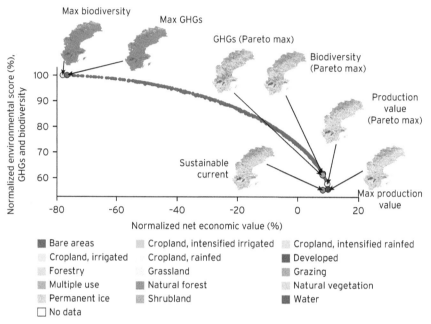

Source: World Bank.
Note: The blue dots trace the efficiency (production possibility) frontier. The interior (brown) dot shows the country's current position, and the various other dots represent achievable places on the frontier that maximize different objectives in the Pareto space. The maps that surround the efficiency frontier show alternative landscapes and intensities of use for Sweden that result in a more efficient use of its natural endowments. GHGs = greenhouse gases.

the Amazon—tend to perform close to their maximum potential on the environmental indicators because they have large land areas devoted to natural forests and so they sequester large amounts of carbon per unit of land and support critical biodiversity. However, many of these countries do not score as well on the economic indicator and thus have room to improve economic productivity, mainly by increasing the intensity of agriculture to close yield gaps (see box 3.1 for a closer look at Liberia). Going beyond this would require extensification that may lead to significant environmental trade-offs unless there is misallocation of land use.

A particularly extreme example in this category is Suriname. Some 93 percent of Suriname's land is in its natural state (that is, not converted to agriculture, cities, commercial forestry, or grazing). Figure 3.5 shows Suriname's efficiency frontier. The country is currently close to achieving its maximum producible GHG sequestration and biodiversity-related services (over 90 percent of the maximum). However, the value of production could

BOX 3.1
Maximizing efficient landscapes in Liberia

The challenge and importance of moving toward efficient landscapes is exemplified in Liberia. This West African nation has among the lowest per capita gross domestic product in the world, US$632 in 2019 or less than US$2 per day on average. This figure stands in stark contrast to the country's original rich natural capital. Its landscape was populated with lush rainforests, rich biodiversity, and fertile soils. But because of vicious cycles of poverty, natural resource degradation, and conflict, much of that natural capital has been degraded or destroyed (see figure B3.1.1, where a map shows the country's current land cover and land use). Much of the forests in the central part of the country were removed for charcoal or shifting agriculture and so are now unproductive shrubland or grassland or devoted to low-intensity agriculture.

The maps that surround the efficiency frontier (blue curve) show alternative landscapes and intensities of use for Liberia that result in a more efficient use of its natural endowments. In the map at the extreme top left, Liberia maximizes its biodiversity through the planting and conservation of natural forests at the expense of most of its economic production. The map at the bottom right shows the opposite; most forests and natural lands are removed and replaced with intensified, rainfed agriculture.

More interesting are the three maps showing the Pareto results. Of these, the leftmost map shows a scenario in which economic production and biodiversity are held constant, but greenhouse gas (GHG) sequestration is maximized. In such a scenario, GHG sequestration

FIGURE B3.1.1
Efficiency frontier: Liberia

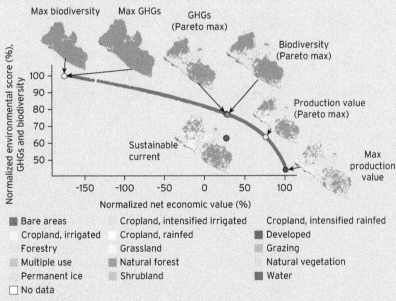

Source: World Bank.
Note: The blue line represents the efficiency frontier. The interior (brown) dot shows the country's current position, and the various other dots represent achievable places on the frontier that maximize different objectives in the Pareto space. The maps that surround the efficiency frontier show alternative landscapes and intensities of use for Liberia that result in a more efficient use of its natural endowments. GHGs = greenhouse gases.

Continued

Box 3.1
Continued

in Liberia increases by 1 billion metric tons of carbon dioxide equivalent (CO_2eq), from 3.6 billion to 4.6 billion. This figure represents over 83 years of business-as-usual annual emissions at the 2030 level.[a]

The center map shows a scenario in which GHG sequestration and economic production are held constant but biodiversity is maximized. This scenario, which is very close to the GHG sequestration Pareto max scenario, assumes an expansion of sustainable forestry and restoration of natural forests, allowing for production gains while safeguarding and restoring biodiversity.

The third Pareto map depicts a scenario in which GHG sequestration and biodiversity are held constant, and economic production from agriculture, grazing, and forestry is maximized. Under this scenario, net economic production could increase from US$174 million (the sustainable current scenario) to US$495 million for an increase of US$321 million without compromising existing biodiversity or increasing greenhouse gas emissions.

a. From Liberia's revised nationally determined contribution (NDC) of August 2021.

FIGURE 3.5
Efficiency frontier of a country with largely intact ecosystems: Suriname

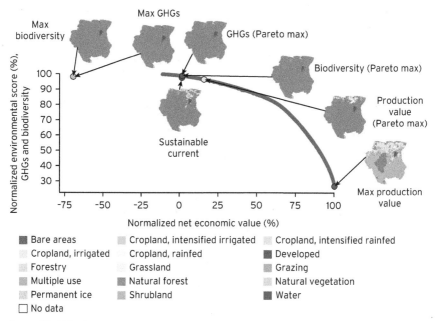

Source: World Bank.
Note: The blue line represents the efficiency frontier. The interior (brown) dot shows the country's current position, and the various other dots represent achievable places on the frontier that maximize different objectives in the Pareto space. The maps that surround the efficiency frontier show alternative landscapes and intensities of use for Suriname that result in a more efficient use of its natural endowments. GHGs = greenhouse gases.

increase significantly (more than tenfold) without environmental trade-offs by shifting from the current configuration to that of maximizing the value of production in the Pareto space. Any increase beyond that point would result in a loss of carbon storage and biodiversity.

Other countries with a large endowment of forests could also find ways to generate growth through nonconsumptive forest uses such as tourism and to improve the economic productivity of land. Many countries in the Congo Basin are in this category. In recent years most of these countries, with the notable exception of Gabon, have turned from net sinks to net sources of GHG emissions.[4] Finding ways to reconcile growth without degrading forest cover in these regions will be pivotal to meeting global climate goals because there is no feasible pathway to these ambitions without addressing deforestation. This report identifies where such opportunities for growth without deforestation lie in these and other countries.

C. Countries where geography is destiny

This group of countries, located close to or on the efficiency frontier in figure 3.3, include a mix of countries that have large deserts, are close to the Arctic, or otherwise have inhospitable terrain. A common characteristic of these countries is extreme climatic conditions that make agriculture difficult and limit the number of plant and animal species that can survive. Thus such countries may perform close to their maximum potential across both environmental and economic metrics. Because of their low population densities, mountainous terrain, extreme cold, or extreme heat with low precipitation such as in deserts, it is unlikely that much of the land in these countries could be sustainably developed for agriculture. Even if their land were converted to agricultural uses, it would likely become unproductive because of a fragile resource base and would involve steep trade-offs. Thus countries in this category will often appear close to their frontier in most of the dimensions because of their geographic constraints. In short, when very little production is possible, these countries will be efficient.

For example, Iceland, the country with the world's highest landscape efficiency score, has a very low population density with rugged terrain and a climate not always conducive to agriculture. Such countries usually improve their environmental scores by retiring land from, for example, grazing, which improves biodiversity conservation and carbon storage but reduces its production value. Conversely, the only way to significantly increase its production value is to increase, say, grazing, which reduces its already limited biodiversity score and carbon storage performance. Thus movements in any single dimension would require significant trade-offs in the other dimensions.

This is illustrated in figure 3.6, which shows Iceland's efficiency frontier and the changes in patterns of production. The sharp kink in Iceland's efficiency frontier indicates that at every point there are sharp trade-offs between the economic and environmental dimensions.

D. Dense, transformed, and traditional agriculture

These mostly low- and lower-middle-income countries have high population densities, have converted large shares of their natural lands to other uses, and are lacking in intensified agriculture. Often, too, the location of agricultural activity may not correlate with agronomic potential. For example, many highly populated arid developing country regions have a high dependence on water-thirsty crops such as rice, sugarcane, and cotton. This group is composed of middle-income countries in Asia and Africa. These countries tend to be quite far from their frontier in both the economic and environmental indicators. By intensifying agriculture and adopting more modern technologies such as improved seeds, fertilizers, and mechanization, they could increase the yield efficiency of converted lands. In many countries, spatial reallocation of production could also improve productivity across multiple dimensions. This reallocation would give

FIGURE 3.6
Efficiency frontier: Iceland

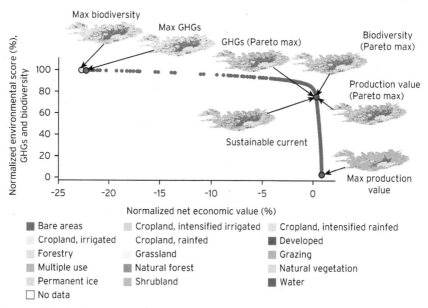

Source: World Bank.
Note: The blue dots trace the efficiency frontier. The interior (brown) dot shows the country's current position, and the various other dots represent achievable places on the frontier that maximize different objectives in the Pareto space. The maps that surround the efficiency frontier show alternative landscapes and intensities of use for Iceland that result in a more efficient use of its natural endowments. GHGs = greenhouse gases.

these countries more freedom either to return current lands to their natural state where they could provide ecosystem services such as carbon sequestration, pollination, flood management, and biodiversity support, or to maintain cultivation and significantly increase their land's economic productivity.

Figure 3.7 illustrates the potential for improvement in landscape efficiency using shifts in the intensive and extensive margin for Haiti. It has a relatively low landscape efficiency score, indicating a large potential for improvement. Haiti has gone through decades of land clearing and land degradation, resulting in a nearly complete loss of its natural forests and a significant loss of the ability of the land to support agriculture. In figure 3.7, this situation is reflected in the sustainable current map, which shows that much of the land is currently grassland, which generates little to no economic production, nor does it support significant levels of biodiversity or carbon sequestration. Therefore, it is not surprising that Haiti is far from its frontier in both the economic and environmental dimensions. Analysis of the efficiency frontier reveals that Haiti could increase its production value by orders of magnitude with no impact on environmental outcomes through

FIGURE 3.7
Efficiency frontier: Haiti

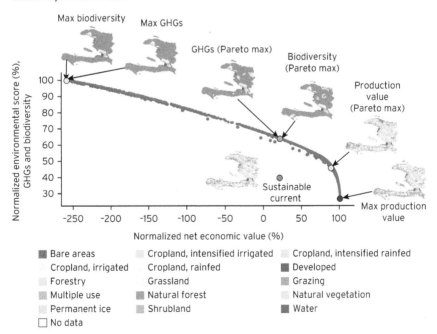

Source: World Bank.
Note: The blue dots trace the efficiency frontier. The interior (brown) dot shows the country's current position, and the various other dots represent achievable places on the frontier that maximize different objectives in the Pareto space. The maps that surround the efficiency frontier show alternative landscapes and intensities of use for Haiti that result in a more efficient use of its natural endowments. GHGs = greenhouse gases.

both significant extensification and intensification of agricultural production. Conversely, by replanting forests and adopting better land management, Haiti could more than double its GHG sequestration without reducing the land's economic production. Moreover, Haiti has many intermediate pathways in which both its economic production and environmental dimensions could increase significantly.

E. Low population density and moderate agricultural intensity

This mix of high-income and low- and middle-income countries tends to have low population densities and large extents of uncultivated terrain, some of which may be devoted to cattle production. Wealthier countries in this group, but also some lower-income countries, tend to have large grasslands, which are not particularly efficient at sequestering carbon or supporting biodiversity, nor do they maximize economic gains. Other countries, such as the Lao People's Democratic Republic, are inefficiently allocating land between economic and environmental sectors.

In Lao PDR, the current landscape score (the brown dot in figure 3.8) lies well inside the efficiency frontier. This country could significantly improve its

FIGURE 3.8
Efficiency frontier: Lao People's Democratic Republic

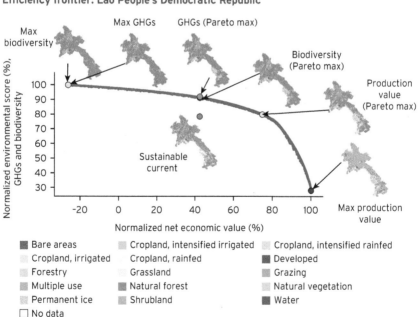

Bare areas
Cropland, irrigated
Forestry
Multiple use
Permanent ice
No data

Cropland, intensified irrigated
Cropland, rainfed
Grassland
Natural forest
Shrubland

Cropland, intensified rainfed
Developed
Grazing
Natural vegetation
Water

Source: World Bank.
Note: The blue line represents the efficiency frontier. The interior (brown) dot shows the country's current position, and the various other dots represent achievable places on the frontier that maximize different objectives in the Pareto space. The maps that surround the efficiency frontier show alternative landscapes and intensities of use for Lao PDR that result in a more efficient use of its natural endowments. GHGs = greenhouse gases.

biodiversity and carbon storage without reducing its monetary returns (vertical movements in figure 3.8). Increases in biodiversity conservation also tend to yield increases in carbon storage and vice versa. These gains can be achieved by (1) relocating agricultural production to areas with higher fertility and away from areas with high carbon storage and biodiversity potential, and (2) intensifying agricultural production to increase yields so that a smaller area will produce the same amount of crops. The landscape that maximizes either carbon storage or biodiversity while maintaining the current value of market returns will require intensifying agriculture to increase yields in two areas near the Thai border, while returning some agricultural land to forest in other parts of the country (figure 3.8).

It is also possible to accommodate significant economic development and still improve biodiversity and carbon storage (movement up and to the right in figure 3.8). In Lao PDR, even larger improvements can be made in production value without losing any biodiversity conservation or carbon storage outputs (horizontal movements in figure 3.8). Indeed, a twofold potential increase in production value could largely come from intensification to close yield gaps. Combining yield increases and movement of agricultural production to areas of high fertility and away from areas of high carbon storage or biodiversity conservation potential could lead to improvements in all dimensions: production value, biodiversity conservation, and carbon storage.

Efficiency gains for achieving global carbon goals

Substantial gains in biodiversity, carbon storage, and production value could be achieved jointly through efficiency improvements in some countries (see maps 3.1 and 3.2). Agriculture, forestry, and other land uses contributed an estimated 23 percent of total GHG emissions over the period 2007–16 (IPCC 2019). Particularly important in the context of climate change is the potential for nature-based solutions (Griscom et al. 2017) to offer carbon storage opportunities without detrimentally affecting other important services offered by the landscape (such as monetary returns and biodiversity). Restoration of natural habitats can increase the amount of carbon sequestered, making land use a sink rather than a source of greenhouse gases. The efficiency frontier can identify the scope for improving carbon sequestration potential by improving land use and land management without diminishing other services.

Within the framework of this study, countries can increase their sequestration and reduce their emissions of CO_2eq in three ways. First, return land to natural habitat from agriculture, grazing, or forestry. In doing so, land formerly used to produce crops, livestock, or timber can increase carbon storage and see lower emissions of methane. To maintain production value, however, offsetting increases would have to occur in the value of production elsewhere by increasing the intensity of production on the remaining economic lands. Second, shift land to more efficient uses. Land that has a high ratio of carbon storage potential to crop production could be shifted to natural habitat, and land with a low ratio could be put into crop production. Similarly, land could be shifted among productive uses (cultivation, grazing, and forestry) to achieve higher combinations of production value and carbon storage. And, third, alter grazing to reduce the amount of methane produced by livestock.

The models used in this analysis indicate that across the 147 countries examined, the current GHG storage capacity is 429 billion metric tons of CO_2eq, which is comparable to the Intergovernmental Panel on Climate Change (IPCC) estimate for 2000 of 466 billion metric tons of CO_2eq (IPCC 2000) for carbon stored in terrestrial vegetation for all lands. By choosing land use and land management to maximize GHG storage, this amount can be increased to 605 billion metric tons of CO_2eq, an increase of 176 billion metric tons (see figure 3.9). Some of this gain in GHG storage would come at the cost of other objectives, such as less production value. Restricting attention to potential gains within the Pareto space brings the feasible maximum potential gain for the 147 countries to 78.1 billion metric tons of CO_2eq, or about 45 percent of the total maximum potential gains (see figure 3.9). If the same average ratio is

FIGURE 3.9
Illustration of maximum potential and Pareto increase in GHG mitigation

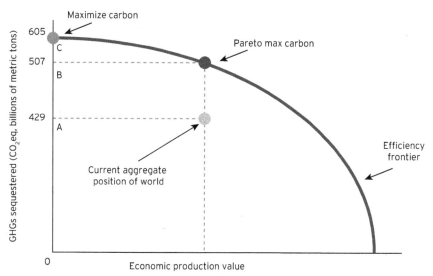

Source: World Bank.
Note: CO_2eq = carbon dioxide equivalent; GHGs = greenhouse gases.

applied to countries not included in this study, the GHG sequestration potential would rise to 85.6 billion metric tons of CO_2eq. To provide context, total annual global emissions of GHG from all sources (fossil fuel burning and land use) are estimated at approximately 50 billion metric tons (Our World in Data 2021). Thus, realizing the increase in GHG mitigation from land use and land management within the Pareto space would be equivalent to 1.7 years of global carbon emissions.

The estimates of GHG mitigation potential are an indication of the total amount mitigated over time (with a 20-year time horizon) by means of changes in land use and land management. In a comparable exercise, Griscom et al. (2017) estimate the potential for sequestration from "nature-based solutions." The 20 land management strategies include changes in agricultural practices, natural habitat conservation, and forest restoration. They estimate that the 20 strategies could sequester 23.8 billion metric tons of CO_2 per year. When constrained to implementing more cost-effective strategies at a carbon price of US$100 per metric ton of CO_2, Griscom et al. (2017) estimate carbon sequestration of 11.3 billion metric tons per year. The ratio of the amount of cost-effective to total potential GHG sequestered is 47 percent, which is similar to the 45 percent ratio of Pareto maximum gains to maximum gains in this study. Aggregating their annual sequestration over a 20-year horizon, the Griscom et al. (2017) estimates generate a savings of 476 billion metric tons (unconstrained by the carbon price) and 226 billion metric tons (constrained by the carbon price). This estimate is about 30 percent higher than prior estimates (IPCC 2014; Smith et al. 2013), mostly because Griscom et al. expand the set of strategies considered. Similarly, the GHG savings reported by Griscom et al. (2017) is higher than the estimates derived in this study because Griscom et al. include a wider set of strategies and do not constrain possibilities to the Pareto space. This possibility is not considered in most simulation exercises, which explains the differences (Peña-Lévano, Taheripour, and Tyner 2019).[5]

In scenarios whose goal is to maximize GHG storage, irrespective of the cost and losses, the additional 176 billion metric tons of CO_2eq stored is achieved by increasing the amount of natural land by almost 50 million hectares, which represents almost a doubling of natural area (a 97 percent increase). Most of the increase in carbon storage occurs in a handful of countries, which include those with the potential to increase agricultural yields while enabling forest restoration. By contrast, in the Pareto space the gain in GHG storage is 78 billion metric tons of CO_2eq. This gain is achieved by increasing the amount of natural land by just over 30 million hectares. Box 3.2 indicates that if land-based GHG sequestration is recognized and rewarded, then low-income countries, because of their relative comparative advantages, would be the greatest beneficiaries. The policy implication is parallel poverty reduction and global environmental goals.

BOX 3.2
The relative gains to low-income countries from improved allocation decisions

An established literature in macroeconomics uses conventional general equilibrium models to estimate the economic losses from factor market misallocation (Adamopoulos and Restuccia 2014; Hsieh and Klenow 2009). A common finding of that literature is that the welfare losses from misallocation are extremely large. This box extends this approach to consider welfare changes from land misallocation in the presence of environmental externalities.

The parsimonious general equilibrium model detailed in section B.6 of the online technical appendix[a] features an economy embedded in nature that recognizes the environmental benefits provided by natural land cover. The model is used to explore a counterfactual in which the greenhouse gas (GHG) sequestration services of forests and landscapes are recognized in factor market allocation decisions and compared with a benchmark where they are not recognized.

The results summarized in table B3.1.1 show that when carbon sequestration from land has economic value, all countries benefit, but low-income countries benefit the most. This result mainly stems from the very different comparative advantages of high- and low-income countries. High-income countries have a comparative advantage in agricultural production and low-income countries in land-based carbon sequestration. By extension, a policy that recognizes and rewards GHG sequestration disproportionately benefits low-income countries. The implication is that such environmental policies would simultaneously contribute to development needs and poverty reduction goals, as well as local environmental objectives through protection of watersheds, pollination services, and other provisioning services, as well as help to achieve global environmental goals through GHG sequestration services.

TABLE B3.1.1
Average welfare gains from policies that recognize GHG sequestration services in factor market allocation decisions

Country income group	Normalized welfare
High income	1.0
Upper-middle income	1.1
Lower-middle income	1.2
Low income	1.4
Lungs of the planet	
Amazon rainforest	1.1
Congo Basin	1.3

Source: World Bank.
Note: Welfare is the relative change in welfare, normalizing high-income countries as 1.0 after a policy change that internalizes the sequestration benefits of land cover through a shadow price on GHGs. The aggregate welfare gains from this policy change in all groups are shown in the online technical appendix, section B.6. By definition, correcting externalities involves a move closer to the optimal outcome.

This finding is of critical development importance because it shows that the current and prospective sequestration potential of land can confer very substantial benefits on low-income countries and would constitute a win-win for both development and global climate change goals. Notable are the welfare gains for countries in the Amazon rainforest and Congo Basin regions, known as the lungs of the planet. These regions experience significant benefits in welfare by recognizing the role of land cover.

a. The online technical appendix (appendix B) is available with the text of this book in the World Bank's Online Knowledge Repository, https://openknowledge.worldbank.org/handle/10986/39453.

Efficiency gains for achieving economic development and food security goals

The efficiency frontier can be used to find the maximum possible increase in production value without loss of biodiversity or GHG storage potential (that is, the Pareto space options). These amounts are then summed across all countries to obtain a global estimate of the potential increase in economic production across sustainable forestry, agriculture, and animal products from improved land use and land management (figure 3.10). The value of economic production could be increased across these sectors by US$535 billion per year if economic production were maximized without regard for the costs of reduced biodiversity and carbon sequestration. In the more restricted Pareto space where there are no environmental losses, the increase is still US$329 billion per year, or 78 percent of the maximum achievable. These results imply that enormous opportunities are available to increase economic outputs, and especially meet growing food security challenges, without further encroaching on the environment and ecosystem services.

FIGURE 3.10
Illustration of maximum potential and Pareto increase in economic production

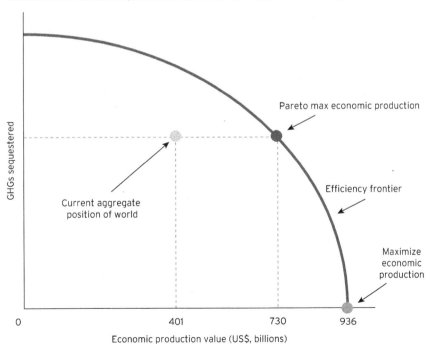

Source: World Bank.
Note: GHGs = greenhouse gases.

Perhaps more important than the value of net production is the impact that increasing efficiency can have on total calories produced. Several studies have attempted to estimate how much population and economic growth will increase the demand for food (Searchinger et al. 2019; Tallis et al. 2018; Tilman et al. 2011; van Vuuren et al. 2015). Although time periods, modeling techniques, and assumptions vary, most studies find that an increase in food production of between 50 and 100 percent will be needed to meet food demand by 2050. Under the scenario in which economic production is maximized in a Pareto way, the results indicate that calorie production would increase by 152 percent, well above even the most pessimistic estimates of what will be needed to feed the world by 2050. This scenario also assumes continuation of the current technology frontier. Advances in agronomy over the next 30 years will almost certainly make achieving these goals easier. On the other hand, climate change will likely shift the efficiency frontier inward in many areas where a changing climate will make agriculture more difficult. Nevertheless, this prediction also demonstrates why, for most countries, achieving food security goals need not require a shift fully to the right—that is, one in which economic production is maximized and environmental services are held constant. Instead, economic and environmental gains can be targeted in tandem, promoting more balanced growth and achieving a fuller suite of global priorities.

Similar to the carbon results, increases in economic production value can be achieved in three ways. First, more land can be devoted to economic production. Second, land can be shifted from less economically productive land use to more economically productive land use. And, third, land can be used more intensively by, for example, increasing the amount of inputs used in cultivation or using grazing patterns that are closer to optimal levels of land use. In the Pareto space, 55.3 percent of the gain is from intensification of economic lands, whereas the residual 44.7 percent is from better spatial planning and extensification, including reallocation of production. Like the carbon results, the increases in economic output are governed by natural potential, land availability, inputs, and management techniques. The gains are from countries across all income groups and regions.

Figure 3.11 shows the distribution by country income group of economic efficiency scores in the Pareto space. Most low- and middle-income countries achieve less than half of their Pareto potential, whereas high-income countries achieve, on average, 70 percent. There is thus considerable scope for lower-income countries to "catch up" in economic production without degrading their environments. Catching up to richer countries would mean enormous benefits in terms of economic growth, rural development, and food security, without the downsides of environmental damages. This finding is consistent with other exercises that investigate differences between actual and potential production and find larger yield and total factor productivity

FIGURE 3.11
Distribution of economic efficiency scores within the Pareto space, by country income group

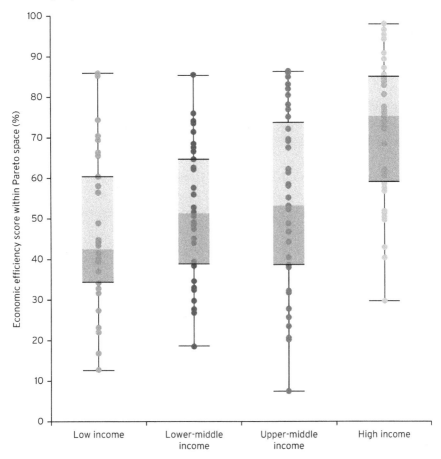

Source: World Bank.
Note: Circles represent individual country scores. The mean value across countries in each income group is indicated by the horizontal line that extends across the box. Inside the box, the upper, light blue portion is the second quartile (25th–50th percentile), and the lower, dark blue portion is the third quartile (50th–75th percentile). Outer lines are useful for identifying outliers.

gaps in lower-income countries. Although potential gains are large, they will require difficult reforms, and, in some contexts, there is insufficient evidence on policy effectiveness.

Currently, the value of the yield gap between high- and low-income countries is US$88.92 per hectare, with high-income countries, on average, producing US$142.37 per hectare and low-income countries producing US$53.47 per hectare. If all countries were to achieve their Pareto maximum for economic efficiency, those yields change to US$129.04 per hectare for low-income countries and US$212.00 per hectare for high-income countries. The result is a proportionately greater increase in benefits accruing to low-income countries relative to the status quo.

Efficiency gains, biodiversity, and ecosystem services

This section examines the dynamics of biodiversity scores. As noted earlier, one of the most reliable indicators for how a country performs on the overall landscape efficiency score is the percentage of land left in its natural state. Use of this indicator is not surprising because undisturbed land will function close to its natural potential in terms of greenhouse gas sequestered and biodiversity supported, putting the landscape closer to the frontier. The results offer some new insights into opportunities for halting the rapid losses of biodiversity.

Figure 3.12 plots countries' biodiversity scores as a share of the maximum attainable when not restricted to the Pareto scenarios against the percentage of land in a seminatural state. "Seminatural state" refers here to land that is not cropland or urban land but could include grazing land or forests. Although the results reveal that countries with higher shares of seminatural land typically perform better on their biodiversity scores, there is significant heterogeneity. Some countries (in the bottom right of the graph) have very high percentages of seminatural land, and yet they perform poorly on the biodiversity score for two possible reasons. First, the lands that have been converted for use in economic

FIGURE 3.12
Biodiversity scores versus land in a seminatural state

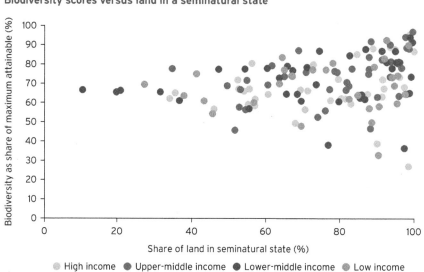

Source: World Bank.
Note: Each dot represents a country in a designated country income group.

activity (crop production, livestock grazing, or forestry) are very valuable in terms of how much biodiversity they can support. For example, in the Middle East's extremely arid biomes, only a small share of the land can support significant biodiversity. If that small share of land is converted to economic uses and loses its biodiversity, the biodiversity score falls significantly, despite most of the land remaining in its natural state. A second possible reason a country may fall in this category is if much of its land has not recovered from previous degradation or deforestation. The land may currently be in an unused state classified as "natural." However, its ability to support biodiversity has been lost, or it has not yet had sufficient time to recover. After sufficient time and perhaps some efforts toward land restoration and the reintroduction of critical species, the land's ability to support biodiversity could be restored.

Countries toward the left side of the graph have converted a large majority of their land to agriculture or urban lands, and yet still support more than 60 percent of their maximum potential biodiversity. There are two possible explanations for such a result. First, the country has preserved its more high-valued biodiversity lands, perhaps by strategically enforcing protected areas (PAs) or perhaps by sheer luck (chapter 4 reviews some of the evidence on PAs). The second possible explanation is that these are countries with low richness of native species and low phylogenetic diversity, so that the number and diversity of species lost on cultivated lands are limited. Nevertheless, the relationships show that development need not always come at the cost of a nation's biodiversity. Through strategic planning, the conversion of land into economic production can be achieved without placing a fatal strain on biodiversity.

Caveats and limitations of the data and methods

Compiling estimates of current performance and efficiency frontiers for all countries requires pushing methods and data to the frontiers of science in many areas. Although the notion of compiling an efficiency frontier is relatively straightforward, actually assembling the data and undertaking the analysis are challenging. It appears that this study is the first such attempt and that global data sets for biodiversity and for the market value of agricultural crops, grazing, and forestry have not yet been assembled. As with any new global analysis, improvements will eventually be needed in both data and methods. Further data collection and advances in methods will no doubt refine the results and improve their accuracy.

This study relies on globally available data so that the analysis is consistent across all countries. However, such an approach does not allow incorporation of specific factors important in some countries that could be analyzed using more detailed local data. For example, land use and land management options were constrained to a relatively small set of 14 options.[6] Because of the limited number of options, it is not possible to model all the land uses or land management practices that might be important in a particular country. The result is conservative estimates of efficiency scores (that is, allowing for more options would result in still larger gaps). Even with this limited number of options, the models used, together with the available data, were often at the limit of what could be reasonably predicted for all outcomes of interest (biodiversity, GHG mitigation, agricultural crop production, grazing, and forestry) under each management option. Annex 3C compares yield gap estimates derived in this report to those of the Global Agro-Ecological Zones product of the Food and Agriculture Organization and finds consistencies as well as differences predictably arising from the sustainability and economic value maximization used in this work. Outliers in that data set are also explained in greater detail.

Several possible improvements deserve special attention going forward in this area of study. Most improvements would arise from investments in better data. For agricultural crop production, grazing, and forestry, data on gross returns are available (revenue), but information on production costs is incomplete. Production cost data was sourced from the Global Trade Analysis Project (GTAP) database,[7] which is perhaps the most widely used and most complete data set on cost shares available on a global scale. (See section B.1.3 of the online technical appendix for full methodological details on how gross returns are converted into net returns by using the factor shares for land in GTAP.)

Grazing and forestry did not include multiple management options, whereas crop production did. For grazing, then, the stocking density is not varied, nor are rotational grazing or other alternative management options considered. For forestry, returns are modeled assuming even-age rotational harvest based on the estimated profit-maximizing rotation age. Thinning or other alternative management options are not considered. Future versions of this approach could allow multiple options for both grazing and forestry. However, doing so will require data and understanding of functional relationships that would allow estimating the impact of alternative management on biodiversity, GHG mitigation, and grazing or forestry returns.

One important way in which countries might be operating well inside their landscape efficiency frontier is when they have a significant portion of degraded land. Part of the effect of degraded lands is captured in areas where (1) the natural vegetation had been forest but is currently grassland or shrubland that is not being used for crop production or grazing (as in Haiti), or (2) the natural vegetation had been grassland or shrubland but is currently desert. However, in the available data the quality of natural forests and grassland is not adequately captured, nor are global data on soil quality systematically available. A very important element of natural capital is quality rather than just quantity, and so future work must try to better represent the aspects of quality that help determine its contribution to biodiversity, GHG mitigation, and production values.

The modeling efforts in this study employed current empirical relationships, which are adequate for understanding small perturbations of current conditions. However, large-scale changes in land use could cause major shifts in these empirical relationships, leading to large changes in the outcomes of interest (see box 1.1 on tipping points). In addition, climate change is likely to cause fundamental changes in ecosystems that will affect all outcomes of interest. Incorporating climate change is another frontier topic that deserves careful attention but is beyond the scope of this report.

The results presented here are based on models that examine the "steady state"—that is, when all variables and land uses are in equilibrium and are unchanging. Nevertheless, reaching that steady state will require a transitional period whether one is building a road, constructing a school, or transitioning landscapes to different land uses. The timing of the transition will vary based on physical and natural properties. Conversion to agriculture may generally be quicker than the conversion to forests. However, young forests tend to absorb more carbon overall because trees are packed more densely when they are small. In addition, where structural works are involved (such as irrigation), there is large variation in the speed of construction across countries. The timing of such transitions is therefore complicated, which is one reason why this study focuses on steady states.

Annex 3A: Additional results

This annex reports additional results based on the work presented in chapter 3.

FIGURE 3A.1
Results by country: Pareto efficiency scores

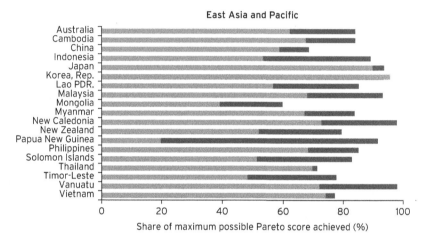

East Asia and Pacific

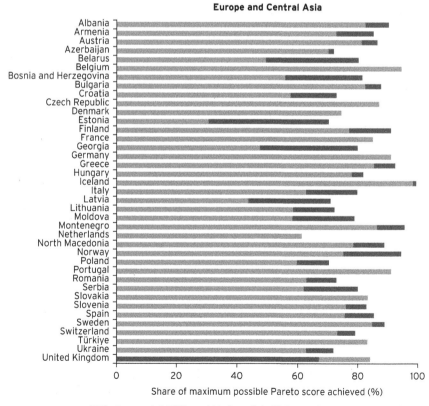

Europe and Central Asia

■ Environmental (GHGs and biodiversity) ■ Economic (net monetary returns)

Continued

FIGURE 3A.1
Continued

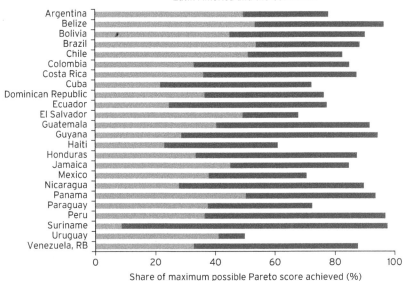

Latin America and the Caribbean

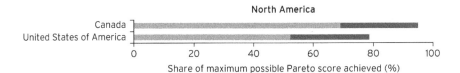

North America

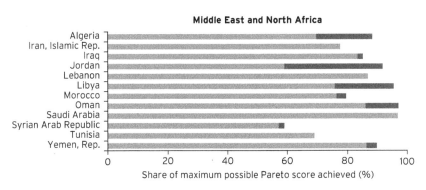

Middle East and North Africa

■ Environmental (GHGs and biodiversity) ▨ Economic (net monetary returns)

Continued

FIGURE 3A.1
Continued

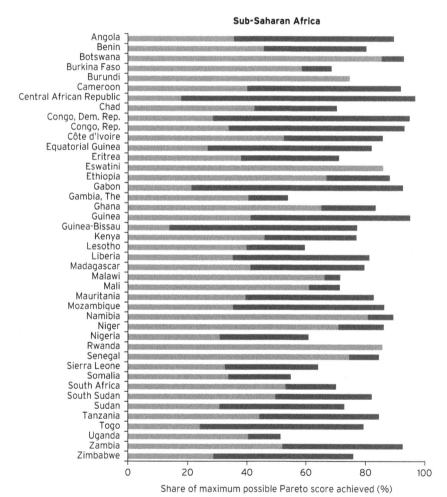

South Asia

Share of maximum possible Pareto score achieved (%)

Sub-Saharan Africa

Share of maximum possible Pareto score achieved (%)

■ Environmental (GHGs and biodiversity)　■ Economic (net monetary returns)

Note: GHGs = greenhouse gases.

Annex 3B: Nonmarket environmental scores: A further analysis of outcomes

This annex examines another aspect of the two nonmarket environmental components of the landscape efficiency score: carbon storage and biodiversity conservation. The aim is to determine the maximum possible outcomes for carbon storage and biodiversity conservation for each country when all land is conserved in its natural condition, which precludes land use for agriculture, grazing, and forestry. Such a scenario is unrealistic, but solving for it shows how much carbon storage and biodiversity conservation are possible, and how close or far to this maximum a country's performance is given its current land use and land management.

The average maximum possible scores across countries by country income group are shown in table 3B.1. The carbon storage and biodiversity scores increase from low-income to lower-middle-income to upper-middle-income countries, but they decrease from upper-middle-income to high-income countries. The lowest average scores for both carbon storage and biodiversity occur in the high-income countries.

For carbon storage and biodiversity conservation, the pattern across income groups is the exact opposite of what has been found in the environmental Kuznets curve literature on air and water pollution (Grossman and Krueger 1991; World Bank 1992). For air and water pollution, expanding industrialization in countries undergoing economic development tends to increase pollution as the countries move from low-income to middle-income. Eventually, when countries become wealthy enough, they begin to devote resources to pollution control so that pollution levels tend to fall as a country moves from middle-income to high-income status. For carbon storage and biodiversity, high-income countries tend to have more land devoted to productive activities and less land remaining in natural vegetation. On average, the percentage of natural land rises from low-income to lower-middle-income to upper-middle-income countries before falling for

TABLE 3B.1
Average carbon storage and biodiversity conservation scores, by country income group

Country income group	Carbon storage (%)	Biodiversity conservation (%)
Low income	60.0	68.0
Lower-middle income	64.8	72.1
Upper-middle income	68.4	73.7
High income	52.4	67.3

Source: World Bank.
Note: These scores represent the share of the maximum possible score achieved by each country in an income group. Those results are then averaged across all countries in an income group to yield the scores shown.

high-income countries (table 3B.2). The percentage of natural land is defined as the total land area minus land area used in agricultural crop production, grazing, managed forests, and urban development divided by total land area. Both greenhouse gas mitigation and biodiversity scores are tightly correlated with the proportion of natural area (figures 3B.1 and 3B.2).

TABLE 3B.2
Share of natural habitat remaining, by country income group

Country income group	Share of natural habitat remaining (%)
Low income	41.1
Lower-middle income	45.3
Upper-middle income	48.1
High income	32.5

Source: World Bank.
Note: Natural habitat is defined as total land area minus land in agriculture, grazing, managed forest, and urban development.

FIGURE 3B.1
Share of carbon storage plotted against the share of maximum possible carbon storage, by country

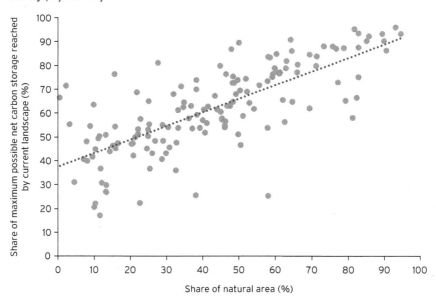

Source: World Bank.
Note: Proportion of a country's natural area is the land area not in crop production, grazing, forestry, or developed, divided by total land area.

FIGURE 3B.2

Share of natural area plotted against the share of maximum possible biodiversity, by country

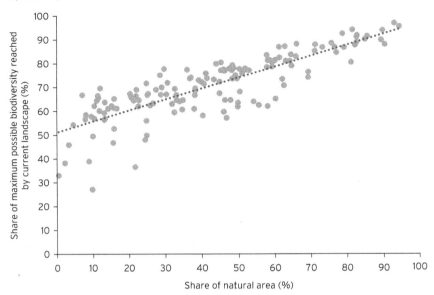

Source: World Bank.
Note: Proportion of natural area in a country is measured by the land that is not in crop production, grazing, forestry, or developed, divided by total land area.

Annex 3C: Comparison of yield gaps calculated from GAEZ and data layers of this study

This annex compares yield gaps calculated from the Global Agro-Ecological Zones (GAEZ) product of the Food and Agriculture Organization and the data layers used for his study. The aim is to identify similarities and explain differences. The comparison also provides a way of assessing whether there are outliers in either set of estimates. However, a direct comparison of yields and yield ceilings across these products is difficult because the data sets and approaches differ widely. The key differences are as follows.[8]

For yield data,

- The study data are subnational; GAEZ data are national.
- The study data mix rainfed and irrigated; GAEZ data separate them.
- The study data report in harvested weight; GAEZ data report in dried weight.

For yield ceiling data,

- The study data are a calculation of economic yield; GAEZ data are a calculation of potential agricultural yield. The two will differ because no account is taken of costs in the yield estimates, suggesting that frequently GAEZ estimates can be expected to exceed those of this study.

- This study focuses heavily on sustainability concerns, which is a binding constraint in the optimization. There is no such constraint in GAEZ, again suggesting that GAEZ estimates will likely exceed those of this study.

- Both make implicit assumptions about the intensive management techniques required to achieve yield ceilings, but these assumptions are different.

- The study data are year-specific; GAEZ data are calculated for 30-year epochs.

- This study's yield ceiling model includes fractional irrigation availability as a parameter; GAEZ provides separate layers for rainfed and irrigated systems.

The data sets are compared using the following calculations:

- The data set from this study is disaggregated to 5-minute resolution to match GAEZ.

- All calculations are limited to those locations where both data sets are defined for both yield and yield ceiling.

- Comparisons are limited to rainfed regions. For the GAEZ data, this simply means using data layers provided by GAEZ that are rainfed specific. For the data sets used in this study, they are limited to those regions where less than 10 percent of cropped area is equipped for irrigation. The map of irrigated area is derived from the MIRCA2000 data sets of monthly irrigated area (Portmann, Siebert, and Döll 2010) using a technique derived by Mueller et al. (2012).

- For both data sets, area-weighted average yield, area-weighted yield ceiling, and production are calculated for each country. The resulting ratio of average yield to average yield ceiling is constrained to between 0 and 1. (Values of exactly 1 or exactly 0 suggest some issues with data quality.)

Figure 3C.1 summarizes the results of this exercise. In the graphs, each data point represents a country. Countries with the smallest production quantities are omitted, and the represented countries represent 95 percent of global production. Overall, the comparisons show considerable agreement for six major crops: wheat, maize, rice, soybean, barley, and rapeseed. The disparities can be explained by the differences in approaches just described. In general, the yield follows a linear cloud just below the 45-degree dotted line in the graph. This outcome, as just noted, is to be expected because agronomic yield potential would typically exceed economic yield potential because the former takes no account of costs. However, some crops (cassava, sugarcane, and oil palm) show very poor agreement. The fact that all of these crops have a large number of points with yield attainment calculated by GAEZ as equal to 1 suggests issues with data quality or the estimate. Likewise, it is unclear why for sorghum the distribution of GAEZ yield attainment remains so low. No explanation is offered.

FIGURE 3C.1

Comparison of yield attainment from GAEZ and landscape efficiency analysis methods, rainfed crops

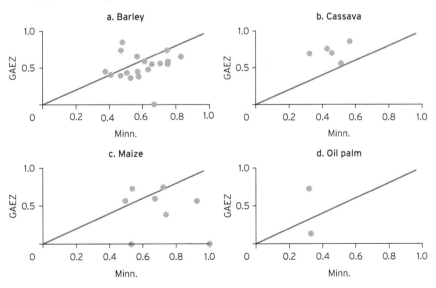

Continued

FIGURE 3C.1
Continued

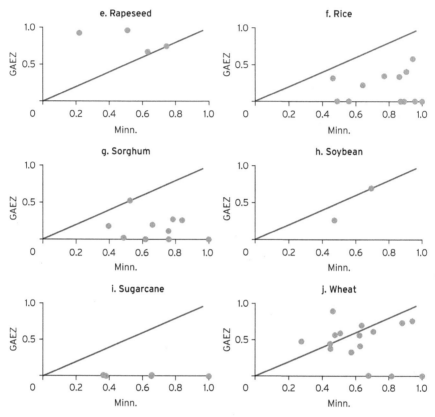

Source: World Bank.
Note: Graphs compare yield attainment for rainfed crops using the GAEZ and this study's methods. Each dot represents a country, and the countries shown are limited to those who together account for 95 percent of global production. Minn. refers to the University of Minnesota, the source of the data used in this study. GAEZ = Global Agro-Ecological Zones (Food and Agriculture Organization).

Notes

1. Maser, C. 2001. *Forest Primeval: The Natural History of an Ancient Forest.* Corvallis, Oregon: Oregon State University Press.

2. Nevertheless, there is significant bunching in the scores. Around 87 percent of countries perform better than a 75 percent landscape efficiency score; 50 percent of countries perform better than an 88 percent score; and 20 percent of countries perform better than a 95 percent score. Only two countries attain a score above 98 percent. This outcome implies that most countries have scope to make significant improvements in one or several of the four dimensions investigated.

3. Annex 3A shows country's scores across these three components as well.

4. Food and Agriculture Organization, https://www.fao.org/redd/news/deforestation-et-degradation-en-afrique-centrale.

5. Another estimate suggests that terrestrial carbon actually saw a net increase between 2000 and 2019, but it puts the total global carbon stock in terrestrial vegetation at quite a bit lower than IPCC, at 380 billion metric tons (Xu et al. 2021). The estimate in this analysis for the maximum increase in carbon that could accrue from reforestation or other restoration, combined with a reduction in methane emissions from grazing, is 175 billion metric tons (from 429 billion metric tons maximum carbon to 604 billion metric tons current carbon), whereas the Pareto efficient increase is 78 billion metric tons (from 429 billion metric tons to 507 billion metric tons). Land-based mitigation measures could sequester 10–15 billion metric tons of CO_2 per year, but cost-effective measures could only provide 8–14 billion metric tons of CO_2 per year, or 2.2–3.8 billion metric tons of carbon per year (Roe et al. 2021). At that rate, it would take 20–35 years to reach the Pareto increase in carbon, which is on the timescale (30 years) considered for these transitions in the optimization.

6. They consist of five land use options (urban, water, crops, grazing, and natural). If the land use is crops, there are 10 land management options, resulting in a total of 14 options.

7. Center for Global Trade Analysis, Purdue University, Global Trade Analysis Project (GTAP) database (dashboard), https://www.gtap.agecon.purdue.edu/databases/default.asp. See also Aguiar et al. (2019).

8. The GAEZ rainfed potential and rainfed yield layers were downloaded March 29, 2022. Potential yield layer URLs were of this form: https://s3.eu-west-1.amazonaws.com/data.gaezdev.aws.fao.org/res02/CRUTS32/Hist/8110H/maiz200b_yld.tif. Rainfed yield layers were of this form: https://s3.eu-west-1.amazonaws.com/data.gaezdev.aws.fao.org/res06/R/2010/mze_2010_yld.tif.

References

Adamopoulos, T., and D. Restuccia. 2014. "The Size Distribution of Farms and International Productivity Differences." *American Economic Review* 104 (6): 1667–97. https://doi.org/10.1257/aer.104.6.1667.

Aguiar, A., M. Chepeliev, E. L. Corong, R. McDougall, and D. van der Mensbrugghe. 2019. "The GTAP Data Base: Version 10." *Journal of Global Economic Analysis* 4 (1): 1–27. https://doi.org/10.21642/JGEA.040101AF.

Griscom, B. W., J. Adams, P. W. Ellis, R. A. Houghton, G. Lomax, D. A. Miteva, W. H. Schlesinger, et al. 2017. "Natural Climate Solutions." *PNAS* 114 (44): 11645–50. https://doi.org/10.1073/pnas.1710465114. (See correction at https://www.pnas.org/content/116/7/2776.)

Grossman, G. M., and A. B. Krueger. 1991. "Environmental Impacts of a North American Free Trade Agreement." NBER Working Paper 3914, National Bureau of Economic Research, Cambridge, MA.

Hsieh, C. T., and P. J. Klenow. 2009. "Misallocation and Manufacturing TFP in China and India." *Quarterly Journal of Economics* 124 (4): 1403–48. https://doi.org/10.1162/qjec.2009.124.4.1403.

IPCC (Intergovernmental Panel on Climate Change). 2014. *Climate Change 2014: Synthesis Report. Contribution of Working Groups I, II and III to the Fifth Assessment Report of the Intergovernmental Panel on Climate Change,* edited by Core Writing Team, R. K. Pachauri, and L. A. Meyer. Geneva, Switzerland: IPCC.

IPCC (Intergovernmental Panel on Climate Change). 2019. *IPCC Special Report on Climate Change, Desertification, Land Degradation, Sustainable Land Management, Food Security, and Greenhouse Gas Fluxes in Terrestrial Ecosystems: Summary for Policy Makers.* Geneva, Switzerland: IPCC.

IPCC (Intergovernmental Panel on Climate Change). 2000. "Land Use, Land-use Change and Forestry, edited by R. T. Watson, I. R. Noble, B. Bolin, N. H. Ravindranath, D. J. Verardo, and D. J. Dokken. Cambridge, UK: Cambridge University Press. https://archive.ipcc.ch/ipccreports/sres/land_use/index.php?idp=3.

Mueller, N. D., J. S. Gerber, M. Johnston, D. K. Ray, N. Ramamkutty, and J. A. Foley. 2012. "Closing Yield Gaps through Nutrient and Water Management." *Nature* 490 (7419): 254–7. https://doi.org/10.1038/nature11420.

Our World in Data. 2021. "Annual Greenhouse Gas Emissions: How Much Do We Emit Each Year?" https://ourworldindata.org/greenhouse-gas-emissions.

Peña-Lévano, L. M., F. Taheripour, and W. E. Tyner. 2019. "Climate Change Interactions with Agriculture, Forestry Sequestration, and Food Security." *Environmental and Resource Economics* 74 (2): 653–75. https://doi.org/10.1007/s10640-019-00339-6.

Portmann, F. T., S. Siebert, and P. Döll. 2010. "MIRCA2000—Global Monthly Irrigated and Rainfed Crop Areas around the Year 2000: A New High-Resolution Data Set for Agricultural and Hydrological Modeling." *Global Biogeochemical Cycles* 24 (1). https://doi.org/10.1029/2008GB003435.

Roe, S., C. Streck, R. Beach, J. Busch, M. Chapman, V. Daioglou, A. Deppermann, et al. 2021. "Land-based Measures to Mitigate Climate Change: Potential and Feasibility by Country." *Global Change Biology* 27 (23): 6025–58. https://doi.org/10.1111/gcb.15873.

Searchinger, T., R. Waite, C. Hanson, and J. Ranganathan. 2019. *Creating a Sustainable Food Future: A Menu of Solutions to Feed Nearly 10 Billion People by 2050.* Washington, DC: World Resources Institute.

Smith, P., H. Haberl, A. Popp, K-H. Erb, C. Lauk, R. Harper, F. N. Tubiello, et al. 2013. "How Much Land-Based Greenhouse Gas Mitigation Can Be Achieved without Compromising Food Security and Environmental Goals?" *Global Change Biology* 19 (8): 2285–302. https://doi.org/10.1111/gcb.12160.

Tallis, H. M., P. L. Hawthorne, S. Polasky, J. Reid, M. W. Beck, K. Brauman, et al. 2018. "An Attainable Global Vision for Conservation and Human Well-being." *Frontiers in Ecology and the Environment* 16 (10): 563–70. https://doi.org/10.1002/fee.1965.

Tilman, D., C. Balzer, J. Hill, and B. L. Befort. 2011. "Global Food Demand and the Sustainable Intensification of Agriculture." *Proceedings of the National Academy of Sciences* 108 (50): 20260–64. https://doi.org/10.1073/pnas.1116437108.

van Vuuren, D. P., M. Kok, P. L. Lucas, A. G. Prins, R. Alkemade, M. van den Berg, L. Bouwman, et al. 2015. "Pathways to Achieve a Set of Ambitious Global Sustainability Objectives by 2050: Explorations Using the IMAGE Integrated Assessment Model." *Technological Forecasting and Social Change* 98: 303–23. https://doi.org/10.1016/j.techfore.2015.03.005.

Xu, L., S. S. Saatchi, Y. Yang, Y. Yu, J. Pongratz, A. A. Bloom, K. Bowman, et al. 2021. "Changes in Global Terrestrial Live Biomass over the 21st Century." *ScienceAdvances* 7 (27). https://www.science.org/doi/10.1126/sciadv.abe9829.

World Bank. 1992. *World Development Report 1992: Development and the Environment.* Washington, DC: World Bank.

Policy Implications for More Efficient Landscapes

*Plans to protect air and water, wilderness and wildlife
are in fact, plans to protect Man.*
Stewart Udall, U.S. Secretary of the Interior, 1961-69[1]

Key messages

- The efficiency scores derived in chapter 3 reveal the large gains that could be harnessed across multiple objectives that vary systematically across countries. But gains will not happen without changes in policies and investments.

- Fortunately, a wide range of policies are available to address the market, policy, and institutional failures that have generated outcomes that have left countries falling behind their full potential. As with all major reforms, there will be winners and losers, and the losers are likely to resist change. Addressing this reality calls for policies that are feasible rather than those that are economically optimal. Where enforcement is weak and the risks of rent-seeking are high, the available policy choices are more constrained.

- Irrespective of country typology, a move toward the efficiency frontier must entail one or more of the following: reallocating resources toward more productive sectors; changing the composition of what is produced; or improving the efficiency of resource use.

- Countries with weak economic productivity but stronger environmental performance should give priority to combining policies that enhance economic productivity without degrading the environment. The mix may include policies that incentivize sustainable intensification, improve land tenure, and reallocate land from lower- to higher-value uses.

- Where economic performance is close to the frontier, there are often opportunities to enhance environmental services by reforming harmful fiscal policies, implementing pay-for-ecosystem service schemes, and adopting conservation tenders.

- In many instances, both economic and environmental performance are far below potential and require policy mixes for sustainable intensification as well as the reallocation of activities.

Introduction

Efficiency gaps in the use of natural resources (land, water, and air) typically emerge because the allocation of these resources is not related to the full environmental benefits they could confer or to the full economic benefits they could generate. As a result, most renewable natural resources are allocated inefficiently, as well as degraded and depleted beyond what is economically justifiable. As noted in chapter 3, the average minimum Pareto scores across countries is 54 percent. Thus most countries can double output in at least one dimension without reducing performance in any other dimensions.

The efficiency scores derived in chapter 3 show that large gains in aggregate productivity and performance across multiple dimensions are possible in many countries. For most low-income countries, significant increases in net economic returns are possible without sacrificing environmental quality. In most high-income countries, substantial increases in greenhouse gas (GHG) mitigation or biodiversity can be made without sacrificing net economic returns. The landscape efficiency scores can be grouped into a typology of countries where similar synergies and trade-offs may prevail between economic benefits and nonmarket gains. If these synergies and trade-offs between these benefits and gains from certain landscape configurations are not transparent and known, policy improvements or shifts in investment are less likely to emerge.

Inefficiencies in resource allocation and use arise not just from market failures. Informational constraints, market frictions, and policies also play a significant role in distorting choices that lead to suboptimal outcomes. For example, one of the unresolved puzzles of agriculture is that smallholder farmers do not adopt profitable new technologies even if they are available and affordable. Thus agricultural performance is often below the technological frontier. A significant literature has identified a litany of barriers to adoption that include credit constraints, risk aversion, and information deficits, as well as more conventional concerns related to constraints in factor markets or output markets (Jack 2013). These constraints may operate on the supply side by limiting the availability of information or financing, or on the demand side by dampening expected profits. For example, with risk aversion, a subsistence farmer may prefer an expected payoff that is lower but more certain than the less certain but, on average, higher payoff from employing unfamiliar technologies. "Ambiguity aversion" leads to status quo bias if known risks are preferred to unknown risks (Kahneman 2003). Credit and liquidity constraints are another common barrier because revenue arrives after harvests, whereas expenditures arise throughout the growing season. Limited access to affordable credit is therefore associated with less use of productive inputs (Njagi et al. 2017). Clearly, then, promoting the intensification of agriculture among smallholders calls for first identifying the barriers to technology adoption and then developing solutions targeting the constraints that apply in that context.

Another crucial factor is land tenure, which shapes many farm decisions, including those related to production, conservation, and investment (Place and Swallow 2000). Secure land tenure enables farmers to invest in long-term improvements to their farms and soils in the expectation that they will reap the benefits of those investments. Formal and informal land rights are therefore key to improving the conditions of the poor in lower-income countries in terms of economic growth, agricultural production, natural resource management, and local governance processes. The existing evidence on the effects of land property rights interventions is mixed and to a considerable degree dependent on initial conditions (Lawry et al. 2014). It suggests that tenure security alone may not be enough to lead directly to higher farmer incomes because its effects vary across regions and depend on other conditions such as the availability of credit, the supply of inputs, and product markets. Numerous qualitative studies have also noted unexpected social impacts from interventions in tenure, with some negative consequences such as displacement or diminished property rights for women (Teklu 2005). None of this is to suggest that tenure is unimportant, but it does highlight the need for careful policy design.

Countries seeking to move toward the efficiency frontier can undergo a variety of transitions that may include adopting new technologies, improving crop yields through intensification, implementing best management practices to boost output, and reallocating resources to their most productive uses considering the multiple dimensions of productivity. But implementing these transitions will not be easy. Not only are political economy barriers to change erected by vested interests, but, as this chapter will argue, there is no single policy panacea. Complementary policies are required because there are always numerous market failures and policy misalignments that interact and cannot be addressed with a single policy instrument. For example, a tax or regulation on the use of a harmful pesticide will be more effective when a less harmful substitute is available. The tax or regulation would then incentivize farmers to switch technologies to the less harmful substitute, whereas if no substitute existed, the tax or regulation could only incentivize farmers to reduce production or pay the tax and continue to pollute.

Apart from the immediate causes of misallocation and inefficiency (such as "wrong" prices and distorted incentives), some indirect drivers of change may have more powerful effects. Often, macroeconomic policies, trade regimes, fiscal policies, and intrusive infrastructure can have large impacts on natural resources that may negate the effects of conservation and sectoral policies (see, for example, Angelsen and Kaimowitz 2001; Rudel 2017). Especially for open-access renewable resources, small perturbations in the macroeconomic and trade environment can have dramatic impacts on resource stocks.[2] The effectiveness of environmental and sectoral policies will then hinge on broader economic forces that are harder to control, calling for a multi-instrument approach that will vary in context, policy design, and implementation capacity. For example, 95 percent of global forest loss occurs in the tropics and is driven by agricultural expansion aimed at clearing forests to grow crops, raise livestock, and produce commercial goods (Ritchie 2021). Forest clearing in the tropics is often a response to demand for commodities consumed in higher-income countries. About 30 percent of these commodities are traded in international markets and are concentrated in particular sectors: beef, soy, and other animal feed.

The following sections highlight the kinds of policy shifts and mixes required across the typology of countries to nudge them closer to their efficiency frontiers.

Policy objectives: Targeting the causes of the problem

How can countries reach their efficiency frontier? For most, multiple pathways to a more efficient state are possible without losing biodiversity, increasing GHG emissions, or reducing economic production. As shown in chapter 3, countries can, on average, almost double at least one beneficial dimension of landscapes without reducing any other dimension. Annex 4A provides a decomposition analysis that shows that a move to the efficiency frontier must entail at least one of the following shifts:

- A reallocation of resources toward more productive sectors that generate higher market or nonmarket returns (for example, from farms to forests or vice versa)

- A change in the composition of what is produced on a landscape with the same configuration of inputs (for example, from cattle ranching to wheat or vice versa)

- Improving the efficiency of resource use for the same outputs produced (for example, more crop per drop of water or more crop per unit of land used).

The specific shift required will vary within the typology identified in chapter 3 and the location of countries within the efficiency frontier.

The wide range of policy instruments available to induce shifts to the efficiency frontier can be divided into three broad categories: direct incentives, disincentives, and economywide enablers.

Table 4.1 summarizes these policies and categorizes them by type and impact. Of the wide range of policies available, the most suitable policy will depend on effectiveness, feasibility of implementation, affordability, and societal acceptability. Because these policy traits will vary by country and even regions within countries, the following section outlines a practical road map to guide policy makers to those options that are realistic and implementable among the many available.

Exploring policy options by country typology

This section offers tailored solutions based on the challenges and characteristics of individual countries according to their placement in the typology of countries in figure 3.3 in chapter 3 (and reproduced here in figure 4.1). The appropriate policies will vary across countries when the core objective is to reach the efficiency frontier.

Type A. This group of countries has high scores on economic efficiency and a relatively low nonmarket environmental score, both in the Pareto space. These typically high-income countries have often already converted a large amount of land to economic uses and invested heavily in agricultural

TABLE 4.1

A categorization of policies for improving resource use efficiency

	Reallocation Shift to more productive sectors	Composition Shift mix of activity within sector	Efficiency Produce more with same or fewer inputs
Direct incentives	• Payment for ecosystem services • Subsidies	• Agricultural extension facilities • Certification (labeling) schemes • Subsidies for desired shifts	• Agricultural extension facilities • Technology transfer • Increasing access to credit and insurance • Ecotourism and other nonconsumptive product development
Disincentives	• Protected areas and other zoning • Land use taxes • Carbon/pollution taxes • Fines	• Removal of environmentally harmful subsidies • Reform of product taxes (such as value added tax system) • Regulations and fees	• Removal of inefficiency-enhancing subsidies and reform of taxes (on externalities) and prices (on underpriced resources)
Economywide policies	• Trade policy • Tax policy • Land tenure	• Trade policy • Strengthening land tenure • Investments in research and development	• Strengthening land tenure • Investments in research and development

FIGURE 4.1

Typology of countries, by environmental indicator and production value

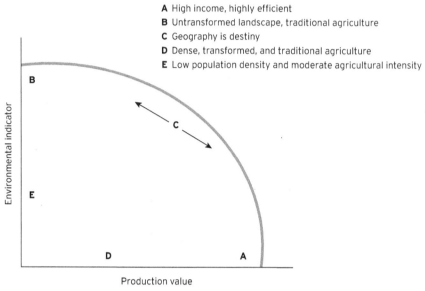

A High income, highly efficient
B Untransformed landscape, traditional agriculture
C Geography is destiny
D Dense, transformed, and traditional agriculture
E Low population density and moderate agricultural intensity

Source: World Bank.

technology advancements. Here, larger efficiency gains can be achieved along the environmental benefits dimension, and smaller gains may be found in economic (marketed) values, both in the Pareto space and even with trade-offs. Trade-offs are generally steeper in this group, and opportunities for enhancing landscape productivity through efficiency moves are more limited.

Policy options may include investing in market-based approaches—such as conservation tenders, payment for ecosystem services (PES) schemes, agrotourism and ecotourism, or biodiversity-friendly products—to improve environmental benefits. The use of beneficial subsidies or direct investments in building capacity and technology to support regenerative agriculture and other nature-based solutions can add further to environmental gains. Finally, in all groups new technology could play a critical role by allowing further increases in productivity that would enable ongoing growth in both the environmental and economic dimensions.

Type B. The comparatively few countries in this group have a relatively low economic score and a high environmental score. In contrast to the type A countries, these countries are characterized by significant amounts of remaining natural land, either undeveloped or protected, but they have low production value scores due to high yield gaps and inefficient land use or land allocation. Large improvements in production value are possible in the Pareto space through intensification and reallocation, and often there are opportunities for small improvements in nonmarket environmental benefits as well. This profile suggests the need for improvements in efficiency by means of policies that boost yields through sustainable intensification. Several countries in this group are in the Congo Basin—the second lung of the planet—which sequesters about eight years of GHGs emitted globally and hosts significant biodiversity.

Finding policies that can harness the available economic gains without adverse environmental impacts remains an important global priority. The mix of required policies might include tackling credit constraints that smallholders in lower-income countries endure, lack of inputs, informational constraints, access to credit and insurance, skill deficits, and secure land tenure. Investments in infrastructure such as irrigation and roads and communications—to better connect farmers to markets in both a physical sense and an informational sense—may also pay large dividends in intensifying agriculture. There is also scope for improving the credibility of certification schemes to enable sustainable harvests from these regions to reach markets that may pay a premium. Because private sector research largely focuses on the commercial farming sector, there is a greater need for public investments in applied research relevant to the poor smallholders in countries in this group that host much of the world's intact forest stocks. However, these policies and investments must be designed and implemented with caution. These countries are at particular risk of the so-called Jevons paradox, whereby intensification increases yields and the profitability of land use, which, in turn, induces expansion of the agricultural frontier into forests and natural habitats. Countries reliant on agricultural commodity exports with large amounts of undeveloped land are at higher risk of such counterproductive trends (Villoria 2019). If the Jevons paradox can be avoided through appropriate policies and regulations, very substantial economic gains can be made through intensification, as well as nonconsumptive and sustainable uses of forest resources with minimal if any environmental spillovers. In several countries in this group, productivity could be increased by as much as 80 percent without environmental losses.

Type C. Very few of the countries analyzed achieved high scores in both the production and environmental dimensions except where geography (natural endowments) constrains production and leaves limited options. These countries have extreme climates such as dry deserts, frozen tundra, or steep terrain where food production is limited by climate and geography. In these countries, any gain in one dimension necessarily requires trade-offs in the other. Appropriate policies could include establishing networks to monitor trends in ecosystem function, removing perverse subsidies that encourage degradation, and investing in regenerative production systems to simultaneously enhance production and environmental benefits. These are universally desirable policy objectives.

Type D. These countries have a high population density and landscapes heavily transformed to economic uses. Many of these countries have relatively low scores in both economic efficiency and the nonmarket environmental benefits generated by the current patterns of land use. Such countries are characterized by large yield gaps and high rates of land degradation, and they may produce goods that generate less value per unit of input than is feasible. In these countries, there are significant opportunities to improve yields and land productivity as well as to restore lands less suited to agriculture to their natural states where they can contribute to the production of public goods such as GHG emission reduction, hydrology, and biodiversity.

The mix of policies needed to enable these shifts will vary, depending on a country's circumstances. Policies may be needed to promote sustainable intensification of agriculture (such as those addressing credit, inputs, insurance, research and development, and extension services); reform distorting subsidies; address market failures in land markets; strengthen land tenure; and address the legacy lock-in effects of historical land use. Once again, investments in applied research are important and could be complemented with support systems at the macro level such as early warning systems; expansion of agriculture value chains; and adoption of digital technologies to help farmers and traders reach new markets. Because of the relative scarcity of land in these countries, government policies should pivot toward encouraging market-oriented value added.

Type E. The significant number of countries in this group have moderate environmental scores and low economic scores. Some of these countries use their land for extensive cattle rearing. Changing the composition of production and switching from ranching to arable agriculture (where this is feasible) will typically generate higher economic payoffs. Some countries can also generate considerable environmental benefits in the Pareto space by reallocating land from producing beef, which carries a high environmental footprint, to arable agriculture, or producing environmental services such as carbon sequestration, water quality and watershed protection, and biodiversity services. Several recent research papers confirm that beef production emits 31 times more carbon dioxide equivalent (CO_2eq) per kilocalorie than equivalent nonanimal alternatives.[3] Conservation tenders, PES schemes, and high-value sustainable agriculture seem especially suitable for these countries. Although the estimates provided take into account transition costs, reallocating land to different uses can be challenging in some situations and may need to be achieved gradually through the patient accumulation of partial successes.

The precise mix of policies needed will vary depending on each country's circumstances and the feasibility of change. Table 4.2 summarizes the types of instruments by the country typology developed in chapter 3, and box 4.1 describes a road map for making policy decisions. Box 4.2 describes a transformative landscape restoration program in Ethiopia.

TABLE 4.2
Summary of policies based on typology of countries

High transformation: high land productivity (type A)	Low transformation: low land productivity (type B)	On the frontier: geography is destiny (type C)	High transformation: low land productivity (type D)	Moderate transformation: moderate land productivity (type E)
• PES • Conservation tenders • Tax incentives	• Certification • Sustainable intensification • Input provision • Skills and education • Land tenure • Reallocation from low- to higher-productivity uses • Sustainable, nonconsumptive forest utilization	• Monitoring ecosystem function • Regenerative investments • Subsidy reform	• PES • Expansion of protected areas • Restore degraded lands (see box 4.2) • Sustainable intensification • Subsidy reform • Insurance • Sustainable, nonconsumptive forest utilization	• Reallocation from low productivity uses (cattle) to higher productivity uses (crops) • Tax incentives • PES

Source: World Bank.
Note: PES = payment for ecosystem services.

BOX 4.1
A policy road map

A policy road map does not prescribe particular policy combinations or how they may be implemented. Instead, it provides guidance for identifying opportunities for improvement and the options available to address them, thereby facilitating the selection of relevant and effective policy choices. Adherence to such a road map also enhances transparency and helps to engage the interest groups, communities, regulators, and other key stakeholders affected by such policies. What follows are the key questions that governments should answer to determine which policies are most suitable among the many available:

1. Where are the efficiency gaps (in the economic space, for biodiversity, for greenhouse gases)?
2. How significant are the likely gains?
3. Which type of country is in the efficiency frontier space (A, B, C, D, or E)?
4. Use "agreement maps" where needed. These maps of land use highlight the areas that remain used in the same way regardless of where the country is placed in the efficiency frontier. In these areas, the best use does not change and often yields high payoffs in their relevant dimension.
5. What shifts are needed? Management options for attaining these shifts should be listed. A Sankey diagram for points on the efficiency frontier will show which policies are most important for achieving the desired change.
6. What policy choices are available for the country type across direct incentives, disincentives, and cross-cutting solutions?
7. For each policy option/combination,
   • How effective is the policy?
   • What are the implementation constraints (political economy, capacity of country, costs of implementation, and so on)?
   • What are the distributional issues (if not covered by the previous question)?
   • What are the risks?
   • Are other co-benefits likely to emerge (such as from subsidy reform)?

BOX 4.2
Landscape restoration in Ethiopia

Since 2008, the World Bank has been supporting efforts by the government of Ethiopia to restore and enhance degraded landscapes. This support has been undertaken through a series of programs,[a] each building on the other and broadening experience gained over time.

MAP B4.2.1
Changes in Normalized Difference Vegetation Index since initial engagement under Sustainable Landscape Management Project II, Ethiopia, 2014

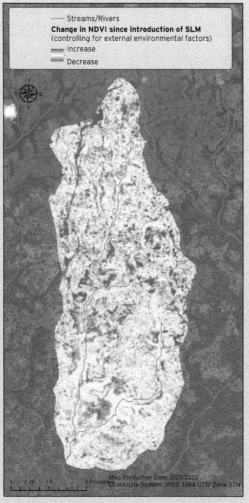

Streams/Rivers
Change in NDVI since introduction of SLM
(controlling for external environmental factors)
Increase
Decrease

Map Production Date: 2/25/2022
Coordinate System: WGS 1984 UTM Zone 37N
0   0.75   1.5   3 Kilometers

Source: World Bank.
Note: Map shows the change in the Normalized Difference Vegetation Index in the Bibir major watershed, Lalo Kile *woreda* (district), Oromia region. The colors represent the changes in the NDVI, a measure of vegetation productivity and a proxy for cropland, grassland, and forest productivity, that can be attributed to sustainable land management practices (that is, NDVI changes after controlling for external environmental factors). SLM = sustainable land management.

Continued

BOX 4.2
Continued

Initially, these programs focused on community-based approaches to supporting sustainable land management practices, such as constructing terraces on farmed hillsides and planting trees. However, over time these initiatives broadened their approach. The current programs adopt approaches that deliver longer-term sustainability through major investments that strengthen land tenure, support climate-smart agricultural practices, improve livelihood security, and build value chain linkages.

The results have been impressive (Map B4.2.1). More than 1.1 million hectares of land are now under sustainable land management practices, and this figure is expected to exceed 3 million hectares by the end of the current round of support. Over 180,000 hectares of forests have been restored through afforestation and reforestation, with more than 123,000 hectares of forests now under participatory forest management with forest cooperatives responsible for managing these forests sustainably.

There is already evidence that these large-scale investments in watershed regeneration and increasing land productivity have led to measurable changes in degraded landscapes. Preliminary analysis of the watershed areas covered by the World Bank-supported programs indicates that 62 percent now have a higher Normalized Difference Vegetation Index (NDVI)[b] than at the start of interventions. NDVI is a broad measure of vegetation productivity, frequently used as a proxy for cropland, grassland, and forest productivity.

Advancement of the restoration of degraded watersheds has required transformative changes. Over 3,000 cooperatives and associations have now been established, and this number will grow to around 6,150. More than 23,000 landless youth have been issued a land title in exchange for restoring land.

a. World Bank, Sustainable Landscape Management Projects (SLMP I, 2009-14; SLMP II, 2014-18); Resilient Landscapes and Livelihoods Project (RLLP I, 2019-24; RLLP II, 2021-25); Climate Action through Landscape Management (CALM, 2019-24); Oromia Forested Landscape Project (OFLP, 2017-22).
b. The NDVI uses remote sensing data to identify the quality and distribution of vegetation. Changes in vegetation can be analyzed using time series observations.

Policy design concerns

The vast literature on policy design issues includes numerous reviews and meta-analyses that serve as useful summaries of the state of knowledge (see, for example, Börner et al. 2020). Instead of reviewing this literature, this section focuses on particular policies for which recent research offers new insights into how to improve the effectiveness of policies. The intention is not to provide an exhaustive overview of the selected policies, but to focus instead on issues that may merit consideration by policy designers.

Direct incentives
Payments for ecosystem services

PES programs provide incentives (either pecuniary or in-kind) for landholders to supply or safeguard the environmental services that flow as a positive externality from their land. These programs come in a variety of forms, including carbon payments (such as REDD+[4]) and payments for hydrological services. These mechanisms are popular throughout China and Latin America, and their implementation is growing in other regions as well, including Africa and Southeast Asia (Mandle et al. 2019; Vogl et al. 2016). These programs allow downstream beneficiaries to pay upstream landholders to change land use and management practices (such as the installation of fencing to keep livestock out of streams, restoration of riparian vegetation, removal of invasive species, and enforcement of protected areas). Such activities and policies improve the ecosystem provisioning of water supply and quality for cities, improve ecosystem provisioning for industrial and agricultural businesses, and enhance rural livelihoods (Mandle et al. 2019; McConnachie et al. 2013; Turpie, Marais, and Blignaut 2008; van Wilgen and Richardson 2012). China, Costa Rica, the United Kingdom, and the United States also are innovators in PES schemes for enhanced forest protection, water quality, agricultural yields, and sandstorm control (Bateman et al. 2019; Mandle et al. 2019; Quesada 2019). PES schemes may require novel mechanisms to provide financial transfers, governance, and management, and the particulars of each are tailored to the sociopolitical circumstances of each country (Brauman et al. 2019; Mandle et al. 2019).

The success of PES schemes is mixed because of poor spatial targeting, insecure land tenure, and problems of adverse selection. The goal of a PES scheme is to encourage the provision of ecosystem services that would not otherwise be provided by the landholder and to obtain services worth more to the public than the private cost of providing them. However, achieving this goal can be difficult because the reservation price at which the landowner is willing to supply the service is private information. More generally, buyers of ecological services know less than landowners do about the costs of contractual compliance. As a result, an informational asymmetry allows landowners to use the private information as a source of market power to extract informational rents and increase the cost of the PES contract. Creating competition among sellers of environmental services is one way to bring down these informational rents through conservation auctions or tenders (Bardsley 2008). Indeed, the emerging evidence suggests that auctions are, in fact, more cost-effective than fixed-price PES schemes (James, Lundberg, and Sills 2021). However, a limitation is that tenders have mainly (but not exclusively) been used in more developed countries where the preconditions of success such as land tenure rights, implementation capacity, and a willingness to participate are more likely to prevail.

There is still much to learn about how to establish the most effective governance, management, and financial transfer mechanisms to support payments for ecosystem services, especially to ensure robust job creation and equitable distribution of benefits. The lessons from existing programs are encouraging, and continued innovation of such mechanisms is a promising pathway to more efficient, sustainable, and just landscape management.

Certification schemes and green labeling

In recent years, mandatory government-led environmental rating systems have gained traction in several countries. At the same time, there has been a proliferation of voluntary eco-labels, such as BREEAM (Building Research Establishment's Environmental Assessment Method) in the United Kingdom and Green Star in Australia. Because supplying greener products generally entails additional costs, any voluntary initiatives that exceed regulatory requirements may come with a green price premium.

Overall, the evidence on the existence and magnitude of a green premium is ambiguous and inconclusive. It is unclear whether producers with a comparative advantage in green production self-select into green schemes, or whether these schemes bring in new firms and incentivize them to change to cleaner production techniques. The evidence from housing markets is not promising. It suggests that making disclosure optional presents a moral hazard problem—the likelihood of disclosure increases in line with the sustainability of the product (Fuerst and Warren-Myers 2018). Numerous studies also report that participating in green supply chains is correlated with better-performing firms (Fen and Zhang 2018). However, once again, the direction of causality remains unclear. It could be argued that green supply chains improve overall economic performance. However, it is also possible that better-performing firms may self-select into green supply chains knowing that they can meet the additional constraints of greener production.

There is also a growing move toward *mandatory* certification schemes, especially for forest products and for processes and products that give rise to climate change concerns. For a mandatory certification strategy to be successful, the eco-label should provide consumers with credible and transparent information. Credibility requires that consumers trust what a label means in terms of environmental protection and that it is immune to manipulation. Media reports about "greenwashing" and corruption have, in general, limited the success of this approach (Garrido, Espínola-Arredondo, and Munoz-Garcia 2020). The Marine Stewardship Council's fisheries certification scheme and rigorous review process is a success story in terms of increasing fishery population viabilities, and forestry and other commodities are using it as a model for ongoing improvements of their schemes (Ruckelshaus, Kareiva, and Crowder 2013).

Overall, there is limited evidence that certification schemes, whether mandated or voluntary, have been especially effective in tackling market failures (Nepstad et al. 2013). Perhaps labeling is a useful complement to other efforts, but it may be insufficient as a stand-alone policy when there are informational asymmetries, risks of adverse selection, and manipulation.

Commercial incentives

Many of the proposed solutions to increasing the efficiency of natural capital will call for additional funding to finance and incentivize the desired changes. Globally, there is a glut of savings in higher-income countries that struggles to find investments that offer investors sufficient economic returns. For example, funds in retirement savings plans grew at around 10 percent in 2021, despite the shock of COVID-19, exceeding US$56 trillion (OECD 2021). An obvious solution is to find ways to channel these financial surpluses from higher-income countries to investment in opportunities in lower-income countries to restore eroding natural capital. But this will not happen automatically because most natural capital assets (whether GHGs, fine particulate matter such as $PM_{2.5}$, or forests) are "common property goods" whose benefits and impacts are shared communally. Thus no one business has sufficient control over a common property resource to gain by investing in it. For a resource to be attractive to private investors, regulations are needed to signal the scarcity value of the resource and create the enabling instruments to ensure it is used efficiently. For example, carbon markets would not exist at their current scale without enabling legislation that provides a "cap and trade" of GHGs. The "cap" is needed to provide an economic signal to investors that the carbon budget[5] is an economically scarce resource, while "trade" facilitates a transfer from lower- to higher-value uses. The tighter the cap, the greater is the scarcity signal, and the higher will be the price. One of the more profitable environmental resources traded is water in Australia; its annual turnover is about US$10 billion (Bjornlund and Rossini 2007). In summary, if there are to be significant financial flows into environmental services, legislation and institutions are needed to turn common property resources into tradable assets that are transferred to their best uses.

Disincentives
Environmental taxes

Pigouvian taxes—that is, environmental taxes on externalities (such as pollution or overharvesting a renewable resource)—are the first-best policy of choice in standard economic models and remain the preferred policy instrument when available. The literature on the advantages of Pigouvian taxes over all other policy instruments is vast and well established. Recent literature based on more complicated models offers a nuanced look at the appropriateness of the Pigouvian tax (Stern and Stiglitz 2021). When there is great uncertainty about the effectiveness of the tax in curbing, for example, pollution, and the pollutant is highly damaging on the margin, quantity controls on pollution levels (a "standard") are the more efficient and effective policy. Moreover, in a world of multiple market failures, optimal interventions will likely involve tools in addition to a corrective tax. Finally, distributional and political economy concerns often make it difficult to bring in new taxes on externalities at a level high enough to change outcomes.

In the context of land use, some governments tax uncultivated land that is deemed to be "unproductive," despite the services such lands might provide. Indeed, several governments in Africa are considering these taxes to boost agricultural output. However, such taxes have perverse and undesirable efficiency effects, leading to the excessive conversion of natural habitats to farming and cattle production. An alternative is a Georgist-style land tax (named after the economist Henry George) that may provide an incentive to make more efficient use of developed land. George argued that, although individuals should own the value of what they produce, the economic rents derived from land—the planet's most finite resource—should not accrue solely to landholders. The "pure" rents accruing to land are often a consequence of exogenous factors (such as scarcity, soil type, or agglomeration economies) that are beyond the landowner's control, and those rents should therefore be used for public benefits. A land value tax (the classic Henry George tax) could be used to redistribute such rents. The implications of such a tax could have profound impacts on the environment as well. It would encourage densification of urban areas and would incentivize landowners to ensure they are making the most efficient use of land. A modification of a Georgist-style tax might be inclusion of the value of lost environmental and ecosystem services in the tax. Thus it would discourage the development of land that has low economic potential but high potential for ecosystem services.

Protected areas (PAs) and other zoning

Biodiversity is in rapid decline, prompting fears of an anthropogenically induced mass extinction of species. To address this crisis, PAs have become the backbone of conservation efforts to prevent the conversion of natural habitats. Critics argue that it is unclear whether this strategy will ensure success. In fact, even though the size of PAs has more than tripled over the last 40 years, biodiversity losses continue to escalate. One issue that compromises effectiveness is the location of PAs. They are often established where they would have the least conflict with land that may have alternative economic uses instead of in locations of high environmental value and where there are high concentrations of threatened species. Simulations suggest that if the new PAs established between 2004 and 2014 had been targeted to areas where the greatest threats have emerged from intrusive infrastructure and an expanding frontier for commodities, then more than 30 times as many species would have been protected (see, among others, Andam et al. 2010; Ferraro, Hanauer, and Sims 2011).

That said, many PAs are effective at protecting biodiversity and habitats and may also reduce poverty and increase the well-being of rural populations. However, if these protections are mainly in distant and nonthreatened locales that host the remnants of endangered species, then their contribution to conservation of these species will seem larger than it actually is. Thus there are concerns about "paper parks" that seem to have no discernable conservation impact (Pringle 2017).

In view of the limited funding for PAs, a debate is under way about the further expansion of PAs versus consolidation to create better outcomes (Kareiva 2010). Notwithstanding these valid concerns, numerous examples demonstrate that, with sufficient management, protected areas can be viable in what might be regarded as high-threat situations. For example, iconic PAs close to cities such as Nairobi still host endangered species despite the threats and challenges posed by an expanding urban footprint. The analysis presented in this report suggests that there is scope for improving and expanding the location of PAs in ways that need not detract from economic progress.

Enabling conditions
The political economy of environmental policy

Even though reform within the Pareto space may confer an overall welfare gain on society, resistance to reform is inevitable, in part because the fruits of any transformation will be unevenly distributed, with winners and losers trying to influence the policy outcome in their favor. The extensive literature on the political economy of environmental policy reform offers insights into the reasons why reform attempts fail so frequently (Gawande and Bandyopadhyay 2000).

Two conclusions seem especially relevant in this context. The literature highlights the asymmetry in lobbying power between those who suffer environmental damage and those who (inadvertently) inflict such damage. The benefits of inflicting environmental damage such as pollution are concentrated and accrue to a small number of people. Conversely, the damage from pollution is nonmonetary, often becomes visible only in the future, and is spread across a large number of people. Furthermore, because collective action involving a large number of people is costly, the polluter will have greater resources and influence to lobby for policy favors. The outcome of this lobbying game will involve excessive environmental damage and often even subsidies to the polluter (Oates, Wallace, and Portney 2003). This asymmetry in bargaining power is heightened when dealing with renewable resources that can be exhausted. As the resource becomes scarcer, supply diminishes, and prices and profits from extraction rise, giving the producer greater influence over those who suffer damage (Barbier, Damania, and Léonard 2015).

Another important finding has emerged from behavioral economics: people tend to be "loss averse," implying that they dislike losing a given sum of money more than they value gaining an equal amount. Because losses are more salient, resistance from those who lose is greater than support from those who gain.

Moreover, when the anticipated losses affect concentrated interests, resistance to reform becomes disproportionately greater. In summary, influential vested interest groups can create substantial institutional and political barriers even when there are benefits that accrue to the economy and the majority of its citizens. These challenges can be exacerbated when channels of communication are captured by the same vested interests.

Common solutions to these problems are compensation and communication aimed at building support coalitions. The form of a coalition differs according to who benefits and who loses. A challenging, unresolved problem is that of credibility and time inconsistency: even if compensation today makes all losers better-off, committing future governments to sustaining those compensatory policies is difficult.

The implication is that there is no simple blueprint for reform because much depends on the distribution of economic and political power, which varies widely across countries (de Mesquita 2004). Successful reform seldom involves first-best options of economic theory. Instead, they may be iterative and determined by the distribution of rents and the influence that these create. For example, eliminating all environmentally harmful subsidies remains the economic ideal, but, in practice, reform has usually occurred by repurposing existing subsidies in ways that are distributionally neutral and more benign in their impacts. Likewise, taxes on externalities tend to be more vigorously opposed than alternative policies such as trade caps or quotas because of distributional objections (Stiglitz 2019). Finally, policies that shift fundamental economic incentives using market forces may be the more effective and lasting way to catalyze reform. For example, technological changes that render harmful practices unprofitable would provide a powerful incentive for reform.

Trade

Where trade affects agricultural prices, deforestation rates could be affected as well. For example, when a country enters international markets, local prices will converge toward international prices. If greater trade liberalization leads to *higher* agricultural prices locally, then deforestation may increase. Conversely, if trade *reduces* local agricultural prices, then deforestation is likely to decrease. Consequently, the impact of trade on deforestation is ambiguous and will depend on a country's characteristics, suggesting that robust empirical evidence is required to determine the overall impact of trade on deforestation.

A recent comprehensive study of 189 countries to determine the overall impact of trade on deforestation found that in tropical lower-income countries, trade liberalization increases net deforestation and shifts it into ecologically sensitive locations (Abman and Lundberg 2020). In a similar vein, another recent paper found that in open-access fisheries, a one standard deviation increase in exports raises the probability of a fishery's collapse the following year by 29 percentage points (Eisenbarth 2022). These empirical results are consistent with a large and established theoretical literature on renewable resources, which predicts that under conditions of open access, trade can be destructive in resource-abundant countries when it promotes overextraction beyond optimal levels (Bulte and Barbier 2005; Copeland and Taylor 2013).

The implication is that trade liberalization should be accompanied by policies to direct expansion of agricultural land away from forests and sensitive habitats. In addition, if policies such as certification can become more credible and effective, they could also help negate incentives for the overextraction of renewable resources.

Conclusions

The world has a tremendous opportunity to transform land use systems in ways that restore life-sustaining ecosystem services and increase agricultural productivity. This report provides the scientific evidence arising from state-of-the-art models to demonstrate that such a transformation is technically feasible and economically affordable.

As with all major reforms, the transformation will inevitably bring many challenges because vested interests resist change, and policy uncertainty will require course corrections. Failure to steer economies toward greater sustainability may entail far greater risks and imperil achieving global goals related to sustainability, as well as more conventional economic objectives that are affected by land productivity.

To support this transformation, this chapter summarizes the broad contours of the desired policy mixes within the Pareto space. The emphasis on reaching the efficiency frontier seems especially apt in this context because countries are more likely to support changes that yield net economic returns to the private sector and environmental benefits to society at large. This chapter identifies policy priorities for five distinct clusters of countries based on their past performance and current state of natural endowments, and it identifies the range of possibilities and the policy shifts needed to achieve these.

Empowering decision-makers with information about the range of opportunities and trade-offs between economic and nonmarket gains from different policies and landscape configurations is more likely to enable change through detailed assessments undertaken at the country level. Meanwhile, addressing the distributional consequences is a first-order concern, not only for normative reasons but also to address the inevitable resistance from vested interests.

Annex 4A: Decomposition analysis and shifting toward the efficiency frontier

The discussion of policy options is motivated by a decomposition of a simple identity that emerges from the models often used in environmental economics. This annex reveals that, in the absence of policies to correct market failures, land will routinely be used less productively than it could be for three reasons. First, there will be an underinvestment in land-saving inputs, implying that marketed economic outputs from land will be lower than is feasible and economically desirable. Second, more land in total will be devoted to agriculture and other marketed uses than is economically optimal because of the presence of unpriced environmental services provided by intact habitats. Third, and as a corollary, the agricultural uses of land (cropping mix) will be more land-intensive than is optimal.

Let A be the fixed amount of land available that can be either used for agriculture, A^{ag}, or left intact as natural habitat, A^{en}. Natural habitat produces environmental services such as biodiversity, hydrological services, and carbon sequestration. Thus $A = A^{ag} + A^{en}$.

There are y_i ($i = 1,....,n$) different types of agricultural outputs (such as crops), with a total value given by $Y = \sum_{i=1}^{n} p_i y_i$. Each crop is produced on land of size A_i^{ag}. The value of output is then given by

$$Y = \sum_i p_i y_i. \tag{4A.1}$$

Let $\delta = \dfrac{A^{ag}}{A}$ be the share of land devoted to agriculture, and let $\theta_i = \dfrac{A_i^{ag}}{A^{ag}}$ be the share of converted cropland devoted to crop type i. Equation (4A.1) can be decomposed as

$$Y = \sum_i p_i \delta A \frac{y_i}{\theta_i A^{ag}}. \tag{4A.2}$$

Equation (4A.2) divides the output identity into three policy-relevant components:

- *Extensification (or scale)*. The term δA describes the scale effect through the extent of conversion of land to agriculture.

- *Intensification (or yield)*. The ratio $\dfrac{y_i}{\theta_i A^{ag}}$ measures productivity or yields through the intensification of agriculture.

- *Composition (or allocation)*. Finally, $q_i A^{ag}$ describes the allocation of different agricultural outputs across land.

The following demonstrates that in the presence of positive environmental externalities there will be an excessive amount of land conversion relative to that economically optimal, an underinvestment in inputs that increase yields, and a suboptimal mix of agricultural outputs. To simplify, consider the case of two types of farm products ($i = 1,2$). Private profits are

$$\pi_i = \sum_i p_i y_i - wL_i - r\theta_i A^{ag} \quad (i = 1,2), \tag{4A.3}$$

where $y_i = f(L_i, q_i A^{ag})$ is a standard production function that is strictly concave and increasing in the relevant range under consideration and L_i is a generic nonland input. The first-order conditions for the optimal choice of land conversion, crop mix, and the other input (L) are given by

$$\frac{\partial \pi_i}{\partial L_i} = p_i \frac{\partial y_i}{\partial L_i} - w = 0 \quad (i = 1,2), \tag{4A.4}$$

$$\frac{\partial \pi_i}{\partial A^{ag}} = p_i \frac{\partial y_i}{\partial A^{ag}} - r = 0 \quad (I = 1,2), \tag{4A.5}$$

$$\frac{\partial \pi_i}{\partial \theta_i} = p_i \frac{\partial y_i}{\partial \theta_i} - rA^{ag} - p_j \frac{\partial y_j}{\partial \theta_i}$$
$$- rA^{ag} \frac{\partial \theta_j}{\partial \theta_i} = 0 \quad (i \neq j \text{ and } i = 1,2). \tag{4A.6}$$

As noted earlier, a fixed endowment of land $A = A^{ag} + A^{en}$ can be used for agriculture or left to generate a flow of environmental services with shadow value of p^{en}. The socially optimal level of land conversion, composition of crop mix, and investment in yields is given by maximizing the welfare function

$$W = p^{en}(A - A^{ag}) + \pi. \tag{4A.7}$$

The first-order conditions are

$$\frac{dW}{dL} = -p^{en} \frac{dA^{ag}}{dL} + \frac{\partial \pi}{\partial L} = 0, \tag{4A.8}$$

$$\frac{dW}{dA^{ag}} = -p^{en} + \frac{\partial \pi}{\partial A^{ag}} = 0, \tag{4A.9}$$

$$\frac{dW}{d\theta_i} = -p^{en} \frac{dA^{ag}}{d\theta_i} + \frac{\partial \pi}{\partial \theta_i} = 0. \tag{4A.10}$$

Total differentiation of (4A.4)–(4A.6) reveals that $\dfrac{dA^{ag}}{dL} > 0$ and $\dfrac{dA^{ag}}{d\theta_i} > 0$.

Comparing (4A.4)–(4A.6) to (4A.8)–(4A.9) yields the following results.

Let superscript $*$ denote the welfare-maximizing choice and $\wedge$ denote profit-maximizing choices. Comparing (4A.4) and (4A.8), it follows that $L^* > \hat{L}$ whenever $\dfrac{dA^{ag}}{dL} < 0$. This follows from the fact that in (4A.4) $\dfrac{\partial \pi}{\partial L} = 0$, while in (4A.8) $\dfrac{\partial \pi}{\partial L} = p^{en}\dfrac{dA^{ag}}{dL} < 0$. By concavity of π, it then follows that $L^* > \hat{L}$. Intuitively, for a single-peaked concave function, whenever $\dfrac{\partial \pi}{\partial Z} > 0$, then $Z^* > \hat{Z}$, and whenever $\dfrac{\partial \pi}{\partial Z} > 0$, then $Z^* < \hat{Z}$.

The remaining proofs are similar and establish that $A^{ag}* < \widehat{A^{ag}}$ and $\theta_i^* \neq \widehat{\theta_i}$. The implication is the need for policies to target these three sources of inefficiency.

Notes

1. Udall, S. 1968. *1976: Agenda for Tomorrow*. New York: Harcourt, Brace and World.

2. See, for example, Eisenbarth (2022), who finds that a small increase in fishery exports of one standard deviation raises the probability of a fishery's collapse in the following year by 29 percentage points. Similar results have been documented in other contexts of common property renewable resources.

3. Comparisons are with plant alternatives. See Crippa et al. (2021); *Economist* (2021); and Xu et al. (2021).

4. Under the auspices of the United Nations, REDD+ refers to the Reducing Emissions from Deforestation and Forest Degradation program.

5. The carbon budget is defined by the Intergovernmental Panel on Climate Change as "the maximum amount of cumulative net global anthropogenic carbon dioxide (CO_2) emissions that would result in limiting global warming to a given level with a given probability, taking into account the effect of other anthropogenic climate forcers."

References

Abman, R., and C. Lundberg. 2020. "Does Free Trade Increase Deforestation? The Effects of Regional Trade Agreements." *Journal of the Association of Environmental and Resource Economists* 7 (1): 35–72. https://doi.org/10.1086/705787.

Andam, K. S., P. J. Ferraro, K. R. E. Sims, A. Healy, and M. B. Holland. 2010. "Protected Areas Reduced Poverty in Costa Rica and Thailand." *PNAS* 107: 9996–10001. https://doi .org/10.1073/pnas.0914177107.

Angelsen, A., and D. Kaimowitz, eds. 2001. *Agricultural Technologies and Tropical Deforestation*. Oxon, UK: CABI.

Barbier, E. B., R. Damania, and D. Léonard. 2015. "Corruption, Trade and Resource Conversion." *Journal of Environmental Economics and Management* 50 (2): 276–99. https:// doi.org/10.1016/j.jeem.2004.12.004.

Bardsley, D. 2008. "Building Resilience into Marginal Agroecosystems? A Global Priority for Socio-ecological Sustainability." Paper prepared for the Berlin Conference on the Human Dimensions of Global Environmental Change, February 22–23, 2008, Berlin. https://hdl .handle.net/2440/56094.

Bateman, I., A. Binner, B. Day, C. Fezzi, A. Rusby, G. Smith, and R. Welters. 2019. "United Kingdom: Paying for Ecosystem Services in the Public and Private Sectors." In *Green Growth That Works: Natural Capital Policy and Finance Mechanisms around the World,* edited by L. A. Mandle, Z. Ouyang, J. E. Salzman, and G. C. Daily, 237–54. Washington, DC: Island Press. https://doi.org/10.5822/978-1-64283-004-0_9.

Bjornlund, H., and P. Rossini. 2007. "An Analysis of the Returns from an Investment in Water Entitlements in Australia." *Pacific Rim Property Research Journal* 13 (3): 344–60. https://doi .org/10.1080/14445921.2007.11104237.

Börner, J., D. Schulz, S. Wunder, and A. Pfaff. 2020. "The Effectiveness of Forest Conservation Policies and Programs." *Annual Review of Resource Economics* 12: 45–64. https://doi .org/10.1146/annurev-resource-110119-025703.

Brauman, K. A., R. Benner, S. Benitez, L. Bremer, and K. Vigerstøl. 2019. "Water Funds." In *Green Growth That Works: Natural Capital Policy and Finance Mechanisms around the World,* edited by L. A. Mandle, Z. Ouyang, J. E. Salzman, and G. C. Daily, 118–40. Washington, DC: Island Press. https://doi.org/10.5822/978-1-64283-004-0_9.

Bulte, E. H., and E. B. Barbier. 2005. "Trade and Renewable Resources in a Second Best World: An Overview." *Environmental and Resource Economics* 30 (4): 423–63. https://doi .org/10.1007/s10640-004-5022-2.

Copeland, B. R., and M. S. Taylor. 2013. *Trade and the Environment.* Princeton, NJ: Princeton University Press.

Crippa, M., E. Solazzo, D. Guizzardi, F. Monforti-Ferrario, F. N. Tubiello, and A. Leip. 2021. "Food Systems Are Responsible for a Third of Global Anthropogenic GHG Emissions." *Nature Food* 2: 198–209. https://doi.org/10.1038/s43016-021-00225-9.

de Mesquita, B. B. 2004. "The Methodical Study of Politics." In *Problems and Methods in the Study of Politics,* edited by I. Shapiro, R.M. Smith, and T.E. Masoud, 227–48. Cambridge, UK: Cambridge University Press.

Economist. 2021. "Treating Beef Like Coal Would Make a Big Dent in Greenhouse-Gas Emissions." October 2, 2021. https://www.economist.com/graphic-detail/2021/10/02 /treating-beef-like-coal-would-make-a-big-dent-in-greenhouse-gas-emissions.

Eisenbarth, S. 2022. "Do Exports of Renewable Resources Lead to Resource Depletion? Evidence from Fisheries." *Journal of Environmental Economics and Management* 112: 102603. https:// doi.org/10.1016/j.jeem.2021.102603.

Fen, C., and J. Zhang. 2018. "Performance of Green Supply Chain Management: A Systematic Review and Meta Analysis." *Journal of Cleaner Production* 183: 1064–81. https://doi .org/10.1016/j.jclepro.2018.02.171.

Ferraro, P. J., M. M. Hanauer, and K. R. E. Sims. 2011. "Conditions Associated with Protected Area Success in Conservation and Poverty Reduction." *PNAS* 108: 13913–18. https://doi .org/10.1073/pnas.1011529108.

Fuerst, F., and G. Warren-Myers. 2018. "Does Voluntary Disclosure Create a Green Lemon Problem? Energy-Efficiency Ratings and House Prices." *Energy Economics* 74 (August): 1–12. https://doi.org/10.1016/j.eneco.2018.04.041.

Garrido, D., A. Espínola-Arredondo, and F. Munoz-Garcia. 2020. "Can Mandatory Certification Promote Greenwashing? A Signaling Approach." *Journal of Public Economic Theory* 22 (6): 1801–51. https://doi.org/10.1111/jpet.12445.

Gawande, K., and U. Bandyopadhyay. 2000. "Is Protection for Sale? Evidence on the Grossman-Helpman Theory of Endogenous Protection." *Review of Economics and Statistics* 82 (1): 139–52. https://doi.org/10.1162/003465300558579.

Jack, B. K. 2013. "Constraints on the Adoption of Agricultural Technologies in Developing Countries." Literature review, Agricultural Technology Adoption Initiative, Abdul Latif Jameel Poverty Action Lab (J-PAL), Massachusetts Institute of Technology, Cambridge, MA, and Center for Effective Global Action (CEGA), University of California, Berkeley.

James, N., L. Lundberg, and E. Sills. 2021. "The Implications of Learning on Bidding Behavior in a Repeated First Price Conservation Auction with Targeting." *Strategic Behavior and the Environment* 9 (1–2): 69–101. https://doi.org/10.1561/102.00000101.

Kahneman, D. 2003. "Maps of Bounded Rationality: Psychology for Behavioral Economics." *American Economic Review* 93 (5): 1449–75. https://doi.org/10.1257/000282803322655392.

Kareiva, P. 2010. "Conservation Science: Trade-In to Trade-Up." *Nature* 466: 322–23. https://doi.org/10.1038/466322a.

Lawry, S., C. Samii, R. Hall, A. Leopold, D. Hornby, and F. Mtero. 2014. "The Impact of Land Property Rights Interventions on Investment and Agricultural Productivity in Developing Countries: A Systematic Review." *Campbell Systematic Reviews* 10 (1): 1–104. https://doi.org/10.1080/19439342.2016.1160947.

Mandle, L. A., Z. Ouyang, J. E. Salzman, and G. C. Daily, eds. 2019. *Green Growth That Works: Natural Capital Policy and Finance Mechanisms around the World*. Washington, DC: Island Press.

McConnachie, M. M., R. M. Cowling, C. M. Shackleton, and A. T. Knight. 2013. "The Challenges of Alleviating Poverty through Ecological Restoration: Insights from South Africa's 'Working for Water' Program." *Restoration Ecology* 21 (5): 544–50. https://doi.org/10.1111/rec.12038.

Nepstad, D. C., W. Boyd, C. M. Stickler, T. Bezerra, and A. A. Azevedo. 2013. "Responding to Climate Change and the Global Land Crisis: REDD+, Market Transformation and Low-Emissions Rural Development." *Philosophical Transactions of the Royal Society B* 368: 20120167. https://doi.org.10.1098/rstb.2012.0167.

Njagi, T., M. Mathenge, E. Mukundi, and M. Carter. 2017. "Maize Technology Bundles and Food Security in Kenya." USAID Feed the Future Innovation Lab for Assets and Market Access Policy Brief. United States Department of Agriculture, Washington, DC.

Oates, A., E. Wallace, and P. R. Portney. 2003. "The Political Economy of Environmental Policy." In *Handbook of Environmental Economics* 1: 325–54. Amsterdam: Elsevier. https://doi.org/10.1016/S1574-0099(03)01013-1.

OECD (Organisation for Economic Co-operation and Development). 2021. *Pension Markets in Focus*. Paris: OECD. http://www.oecd.org/finance/pensionmarketsinfocus.htm.

Place, F., and B. M. Swallow. 2000. "Assessing the Relationship between Property Rights and Technology Adoption in Smallholder Agriculture: A Review of Issues and Empirical Methods." CAPRI Working Paper, International Food Policy Research Institute, Washington, DC.

Pringle, R. M. 2017. "Upgrading Protected Areas to Conserve Wild Biodiversity." *Nature* 546 (2017): 91–99. https://doi.org/10.1038/nature22902.

Quesada, A. U. 2019. "Costa Rica: Bringing Natural Capital Values into the Mainstream. In *Green Growth That Works: Natural Capital Policy and Finance Mechanisms around the World,* edited by L. A. Mandle, Z. Ouyang, J. E. Salzman, and G. C. Daily, 195–212. Washington, DC: Island Press.

Ritchie, H. 2021. "Cutting Down Forests: What Are the Drivers of Deforestation?" Our World in Data. https://ourworldindata.org/what-are-drivers-deforestation#note-1.

Ruckelshaus, M., P. Kareiva, and L. Crowder. 2013. "The Future of Marine Conservation." In *Marine Community Ecology and Conservation,* edited by M. Bertness and B. Silliman, 517–43. New York: Sinauer Associates.

Rudel, T. K. 2017. "The Dynamics of Deforestation in the Wet and Dry Tropics: A Comparison with Policy Implications." *Forests* 8 (4): 108. http://dx.doi.org/10.3390/f8040108.

Stern, N., and J. E. Stiglitz. 2021. "The Social Cost of Carbon, Risk, Distribution, Market Failures: An Alternative Approach." NBER Working Paper 28472, National Bureau of Economic Research, Cambridge, MA.

Stiglitz, J. 2019. "Addressing Climate Change through Price and Non-Price Interventions." *European Economic Review* 119 (C): 594–612. https://doi.org/10.3386/w25939.

Teklu, A. 2005. *Research Report 4: Land Registration and Women's Land Rights in Amhara Region, Ethiopia.* International Institute for Environment and Development, London.

Turpie, J. K., C. Marais, and J. N. Blignaut. 2008. "The Working for Water Programme: Evolution of a Payments for Ecosystem Services Mechanism that Addresses Both Poverty and Ecosystem Service Delivery in South Africa." *Ecological Economics* 65 (4): 788–98. https://doi.org/10.1016/j.ecolecon.2007.12.024.

van Wilgen, B. W., and D. M. Richardson. 2012. "Three Centuries of Managing Introduced Conifers in South Africa: Benefits, Impacts, Changing Perceptions and Conflict Resolution." *Journal of Environmental Management* 106: 56–68. https://doi.org/10.1016/j.jenvman.2012.03.052.

Villoria, N. B. 2019. "Technology Spillovers and Land Use Change: Empirical Evidence from Global Agriculture." *American Journal of Agricultural Economics* 101 (3): 870–93. https://doi.org/10.1093/ajae/aay088.

Vogl, A. L., P. J. Dennedy-Frank, S. Wolny, J. A. Johnson, P. Hamel, U. Narain, and A. Vaidyae. 2016. "Managing Forest Ecosystem Services for Hydropower Production." *Environmental Science and Policy* 61 (July): 221–29. https://doi.org/10.1016/j.envsci.2016.04.014.

Xu, X., P. Sharma, S. Shu, T.-S. Lin, P. Ciais, F. N. Tubiello, P. Smith, et al. 2021. "Global Greenhouse Gas Emissions from Animal-Based Foods Are Twice Those of Plant-Based Foods." *Nature Food* 2 (9): 724–32. https://doi.org/10.1038/s43016-021-00358-x.

Efficiency Frontier for Air Quality

*Gold, on the contrary, though of little use compared with air or water,
will exchange for a great quantity of other goods.*
David Ricardo, British political economist[1]

Key messages

- Outdoor air pollution claims over 4 million lives each year and causes a host of other health-related problems that spill over into the economy.

- On average, improving the efficiency of air pollution policies and spending turns out to be a remarkably cost-effective way to save lives—less than US$40,000 per life saved.

- Although richer countries are more efficient in their air pollution spending and control, there is high variation within country income groups.

- Implementing policies for reducing air pollution more efficiently would produce a 60 percent cost saving, while delivering the same health benefits.

- Alternatively, had countries spent the same amount of money to abate fine particulate matter ($PM_{2.5}$), but implemented the most efficient policies, they would have prevented an additional 366,000 premature deaths each year.

- Inefficiencies often arise because the wrong pollutant has been targeted; an inappropriate technology is being used; policies are permissive; or sources of pollution that cost less to abate are overlooked.

Introduction

Air pollution has been a festering issue at least since the onset of the Industrial Revolution in the nineteenth century. Clean air is an important component of natural capital, indispensable for healthy lives, the protection of biodiversity, and the productivity of ecosystems and agricultural systems. Unlike other forms of natural capital that have substitutes in the form of physical capital—for example, the wastewater treatment plants that can substitute for the filtration benefits of forests or the seawalls that can substitute for the flood protection benefits of mangroves—there are no known substitutes for clean air (Greenstone and Hanna 2014), making its protection and management even more critical.

Economic activities, while lifting billions of people out of poverty and raising living standards worldwide, inadvertently release large quantities of harmful substances into the atmosphere with serious negative impacts on human health, well-being, economic productivity, natural ecosystems, and crop yields. Globally, about 4 million cases of premature deaths a year can be attributed to poor outdoor air quality (Burnett et al. 2018; Watts et al. 2019; WHO 2016). Air pollution is also implicated in acute respiratory infections, blindness, heart diseases, and low birth weight, which can affect the quality and longevity of life of millions of people (Branca and Ferrari 2002). It has been estimated that exposure to ambient and household air pollution cost the world economy some US$5.11 trillion in welfare losses in 2013 (World Bank 2016). This burden is exacerbated by significant losses in staple crops from reduced agricultural productivity (Van Dingenen et al. 2009) and diminished biodiversity and ecosystems services. Although all of these impacts are widely documented and recognized, not all are readily monetized or recorded in conventional measures of economic progress based on the gross domestic product (GDP).

Because of the nonsubstitutability of air pollution and its critical role in protecting the quality and longevity of human lives and the economy, policies and investments must protect this common pool resource and prevent its degradation. Accordingly, this chapter assesses the efficiency of spending on air quality management. Similar to the approach used in previous chapters, it develops an efficiency frontier to examine whether countries are using their resources on air quality management in ways that deliver maximum sustainable benefits. It then develops scores for efficiency and ambition to complement similar indexes for land use and other environmental services.

The approach

This chapter describes the efficiency frontier between a country's expenditures on air quality management and the health impacts avoided by means of these investments for a sample of 63 countries. The efficiency frontier traces the maximum number of lives that could have been saved for given levels of pollution control costs. Or equivalently, the frontier traces the lowest costs at which a given number of lives could have been saved. In addition, this chapter reveals scores for the ambition levels of each country—that is, the maximum number of lives that could be saved if there were no budgetary constraints (box 5.1). Comparing a country's current environmental performance with the maximum achievable results is a useful indication of the level of policy ambition.

BOX 5.1
Efficiency scores for air quality management

The efficiency score for air quality management and the environmental score are illustrated in figure B5.1.1. Prevented premature deaths are cited as an environmental outcome on the vertical axis and pollution control costs on the horizontal axis. Current performance is point **Z**. The efficiency frontier shows the maximal possible combinations of the environmental outcomes and the pollution control costs that accrue from decisions on air quality management. The efficiency frontier is found using the GAINS optimization (see annex 5A).

The country's current performance **Z** lies well inside the efficiency frontier, indicating that improvements in both dimensions—environmental outcomes and pollution control costs—are possible. A country can move closer to the frontier either by changing pollution

FIGURE B5.1.1
Air pollution: Relationships among various performance metrics

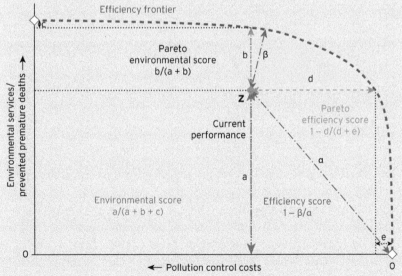

Source: World Bank.

Continued

BOX 5.1
Continued

controls while maintaining the same health outcome or by changing the health outcome for constant pollution control costs. The shaded area in the figure shows the possible Pareto improvements (win-wins) in which the outcome in both dimensions could be improved.

Formally, for a given performance Z

$$\text{efficiency score} = 1 - \frac{\beta}{\alpha}, \tag{B5.1.1}$$

where α is the Euclidean distance between the coordinates of the current outcome and the minimum possible score, and β is the Euclidean distance between the coordinates of the current outcome (what has been achieved) and the coordinates of the closest point on the efficiency frontier (what could be achieved). The minimum possible scores for pollution control costs in a country and for environmental outcome (avoided premature deaths within the same country) are 0.

An environmental ambition score is defined as the share to which a given performance Z realizes the maximum possible environmental improvement—that is,

$$\text{environmental score} = \frac{a}{a + b + c}. \tag{B5.1.2}$$

An alternative set of performance measures compares current performance in one dimension relative to what can be achieved without sacrifice in the other dimension. This is termed a Pareto improvement in which one output can be increased without sacrifice of another outcome, so that

$$\text{Pareto efficiency score} = 1 - \frac{d}{d + e}, \tag{B5.1.3}$$

and

$$\text{Pareto environmental score} = \frac{b}{a + b}. \tag{B5.1.4}$$

These scores measure the amount achieved relative to the amount that could be achieved without sacrifice if resources are not used as efficiently as they could be used or if inputs are not allocated in ways that can maximize outputs.

The efficiency frontier is derived from calculations using the Greenhouse Gas–Air Pollution Interactions and Synergies (GAINS) model (Amann et al. 2011).[2] The scores reveal insights into how efficiencies can be improved. The analysis is conducted for 63 countries across all income levels, covering 86 percent of the global population and 45 percent of global GDP. In 2015, 84 percent of all global cases of premature deaths attributable to poor air quality occurred in these countries.

The focus in this analysis is on fine particulate matter, $PM_{2.5}$, the pollutant identified as especially harmful to human health (GBD 2015 Risk Factors Collaborators 2016; GBD 2017 Risk Factors Collaborators 2018). $PM_{2.5}$ in ambient air is generated from so-called "primary" sources of emissions (such as soot and mineral dust), as well as secondary particles that are formed in the atmosphere from gaseous precursor emissions: sulfur dioxide (SO_2), nitrogen oxides (NO_x), ammonia (NH_3), and volatile organic compounds (VOCs). Meanwhile, at the outset it is useful to note the following caveats when interpreting the results:

- The analysis is directed at only a subset of countries for which modeled data are available, focusing on lower-income ones.

- The assessment is limited to premature mortality attributable to human exposure to fine particulate matter in ambient air. The only health endpoint it considers is premature mortality. It does not consider other health endpoints such as morbidity or reduced labor productivity. That said, $PM_{2.5}$ is the criteria source pollutant that has by far the largest health and economic consequences.

- The analysis is confined to ambient air quality. It does not take into account additional benefits that emerge through reduced indoor air pollution from less use of solid fuels in households. Likewise, the analysis does not take into account negative impacts on agricultural crops, forests, and natural ecosystems (through, for example, acidification and eutrophication of freshwater and soils) and does not quantify threats on ecosystems services (such as biodiversity and pollination) from air pollution.

- Although this study considers primary $PM_{2.5}$ as well as the formation of secondary $PM_{2.5}$ in the atmosphere, it quantifies only health benefits that occur within the same country, thereby ignoring additional benefits that occur downwind of other countries. Because the typical transport distance of $PM_{2.5}$ in the atmosphere is 300–1,500 kilometers, this limitation is important for smaller to medium-size countries. For example, in European countries 20–30 percent of the health benefits occur outside the country in which investments are made (Amann et al. 2021). Nevertheless, this limitation was applied because policy decisions on domestic air quality tend to be based on expected domestic benefits.

- The cost evaluation considers pollution reductions that emerge from technical emission controls and fuel substitution (such as substituting solid fuels for cooking). The evaluation does not take fully into account the emission reduction potentials and costs of measures that interact with or were originally taken for other policy priorities for which emission reductions may be an unintended side effect. Such measures include structural changes in the energy system (such as fuel substitution) and new technologies that may be efficiency enhancing, as well as policies leading to behavioral changes (for example, changes in mobility and different consumption patterns).

Finally, it is important to note that being on the efficiency frontier does not necessarily mean that the chosen policy represents the optimal outcome (where marginal benefits and marginal costs are equalized). In fact, a large body of literature (WHO 2015) indicates that even in countries with highly advanced pollution controls, such as the United Kingdom, United States, and member states of the European Union (EU), the marginal benefits of current measures exceed the marginal pollution control costs by a wide margin. Thus even if countries attain a high efficiency score (which means the resources are spent in a cost-effective way to achieve a given level of air quality), the net economic benefits would be enhanced through more stringent pollution controls.

How well do countries perform?

The current pollution abatement technologies and practices prevent about 43 percent of premature mortalities, compared with a scenario in which no abatement action would have been taken. According to the GAINS analysis, the 63 countries in the sample in this study spent about US$220 billion (0.6 percent of their collective GDP) on air pollution controls. However, there are large variations across countries, even within the same income group (figure 5.1).

These investments prevent some 1.9 million premature deaths within the countries undertaking the investments, compared with a counterfactual situation with no control measures. However, the remaining (unabated) emissions

FIGURE 5.1
Air pollution: Expenditures as a share of GDP, by country income group, 2015

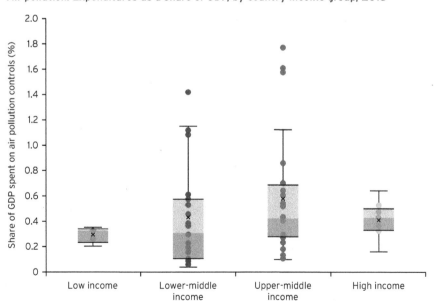

Source: World Bank.
Note: The upper and lower bounds of a box define the upper and lower quartiles of the distribution—that is, 75th and 25th percentiles. The horizontal bar inside the box indicates the median of the distribution, and the x indicates the mean value. The whiskers indicate the maximum and minimum values, not taking into consideration outliers. The dots are observations. GDP = gross domestic product.

currently account for 2.5 million premature deaths in these countries. Thus, on average, control measures are responsible for reducing premature deaths by 43 percent. These estimates are conservative, however, because they do not take into account either the transboundary health benefits occurring downwind of the emitting countries or the health benefits of the reduced indoor pollution arising from the use of cleaner household fuels.

The current pollution abatement mix is inefficient, and this inefficiency has a substantial price tag. A comparison of current positions relative to what could be achieved along the efficiency frontier reveals significant inefficiencies of spending (figure 5.2):

- The same health benefits (that is, 1.9 million prevented premature deaths) could have been achieved for one-third of the cost (US$75 billion). Thus the economic cost of inefficiency amounted to US$145 billion in 2015—that is, 0.39 percent of the combined GDP of these 63 countries.

- As a corollary, if each country had spent the same resources in the most efficient way, the US$220 billion expenditure could have prevented 2.3 million premature deaths (about 20 percent more than the 1.9 million deaths), implying that about 366,000 more premature deaths could have been prevented had the current spending been allocated across efficient pollution abatement options.

The estimates just presented refer to the 63 countries taken as a whole. However, a country-by-country analysis reveals large differences between countries. This variation across similar countries provides a path to how to enhance the efficiency of the resources spent on air quality management.

FIGURE 5.2
Air pollution: Collective performance of sample of 63 countries in relation to their efficiency frontiers, 2015

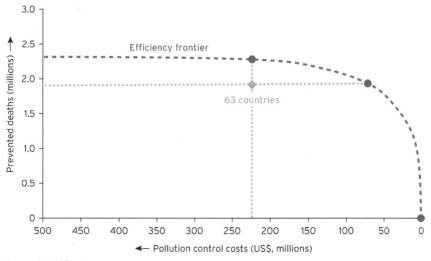

Source: World Bank.

Efficiency and environmental scores that measure policy ambitions

Efficiency scores and income

Efficiency scores, which measure the distance of a country's performances to the efficiency frontier, show large variations across countries, ranging from 12 to 96 percent. As shown in figure 5.3, in general more developed countries— lower-middle-income countries (LMICs), upper-middle-income countries (UMICs), and high-income countries (HICs)—perform significantly better than low-income countries (LICs). However, like the landscape analysis, the variation within country income groups is larger than the variation across groups. Specifically, although the variation in means across groups ranges from 35 to about 85 percent, the scores of the low-income group exhibit the largest variation, ranging from 15 to about 70 percent.

Notably, all income groups display good examples of both highly efficient resource use and low-efficient resource use. For example, among LMICs, UMICs, and HICs are countries with pollution abatement efficiencies of more than 95 percent, as well as countries with pollution abatement efficiencies

FIGURE 5.3
Air pollution: Efficiency scores, by country income group

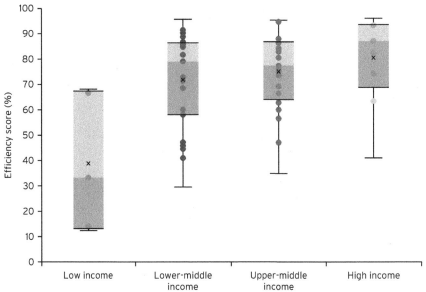

Source: World Bank.
Note: The upper and lower bounds of a box define the upper and lower quartiles of the distribution—that is, 75th and 25th percentiles. The horizontal bar inside the box indicates the median of the distribution, and the x indicates the mean value. The whiskers indicate the maximum and minimum values, not taking into consideration outliers. The dots are observations.

of 30–40 percent. Some LICs are 70 percent efficient, and others are merely about 10 percent efficient.

Environmental scores and income

The environmental score quantifies the level of *ambition* in a country by measuring the extent to which the country realizes the potential air quality improvements that, in principle, would be achievable. For example, a score of over 70 percent for the average high-income country means that this average country has been able to reduce more than 70 percent of the preventable causalities from air pollution through the most ambitious policy interventions. Thus the environmental score expresses how ambitious a country is in abating air pollution.

Figure 5.4 shows that although environmental scores tend to increase with a country's income level, there is still significant variation within each income group. This finding indicates that there is only a loose statistical relationship between ambition in reducing air pollution and income level. However, the low-income countries do have extremely low levels of ambition, implying that there are large (and perhaps cost-effective) opportunities to save lives through improvements in air quality in these countries. This issue is explored further in the policy section of this chapter.

FIGURE 5.4
Air pollution: Environmental scores, by country income group

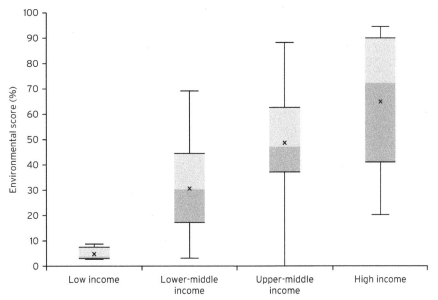

Source: World Bank.
Note: The upper and lower bounds of a box define the upper and lower quartiles of the distribution—that is, 75th and 25th percentiles. The horizontal bar inside the box indicates the median of the distribution. The whiskers indicate the maximum and minimum values, not taking into consideration outliers. The x indicates the statistical mean.

Ambition and efficiency

The overall statistical correlation between the efficiency and environmental scores themselves ($R^2 = 0.42$) suggests that ambitious countries generally clean up in more efficient ways. On the other hand, there is almost no correlation between efficiency and income ($R^2 = 0.08$), suggesting that efficiency is not affected by levels of development, similar to the landscape efficiency scores (figure 5.3).

A better understanding of how efficiencies can be enhanced is gained by assessing two important insights emerging from the large variation in efficiency scores among countries with similar environmental (ambition) scores (figure 5.5). First, good-practice examples with efficiencies of more than 90 percent occur across the full range of environmental scores, revealing that the efficient use of resources for air quality management is possible for less ambitious as well as more ambitious countries. Second, the spread of efficiency scores declines with increasing ambition, indicating large potentials for efficiency gains, especially in the less ambitious countries. Such countries can enhance their environmental performance as well, and they can do so without additional costs by implementing more efficient environmental policies and measures. This point is discussed in more detail in the final section of this chapter.

FIGURE 5.5
Air pollution: Efficiency and environmental scores, by country income group

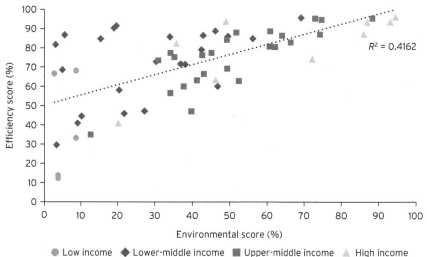

Source: World Bank.
Note: The figure compares countries' environmental scores with their efficiency scores. The color and shape of the marker indicate a country's income level, according to the World Bank.

A typology of countries and priority directions for improving efficiency

Many countries could improve their air quality without placing an additional burden on their economy. Meanwhile, many good-practice examples of efficient air quality management can be found in countries at all stages of development. To derive generic priority directions for efficiency improvements from good practices, three types of countries are distinguished based on their efficiency and environmental scores (figure 5.6):

- Type A: high efficiency scores, high environmental scores
- Type B: high efficiency scores, low environmental scores
- Type C: low efficiency scores, low environmental scores.

This framework can be used to identify the necessary policy mixes in countries to promote both sustainability and the efficient use of capital.

Type A: High efficiency scores and high environmental scores

Type A countries combine high efficiency scores with high environmental scores (ambition) (see figures 5.6 and 5.7). These countries include high-income (Canada, Germany, and the Republic of Korea) and upper-middle-income

FIGURE 5.6

Air pollution: Country types (A, B, and C) based on efficiency and environmental scores, by country income group

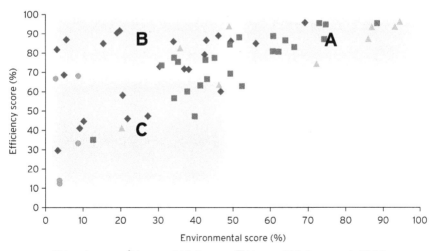

Source: World Bank.

FIGURE 5.7
Air pollution: Location of type A countries vis-à-vis the efficiency frontier

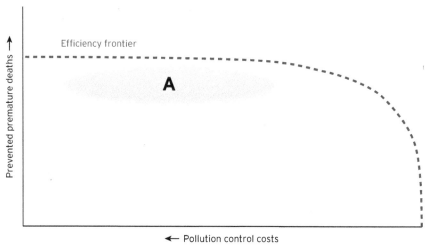

Source: World Bank.

(China, Mexico, South Africa, Thailand, and Türkiye, among others). Within this group, the best performers reach efficiency scores of up to 95 percent. The scores of other countries barely exceed 60 percent, indicating significant scope for efficiency enhancements by emulating relevant examples.

At high environmental scores, marginal costs increase steeply, implying that in many cases alternative portfolios of measures could achieve the same impact at significantly lower cost.

This study identifies four common reasons for inefficiencies in type A countries:

1. More cost-effective gains can be made *in frequently overlooked sectors* such as household burning of biomass for cooking and heating and agriculture. In addressing air pollution problems, many countries have focused on conventional sectors with large point sources that often require more costly interventions and ignore less familiar sources of pollution. After implementation of effective controls of road transport and large point source emissions (indicated by high environmental scores), other sectors emerge as dominant contributors to $PM_{2.5}$ (as shown in systematic source apportionment studies—see Van Dingenen et al. 2004; Zheng et al. 2019). Depending on the country, these "other sectors" may include solid fuel combustion in the residential sector (for example, wood burning in "pleasure" stoves), open burning of crop residue, nonroad mobile machinery, and midsize combustion plants. Source apportionment studies have also uncovered a critical share of secondary $PM_{2.5}$ in total $PM_{2.5}$ concentrations in ambient air

(typically 40–60 percent). Secondary $PM_{2.5}$ is formed through chemical reactions from precursor emissions—that is, sulfur dioxide, nitrogen oxides, and nonmethane volatile organic compounds. In many situations, the formation of secondary $PM_{2.5}$ is brought about by the availability of ammonia, which is mainly emitted from agricultural activities (manure management and fertilizer application). Many type A countries have managed to reduce pollution in a cost-effective way by harmonizing further (and sometimes costly) measures to tackle remaining primary $PM_{2.5}$ emissions from road transport and large point sources, but they often neglect controls of precursor emissions that form secondary $PM_{2.5}$. Correction of this neglect requires widening the scope of air quality management from the conventional sectors (transport, power, and industry) to other sectors such as households and agriculture.

2. Countries have not caught up with the need to *shift from focusing on peak pollution days to focusing on annual exposure.* In recent decades, epidemiological evidence on the determinants of the health impacts of air pollution has demonstrated the importance of long-term exposure to $PM_{2.5}$ when compared with episodic peak exposures (Burnett et al. 2018; WHO 2013). Based on this scientific finding, many countries have moved from directing air quality management toward peak concentrations, which are often highly visible and occur during short episodes or at the worst-polluted locations, toward long-term exposure of the total population to $PM_{2.5}$. These countries have complemented their existing legal frameworks for compliance with given air quality standards (and in the most polluted situations) with approaches to reduce exposure of the entire population to $PM_{2.5}$. The approaches used include caps on the various precursor emissions and consideration of the impacts of the various sources on population exposure. This shift has increased significantly the efficiency of efforts for public health.

3. Because $PM_{2.5}$ is highly mobile and crosses jurisdictions, *cooperative approaches produce greater efficiency* than do purely unilateral efforts at pollution control. Fine particulate matter, which remains in the atmosphere for up to a week, can be transported from several hundred to 1,000 kilometers. Thus at any location a significant share of $PM_{2.5}$ found in ambient air originates from remote sources in other regions or in other countries. Because of the steep increase in the marginal costs of pollution controls at high environmental scores, many countries have enhanced cost-effectiveness by adopting regionally coordinated approaches to air quality management. By revealing information about the mutual benefits of cooperation and acting on that information, countries can replace the costliest domestic efforts with cheaper measures at upwind emission sources. Good examples of regional cooperation within countries can be found in China (Song et al. 2020), in EU

member countries (Maynard and Williams 2018), outside the EU through the Convention on Long-range Transboundary Air Pollution (Fowler et al. 2020), and in the United States such as through the Clean Air Act's "good neighbor" provision.

4. Several countries chose command and control over economic measures that would have resulted in the *adoption of more efficient and advanced pollution abatement technology*. The high environmental efficiencies of these countries imply that many sources at close to the maximum technical potentials limit opportunities for efficiency gains. It is well established that pollution taxes are more cost-effective than command and control approaches at reducing pollution in many situations. Regulations based on decrees to use the "best available technologies" may miss options that would achieve the same emission reductions at lower cost. For that reason, countries with ambitious pollution control objectives have introduced emission taxes (such as for SO_2, NO_x, and VOCs) that provide economic incentives to select the most effective options for their specific situations. Examples are Denmark (Millock, Nauges, and Sterner 2004), Sweden (Söderholm et al. 2021), and a few other European countries (Sterner and Köhlin 2004). In Sweden, those revenues are used to reimburse the taxed plants that emit low volumes of NO_x in order to incentivize energy efficiency and reduce any potentially negative impact on competitiveness (Sterner and Höglund Isaksson 2006).

To identify the specific types of policy interventions that increase efficiency, many of these countries have established scientific infrastructure that provides a shared knowledge base on the benefits and cost-effectiveness of the available options. In the largest countries (for example, China and the United States), this infrastructure has been established at the national level, while smaller countries, such as some in Europe, have developed regional networks. Examples are those under the Convention on Long-range Transboundary Air Pollution.

Despite high environmental ambitions and the cost-effective use of resources, it is not certain that the high ambition levels correspond to the socially optimum use of resources. In practice, some of the current inefficiencies may reflect path dependencies and past choices. For example, if a country was an early adopter of pollution control technology, the chosen technology would likely be overtaken by more advanced technologies (such as new desulfurization plants and catalytic converters) with superior environmental or economic performance. Although the current methodology does not discount early adoption, reassessing national environmental standards in view of technological progress might be beneficial.

Type B: High efficiency scores and low environmental scores

Type B countries are characterized by relatively low environmental scores (ambition), which those countries achieve in relatively efficient ways. These countries are located close to the low-ambition range of the efficiency frontier (see figures 5.6 and 5.8). This group includes many middle-income countries (for example, Bangladesh, Chile, India, Indonesia, Pakistan, Peru, the Philippines, Saudi Arabia, and the West Balkan countries).

Type B countries often focus on the *lower-hanging fruits of pollution controls.* Basic pollution controls are frequently limited to a small number of key sectors (such as particle filters for large point sources burning coal), where pollution abatement is relatively less expensive with well-established technologies. However, despite their economic efficiency, such measures are often not commensurate with the scale of the pollution problems arising from rapid economic growth. This is especially true for cities (WHO 2018) with significant burdens on public health (Burnett et al. 2018; Watts et al. 2019; WHO 2016) and with high productivity losses and health costs (World Bank 2016).

In such cases, it is likely that the chosen ambition levels are far from socially optimal levels. Based on the findings for countries with much higher ambition levels, the marginal benefits of available measures are likely to exceed their marginal costs by a wide margin. Thus, while acknowledging the efficiency of current policies, these countries urgently need to enhance their environmental scores. This effort will involve additional costs because the current efforts are

FIGURE 5.8
Air pollution: Location of type B countries vis-à-vis the efficiency frontier

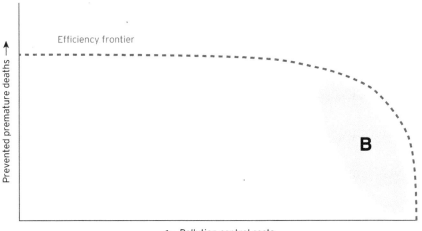

Source: World Bank.

close to the efficiency frontier. Maintaining high efficiency for the additional air quality improvements will be critical but challenging.

Many type B countries have a limited understanding of the *regional nature* of $PM_{2.5}$ pollution. As noted, a considerable share of $PM_{2.5}$ originates from distant sources outside a jurisdiction. Many strategies for urban air quality management in these countries neglect this feature by embarking on costly local measures instead of entering into cooperative agreements with the surrounding regions.

More ambitious pollution controls in these countries will require *extending the scope of pollution controls* to emission sources that require more complex interventions and detailed analyses. Systematic source apportionment studies for a population's exposure to $PM_{2.5}$ can reveal sources that are of particular importance in a given country. Depending on the local situations, these sources could include the household use of solid fuels for cooking and heating (within and outside cities), open burning of municipal waste and agriculture residues, industrial midsize combustion plants (such as brick kilns), industrial activities such as cement production, nonroad mobile agricultural and construction machinery, as well as road transport, which makes particularly large contributions to concentrations along busy streets in urban areas. In addition, reducing high concentrations of secondary $PM_{2.5}$ will require balanced cuts of the precursor emissions of secondary particles (SO_2, NO_x, VOC, and NH_3).

Tackling such sources requires prioritizing resources for pollution control because the measures already adopted will produce limited efficiency gains. Political will and support can emerge from appreciation of the benefits of clean air and from understanding the cost-effectiveness of involving additional sectors and stakeholders in air quality management. At the same time, the large variety of measures in different sectors with diverse stakeholders carries with it the danger of unproductive or counterproductive investments that could compromise economic efficiency.

Countries at comparable development levels have managed to simultaneously achieve high environmental and efficiency scores. Common features of these successful countries include comprehensive stocktaking of their current sources of pollution; an unbiased, comprehensive assessment of the air quality improvements offered by various approaches; a robust shared knowledge base on the cost-effectiveness of alternative interventions under local conditions; and a political commitment to engage in sectors that could deliver cost-effective contributions.

Type C: Low efficiency scores and low environmental scores

Type C countries, predominantly low-income and lower-middle-income, perform far from the efficiency frontier (figures 5.6 and 5.9). Notably, there are large differences in the efficiency scores even between countries with similar incomes

FIGURE 5.9
Air pollution: Location of type C countries vis-à-vis the efficiency frontier

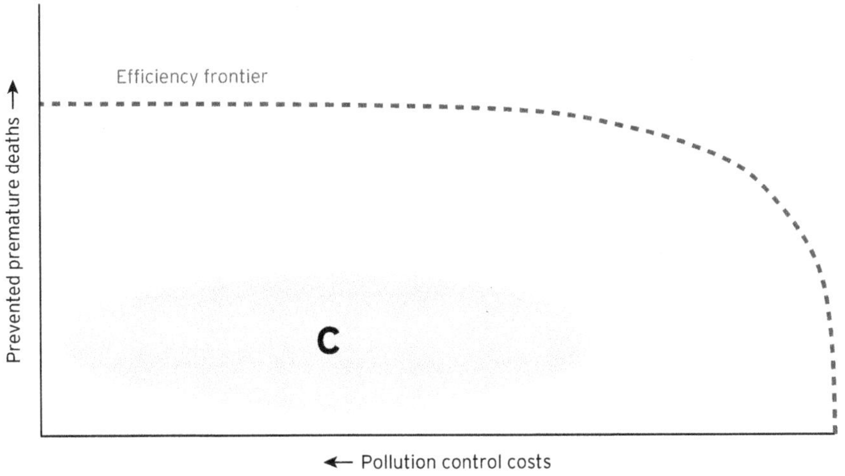

Source: World Bank.

and environmental scores. For example, efficiency scores of low-income countries range from 15 percent to almost 70 percent, indicating a large potential for efficiency improvements.

Typically, countries in this group have taken only very *basic measures* to control air pollution, despite the serious pollution levels and significant burden on public health and economic performance pointed out by numerous studies (WHO 2018). However, unlike the measures used in type B countries, the measures used in type C countries do not address sources that offer the most cost-effective potential.

Often, expertise and understanding of the specific air quality situation and possible cost-effective responses are underdeveloped. The GAINS model finds that measures adopted by these countries tend to be inspired by examples from other countries at different development stages and with different challenges for air quality management. As a consequence, significant resources are often spent on measures that have relatively little impact on population exposure (such as on technically advanced control of road vehicle emissions), while cost-effective air quality improvements that tackle other sources of emissions remain untapped (such as solid-fuel combustion in households, waste management, and open burning of agricultural residues). Not only are interventions often suboptimal in such situations, but efficiency is further impaired by poor monitoring, compliance, and enforcement mechanisms, which further increase the costs of pollution reduction. This is an example of where emulating success can lead a country astray.

In type C countries, a move toward the efficiency frontier would deliver large economic and health benefits. Because current performance is located far from the efficiency frontier, big opportunities exist for simultaneously improving both the efficiency and environmental scores. Thus more efficient strategies for air quality management can combine measures that work in two directions.

First, higher environmental scores without large additional investments in infrastructure can be achieved through better governance—that is, stronger monitoring, compliance, and enforcement mechanisms. Where compliance and enforcement are limited, relatively costly measures, such as advanced road vehicle controls, will fail to deliver their intended air quality benefits.

Second, economic efficiency scores can be increased by tailored measures that include a much wider set of sources at lower costs. However, because these countries have low environmental scores, additional measures should not replace existing efforts. Depending on local conditions, such measures might include enhanced access to clean household fuels to replace solid-fuel use in households, improved waste management practices, bans on burning agricultural residues, and more efficient and cleaner brick kilns. Many of these measures will involve small enterprises that may lack the resources to adopt cleaner technologies, suggesting the need for measures carefully aligned with affordability.

It is also important to compare the cost-effectiveness of possible additional controls (such as for road transport emissions, which tend to be more expensive than interventions in other sectors) with the potential benefits and costs of measures that could be taken in the other sectors. Focusing on public health benefits, such a comparison will need to consider the impacts of potential measures on the entire population of a country and not just the impacts on pollution hot spots (such as busy street crossings in cities) where air quality monitors may be located.

Like type B countries, type C countries typically have only a limited understanding of the regional nature of $PM_{2.5}$ pollution. Many strategies for urban air quality management in these countries neglect transboundary pollution. As a result, they focus on costly local measures instead of entering cooperative agreements with surrounding regions.

Some of the most challenging constraints lie in misaligned incentives. Polluting activities are often heavily subsidized by governments (such as coal combustion in the energy sector and fuel prices). Reducing such subsidies and possibly imposing taxes on polluting fuels (such as a carbon tax) will make the status quo economically less attractive to enterprises and consumers and support a move toward cleaner fuels. Caution may be warranted, however, because reforms aimed at introducing fuel taxes or removing fuel subsidies have been met with stiff opposition that sometimes spills over into public protests. Successful subsidy reforms have often called for ensuring there are credible compensation mechanisms for those who may lose from the reforms. Such compensation mechanisms can help build a broad coalition in favor of reform. In addition, beginning with small changes rather than radical reforms is less likely to spark dissent.

Improving efficiency and ambition will entail tackling less familiar sources of pollution by households and farmers. Changing behaviors can be challenging, but examples of success can be emulated. The tools based on these behavioral nudges do not displace economic policy approaches that target incentives. Instead, such tools complement and enhance economic policy approaches. Some of these approaches may cost little and can be carried out fairly quickly because they depend on nuances in messaging and policy design, whereas others may take longer, especially when changes in attitudes and values are involved.

Many of the measures to improve air quality deliver other benefits as well. For example, access to clean cooking fuels, in addition to its health benefits, reduces the time spent (mostly by women) to collect biomass and diminishes the emissions of short-lived climate pollutants (such as black carbon) that increase near-term global temperatures. Abolishing the open burning of municipal waste requires effective waste management systems with important benefits for other environmental media, development, and resource use. Diversion of agricultural residues from open burning to other productive uses such as co-firing in larger plants to replace fossil fuels can deliver economic benefits and create additional income for rural populations. Comprehensive appraisals of the full range of benefits of such measures will be important for the design of effective policy instruments and adoption by the population.

Finally, knowledge gaps can lock countries into low-performance conditions. The design of policies and measures that could move countries toward the efficiency frontier requires a thorough understanding of the local air pollution situation and of cost-effective interventions that work under particular conditions. Often, there is only limited understanding of the current level of pollution beyond a few monitoring stations in capital cities, and little is especially known about the levels in rural areas. Emission inventories, if they exist, are frequently incomplete. Moreover, expertise may be lacking on environmental economics, health effects, and the social factors that determine consumer behavior. Thus enhancing the relevant expertise in countries will be essential and will be an urgent prerequisite for moving toward the efficiency frontier. Regional networks of experts sharing local experiences and working toward cooperative solutions can accelerate development of the relevant knowledge.

Priorities for efficiency improvements

Based on the analysis just described, the priority directions for moving toward the efficiency frontier are summarized in table 5.1.

TABLE 5.1
Air pollution: Priority directions for moving toward the efficiency frontier, by country type

Type A	Type B	Type C
Priority directions for efficiency improvements		
• Adjust the ambition level to optimize the use of societal resources by equalizing marginal benefits and costs. • Where necessary and possible, further increase efficiency.	• Enhance the environmental ambition to optimize the use of societal resources. • Shift focus of air quality management to public health benefits.	• Move toward the efficiency frontier by enhancing environmental and efficiency scores. • Shift the focus of air quality management to public health benefits.
Focus areas		

• Balance control efforts across a wider range of source sectors, considering, among other things,
  ○ Household wood stoves
  ○ Agricultural residue burning
  ○ Precursors of secondary particulate matter ($PM_{2.5}$), including ammonia from manure management and fertilizer application.
• Pursue transboundary cooperation with neighboring countries to reduce the need for measures with high marginal costs.
• Avoid trade-offs and capture synergies with other policy priorities such as greenhouse gas (GHG) mitigation.
	• Widen pollution control efforts to sectors beyond road transport and large point sources to, among other things,
	  ○ Solid-fuel cookstoves
	  ○ Agricultural residue burning
	  ○ Municipal solid-waste management.
	• Improve monitoring, compliance, and enforcement mechanisms.
	• Avoid trade-offs and capture synergies with other policy priorities (such as GHG mitigation and social aspects).
		• Enhance governance.
		• Improve monitoring and compliance mechanisms.
		• Widen pollution control efforts to sectors beyond road transport and large point sources to, among other things,
		  ○ Solid-fuel cookstoves
		  ○ Agricultural residue burning
		  ○ Municipal solid-waste management.
		• Avoid trade-offs and capture synergies with other policy priorities (such as poverty alleviation, development, and climate change).

Relevant instruments		
• Adopt pollution taxes instead of strict performance standards. • Pursue international cooperation.	• Revisit existing fuel subsidy systems and consider alternative tax/subsidy systems that make socially desirable investments attractive to consumers and enterprises.	• Revisit existing fuel subsidy systems and consider alternative tax/subsidy systems that make socially desirable investments attractive to consumers and enterprises. • Establish enforcement mechanisms.

Continued

TABLE 5.1
Continued

Type A	Type B	Type C
Knowledge gaps		
• Expertise on cost-effective air quality management to address precursor emissions of secondary $PM_{2.5}$	• Air quality monitoring representative of population exposure (for example, in residential and rural areas) • Local health impacts of air pollution • Source apportionment of $PM_{2.5}$ in ambient air	• Air quality monitoring representative of population exposure (for example, in residential and rural areas) • Local health impacts of air pollution • Source apportionment of $PM_{2.5}$ in ambient air
	• Comprehensive emission inventories beyond large point sources and road transport • Environmental economics of cost-effective measures and instruments • Social aspects of pollution • Co-benefits with other policy priorities	• Comprehensive emission inventories beyond large point sources and road transport • Environmental economics of cost-effective measures and instruments • Social aspects of pollution • Co-benefits with other policy priorities

Source: World Bank.

Annex 5A: GAINS model methodology explained

This annex provides details on the GAINS model that was used to estimate the results described in this chapter. A more comprehensive presentation of the optimization method of the GAINS model appears in Wagner et al. (2013).

Impact calculations

Comprehensive atmospheric chemistry and transport models have traditionally been used to calculate concentration levels of air pollution. These models simulate a complex range of chemical and physical reactions. For example, the Unified EMEP Eulerian model (Simpson and Tuovinen 2014) describes the fate of emissions in the atmosphere. It considers more than 100 chemical reactions involving 70 chemical species with time steps down to 20 seconds, including numerous nonlinear mechanisms. However, the joint analysis using the economic and ecological aspects of the GAINS model, and especially the optimization task, calls for computationally efficient source–receptor relationships. For this purpose, reduced-form representations of the full models in the form of response surfaces have been developed. They describe the response of impact-relevant air quality indicators using mathematically simple formulations. Functional relationships describe changes in annual mean $PM_{2.5}$ concentrations. The (grid- or country-specific) parameters of these relationships have been derived from a sample of several hundred runs of a full atmospheric chemistry model with systematically perturbed emissions of the individual sources around a reference level.

The principle of the atmospheric calculations in the GAINS model are described by Amann et al. (2011). Because of the evolution of the GAINS model over time, some details of the formulation (such as grid resolution) differ in European versus non-European regions. Details for Europe are described by Kiesewetter et al. (2015). A description for non-European regions can be found in the supplementary material to Amann et al. (2021). A description of the ambient $PM_{2.5}$ concentration modeling follows.

Index i denotes the emitting country. When it is necessary to draw a distinction between the emitter/source and receptor country, the receptor country is denoted by index k. The emission sector is denoted as s and fuel as f. Concentrations are calculated on a grid, distinguishing emissions from near-ground (low-level) sources (residential combustion, traffic, municipal waste burning) and all other sources. Contributions from low-level emissions of primary particulate matter are calculated at a higher resolution ($0.125° \times 0.0625°$ or roughly 7×7 kilometers in Europe, and $0.1° \times 0.1°$ or roughly 10×10 kilometers outside Europe). The long-range component that stems from high-level sources and secondary particles is modeled at a coarser resolution of $0.5° \times 0.25°$ in Europe (roughly 28 kilometers) and $0.5° \times 0.5°$ elsewhere. The transfer coefficients for low-level sources include information on the urban-rural split of activities in some sectors (such as use of different fuels for cooking) and are therefore inherently activity- and sector-specific.

The concentration is calculated as

$$average\ ambient\ PM_{2.5}\ concentration\ (k) = \Sigma_{i,s,f,p}\ T_{iksfp}\ E_{isfp},$$

where E_{isfp} denotes the emissions of pollutant p from country i, sector s, and activity (fuel) f, and T_{iksfp} is the source-receptor matrix (or transfer matrix) for pollutant p from activity (fuel) f and sector s in emitting country i to receiving country k. Exposure to $PM_{2.5}$ concentration is then calculated by multiplying the concentration map with the population map for a given country and aggregating to the national scale. In practice, the calculations are performed on a high-resolution grid scale, and through appropriate aggregation this simple form can be established.

The impact calculations conducted in this project use a linear interpolation between endpoints defined by the current legislation scenario and the maximum feasible reduction (MFR) scenario. For both scenarios, total premature deaths attributable to ambient $PM_{2.5}$ were calculated using the full health impact calculation module in GAINS, as described shortly. The relation between $PM_{2.5}$ exposure and premature deaths at these endpoints was then used to derive a coefficient $f(k)$ describing the change of premature deaths per unit of exposure so that

$$premature\ deaths\ (k) = premature\ deaths\ MFR\ (k)$$
$$+ f(k) \times [exposure\ (k) - exposure\ MFR\ (k)].$$

Premature deaths from total ambient $PM_{2.5}$ for regions other than Europe are calculated using the methodology of the World Health Organization (WHO) assessment of the burden of disease from ambient air pollution (WHO 2016), which relies on disease-specific integrated exposure response relationships developed in the Global Burden of Disease 2013 study (GBD 2015 Risk Factors Collaborators 2016).

The population attributable fraction PAF_{dka} of air pollution–related deaths from disease d in region k and age a is calculated as

$$PAF_{dka} = \frac{\sum_i \frac{pop_{ki}}{pop_k}(RR_{dai} - 1)}{1 + \sum_i \frac{pop_{ki}}{pop_k}(RR_{dai} - 1)}, \tag{5A.1}$$

where i represents the 0.1° grid cells hosting population pop_{ji} belonging to region j. RR_{dai} is the disease and (possibly) age-specific relative risk as calculated from the integrated exposure response functions for $PM_{2.5}$ concentration levels in that spatial unit.

Premature deaths are calculated by multiplying the PAF_{dka} from equation (5A.1) with age-specific baseline cases of deaths d_{dka} from disease d in region k so that

$$pd_{dka} = PAF_{dka} \cdot d_{dka}. \qquad (5A.2)$$

Age-specific numbers of deaths from individual diseases are estimated from published numbers for 2010 in the Global Burden of Disease (GBD) 2013 project, which were obtained from the GBD data query tool. Age-specific projected total deaths for each GAINS region are taken from the United Nations' World Population Prospects 2017 (United Nations 2017). It is assumed that although total age-specific deaths vary according to the United Nations projections, the relative shares of individual diseases contributing to age-specific deaths remain unchanged in the future.

For Europe, calculations of premature deaths follow the WHO Europe methodology and apply exposure–response relationships for all-cause mortality of those over 30 years of age in a population, as reported under the REVIHAAP assessment (WHO 2013).[3] Equations (5A.1) and (5A.2) are applied without further age differentiation to total deaths of those over 30 years of age using the approximation $pd_k \approx \beta \cdot PM_k \cdot d_k$ with $\beta = 0.00588$, PM the population-weighted mean anthropogenic $PM_{2.5}$, and dk the number of nonaccidental deaths of those over 30 years of age in each region k.

Optimization: Objective, constraints, potentials

The optimization problem in the GAINS model is formulated as a linear programming problem and is solved with a commercial solver (GAMS-CPLEX). The decision variables in the GAINS model are essentially the shares that describe the extent to which a given activity (such as a coal-fired power plant) is subject to various emission control strategies. In practice, the model spans a rather large configuration space that takes into account the possible combinations of technologies, the possible transitions from one technology to another, the multipollutant nature of some sources, and a number of other factors.

In a typical optimization run for this study, the objective function minimized is the total cost for emission control measures in a country, subject to the constraint that a particular target for mortality or population-weighted concentration is achieved in that country. The target value for the exposure is iteratively set and solved for, starting from the lowest ambition level—either the no control emissions (NOC) scenario or the current legislation emissions (CLE) scenario—and gradually increased, typically in 30 steps, to the highest ambition level still feasible.[4] Each iteration starts afresh with a new target and no knowledge of the outcome of the previous run. Thus at each ambition level, the model is free to select an optimal solution that is not path-dependent in the sense that it does not depend on the solution taken at another point on the cost curve. Therefore, as one moves up the cost curve there is also no lock-in effect.

Positively speaking, leapfrogging is possible in the model—that is, it is not necessary to deploy less efficient technologies before moving up the curve and deploying more efficient ones. For example, the optimization reflects that it is possible to introduce, for example, a Euro-6 standard for vehicles without having already imposed Euro-1 through Euro-5 standards. The standard considered cost-effective depends on the ambition level for the health benefits.

The deployment of technologies may nevertheless be limited. This limitation is represented by decision variables that are subject to a variety of constraints. First, a technology is subject to upper limits. For example, only a fraction of all activities related to a source of pollution are subject to control. For example, if a power plant is situated on a confined plot, it may physically not be possible to install a selective catalytic reduction (SCR) device around it to reduce NO_x emissions. Thus the maximum application rate of the SCR technology for the whole country may be less than 100 percent and will have to be calculated accordingly. Second, there may be a lower bound on the application rate of a technology, perhaps stemming from a path dependence. For example, if an investment-intensive, medium-efficient new installation was built recently, from an economic point of view it might not be replaceable today by a better and more expensive technology (unless referring to an additive upgrade). Lower bounds on decision variables in GAINS typically reflect capital turnover dynamics, but, as indicated earlier, these constraints are relaxed for the present study. Relaxation of the lower bounds gives the model more flexibility and allows consideration of full emission reduction potentials in all sectors, independently of the past investment schedule. Thus premature scrapping of existing—already implemented—pollution controls before the end of their technical lifetime is explicitly allowed.

This study has also introduced measures motivated by other objectives or have very localized effects. For example, the electrification of buses could have a significant effect on air quality if the counterfactual for comparison is a bus running on diesel with a high sulfur content and not subject to any NO_x or PM control. In addition, electrification of buses has GHG benefits and does not depend on fuel quality standards implemented at the national scale. Thus it could be implemented locally. However, as a pure air pollution reduction measure this measure may be fairly expensive, compared with introducing on a national scale an advanced Euro emission standard coupled with low-sulfur fuel. Thus electrification as an emission reduction measure typically exhibits high marginal costs and low emission reduction potentials on a national scale relative to efficient end-of-pipe emission control devices. Similar arguments hold for control measures in the waste and other sectors. Their effect, as a result of a change in the underlying production and consumption system, is often more fruitfully analyzed as alternative (exogenous) states of that system without associating the costs for these system changes to the air pollution control domain.

In summary, local or island solutions that address very specific national or regional circumstances are not represented in sufficient detail in the global GAINS model used in this study for country comparisons. However, in the national and subnational versions and with input from the respective country experts, more sophisticated and tailored options could be explored.

Notes

1. Ricardo, D. 1817. *On the Principles of Political Economy and Taxation.* https://www.marxists .org/reference/subject/economics/ricardo/tax/ch01.htm.
2. The methodology of the GAINS model is described in annex 5A.
3. Details are provided by Kiesewetter et al. (2015).
4. This highest ambition level corresponds to the lowest level in exposure/concentration. In GAINS, this is called the maximum technically feasible reduction scenario. Together with the starting point (CLE or NOC), it limits the space of feasible scenarios. It is typically not associated with zero emissions. Instead, it reflects the level of residual pollution after all technically feasible measures have been taken. Reducing emissions further would imply taking very different types of measures, such as relocating certain activities such as industrial production to other countries. Such measures are not considered here.

References

Amann, M., I. Bertok, J. Borken-Kleefeld, J. Cofala, C. Heyes, L. Höglund-Isaksson, Z. Klimont, et al. 2011. "Cost-Effective Control of Air Quality and Greenhouse Gases in Europe: Modeling and Policy Applications." *Environmental Modelling and Software* 26 (12): 1489–1501. https://doi.org/10.1016/j.envsoft.2011.07.012.

Amann, M., J. Borken-Kleefeld, G. Kiesewetter, J. Cofala, Z. Klimont, P. Rafaj, C. Heyes, et al. 2021. *Support to the Development of the Second Clean Air Outlook of the European Union.* Brussels, Belgium: European Commission Directorate General Environment; Laxenburg, Austria: International Institute for Applied Systems Analysis. https://ec.europa.eu /environment/air/pdf/CAO2-MAIN-final-21Dec20.pdf.

Branca, F., and M. Ferrari. 2002. "Impact of Micronutrient Deficiencies on Growth: The Stunting Syndrome." *Annals of Nutrition and Metabolism* 46 Suppl. 1: 8–17. https://doi .org/10.1159/000066397.

Burnett, R., H. Chen, M. Szyszkowicz, N. Fann, B. Hubbell, C. A. Pope, J. S. Apte, et al. 2018. "Global Estimates of Mortality Associated with Long-Term Exposure to Outdoor Fine Particulate Matter." *PNAS* 115 (38): 9592–97. https://doi.org/10.1073/pnas.1803222115.

Fowler, D., P. Brimblecombe, J. Burrows, M. R. Heal, P. Grennfelt, D. S. Stevenson, A. Jowett, et al. 2020. "A Chronology of Global Air Quality." *Philosophical Transactions of the Royal Society A: Mathematical, Physical and Engineering Sciences* 378 (2183): 20190314. https:// doi.org/10.1098/rsta.2019.0314.

GBD 2015 Risk Factors Collaborators. 2016. "Global, Regional, and National Comparative Risk Assessment of 79 Behavioural, Environmental and Occupational, and Metabolic Risks or Clusters of Risks, 1990–2015: A Systematic Analysis for the Global Burden of Disease Study 2015." *Lancet* 388: 1659–1724. https://doi.org/10.1016/S0140-6736(16)31679-8.

GBD 2017 Risk Factors Collaborators. 2018. "Global, Regional, and National Comparative Risk Assessment of 84 Behavioural, Environmental and Occupational, and Metabolic Risks or Clusters of Risks for 195 Countries and Territories, 1990–2017: A Systematic Analysis for the Global Burden of Disease Study 2017." *The Lancet* 392 (10159): 1923–94. https://doi.org/10.1016/S0140-6736(18)32225-6.

Greenstone, M., and R. Hanna. 2014. "Environmental Regulations, Air and Water Pollution, and Infant Mortality in India." *American Economic Review* 104 (10): 3038–72. https://doi.org/10.1257/aer.104.10.3038.

Kiesewetter, G., J. Borken-Kleefeld, W. Schöpp, C. Heyes, P. Thunis, B. Bessagnet, E. Terrenoire, et al. 2015. "Modelling Street Level PM10 Concentrations across Europe: Source Apportionment and Possible Futures." *Atmospheric Chemistry and Physics* 15 (3): 1539–53. https://doi.org/10.5194/acp-15-1539-2015.

Maynard, R. L., and M. L. Williams. 2018. "Regulation of Air Quality in the European Union." In *Regulatory Toxicology in the European Union*, edited by Tim Marrs and Kevin Woodward, 539–56. London, UK: Royal Society of Chemistry. https://doi.org/10.1039/9781782622222-00539.

Millock, K., C. Nauges, and T. Sterner. 2004. "Environmental Taxes: A Comparison of French and Swedish Experience from Taxes on Industrial Air Pollution." *CESifo DICE Report* 2 (1): 30–34. https://fo.de/en/publikationen/2004/article-journal/environmental-taxes-comparison-french-and-swedish-experience.

Simpson, D., and J. P. Tuovinen. 2014. "ECLAIRE Ecosystem Surface Exchange Model (ESX)." In *Transboundary Particulate Matter, Photo-oxidants, Acidifying and Eutrophying Components. EMEP Status Report 1/2014*, 147–54. Oslo: Norwegian Meteorological Institute.

Söderholm, P., A -K. Bergquist, M. Pettersson, and K. Söderholm. 2021. "The Political Economy of Industrial Pollution Control: Environmental Regulation in Swedish Industry for Five Decades." *Journal of Environmental Planning and Management* 1–32. https://doi.org/10.1080/09640568.2021.1920375.

Song, Y., Z. Li, T. Yang, and Q. Xia. 2020. "Does the Expansion of the Joint Prevention and Control Area Improve the Air Quality? Evidence from China's Jing-Jin-Ji Region and Surrounding Areas." *Science of the Total Environment* 706 (March): 136034. https://doi.org/10.1016/j.scitotenv.2019.136034.

Sterner, T., and L. Höglund-Isaksson. 2006. "Refunded Emission Payments Theory, Distribution of Costs, and Swedish Experience of NO$_x$ Abatement." *Ecological Economics* 57 (1): 93–106. https://doi.org/10.1016/j.ecolecon.2005.03.008.

Sterner, T., and G. Köhlin. 2004. "Environmental Taxes in Europe." SSRN Scholarly Paper ID 461537. Rochester, NY: Social Science Research Network. https://papers.ssrn.com/abstract=461537.

United Nations. 2017. *World Population Prospects: The 2017 Revision, Key Findings and Advance Tables*, edited by Department of Economics and Social Affairs PD. New York: United Nations.

Van Dingenen, R., F. J. Dentener, F. Raes, M. C. Krol, L. Emberson, and J. Cofala. 2009. "The Global Impact of Ozone on Agricultural Crop Yields under Current and Future Air Quality Legislation." *Atmospheric Environment* 43 (3): 604–18. https://doi.org/10.1016/j.atmosenv.2008.10.033.

Van Dingenen, R., F. Raes, J-P. Putaud, U. Baltensperger, A. Charron, M-C. Facchini, and S. Decesari. 2004. "A European Aerosol Phenomenology—1: Physical Characteristics of Particulate Matter at Kerbside, Urban, Rural and Background Sites in Europe." *Atmospheric Environment* 38 (16): 2561–77. https://doi.org/10.1016/j.atmosenv.2004.01.040.

Wagner, F., C. Heyes, Z. Klimont, and W. Schöpp. 2013. "The GAINS Optimization Module: Identifying Cost-effective Measures for Improving Air Quality and Short-term Climate Forcing." Interim Report IR-13-001, International Institute for Applied Systems Analysis, Laxenburg, Austria.

Watts, N., M. Amann, N. Arnell, S. Ayeb-Karlsson, K. Belesova, M. Boykoff, P. Byass, et al. 2019. "The 2019 Report of The Lancet Countdown on Health and Climate Change: Ensuring That the Health of a Child Born Today Is Not Defined by a Changing Climate." *Lancet* 394 (10211): 1836–78. https://doi.org/10.1016/S0140-6736(19)32596-6.

WHO (World Health Organization). 2013. *Review of Evidence on Health Aspects of Air Pollution— REVIHAAP Project*. Technical report. Bonn, Germany: WHO Regional Office for Europe. http://www.euro.who.int/__data/assets/pdf_file/0004/193108/REVIHAAP-Final-technical-rep.

WHO (World Health Organization). 2015. "Economic Cost of the Health Impact of Air Pollution in Europe: Clean Air, Health and Wealth." Copenhagen, Denmark: WHO Regional Office for Europe.

WHO (World Health Organization). 2016. "Ambient Air Pollution: A Global Assessment of Exposure and Burden of Disease." Geneva, Switzerland: WHO. https://www.who.int/phe/publications/air-pollution-global-assessment/en/.

WHO (World Health Organization). 2018. "WHO Global Urban Ambient Air Pollution Database (Update 2018)." Geneva, Switzerland: WHO. https://www.who.int/airpollution/data/cities/en/.

World Bank. 2016. *The Cost of Air Pollution: Strengthening the Economic Case for Action*. Washington, DC: World Bank. http://documents.worldbank.org/curated/en/781521473177013155/The-cost-of-air-pollution-strengthening-the-economic-case-for-action.

Zheng, H., B. Zhao, S. Wang, T. Wang, D. Ding, X. Chang, K. Liu, et al. 2019. "Transition in Source Contributions of PM2.5 Exposure and Associated Premature Mortality in China during 2005–2015." *Environment International* 132 (November): 105111. https://doi.org/10.1016/j.envint.2019.105111.

CHAPTER 6

Country Spotlights

Key messages

- This chapter illustrates the insights and utility of the tools and frameworks presented in this report. It does so by means of several case studies of countries in different geographic regions and across diverse geographies, at different levels of development, and with widely differing capacities to implement policies.

- The exercises pinpoints (1) the magnitude of efficiency gaps; (2) the gains achievable from closing these gaps; (3) the types of changes necessary; and (4) where these changes need to be made within each country.

- Given the long menu of policy choices and management options available for generating such changes, the chapter illustrates how the policy filter introduced in box 4.1 can be used to select the most suitable mix of policies. It does this by examining the costs of policy implementation, the complexity and effectiveness of a policy, the feasibility of implementing a policy in a country, and the risks and co-benefits of a policy. The approach therefore aims to facilitate the selection of relevant and effective policy choices.

Introduction

This chapter provides several examples of how the tools developed in this report can guide country strategies that enhance sustainability. The countries under the spotlight are Azerbaijan, the Lao People's Democratic Republic (Lao PDR), and Liberia. In addition, box 6.3 describes an application of the landscape approach in China and box 6.4 an application of the efficiency frontiers for air pollution in the Arab Republic of Egypt. Each country is distinctive, and the differences among countries illustrate the pathways available to enhancing efficiency and productivity, the shifts needed to realize these gains, and the policies that could incentivize and catalyze these changes. These factors will vary by type of country (see the country typology in chapter 3 and box 6.1), as well as by country-specific characteristics. The country spotlights also illustrate that some changes are far-reaching and will take time, as do all significant reforms. These examples also suggest that often there may be merit in gradualism when it permits course corrections and adaptive adjustments of policies. The policy road map in box 4.1 in chapter 4 identifies the most appropriate policy mix based on an assessment and ranking of the costs of the policy intervention, the complexity of the intervention, the feasibility of implementation, the distributional impact, and the evidence of policy effectiveness. These foundational criteria can guide decision-makers on the trade-offs between alternative policy packages.

BOX 6.1
A primer on the resource efficiency frontier

Most renewable resources are common property assets, and although they may be vital for production and survival, they are neither used efficiently nor allocated to their best uses. The resource efficiency frontier (the green curve in figure B6.1.1) tracks the maximum environmental goods and income that these resources could generate if they were used and allocated efficiently.

Most countries are inefficient and lie within the frontier. According to this study's estimates, five types of countries emerge relative to each country's own efficiency frontier.

FIGURE B6.1.1
Typology of countries, by environmental indicator and production value

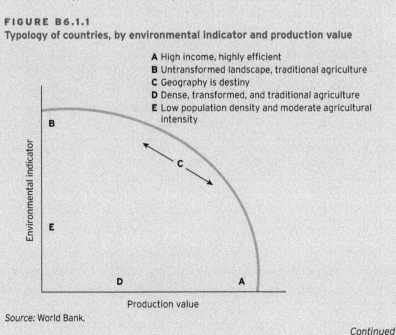

A High income, highly efficient
B Untransformed landscape, traditional agriculture
C Geography is destiny
D Dense, transformed, and traditional agriculture
E Low population density and moderate agricultural intensity

Source: World Bank.

Continued

BOX 6.1
Continued

- *Type A: high-income, highly efficient countries.* This group includes most advanced economies that tend to be close to their maximum potential in terms of economic indicators. However, they do not necessarily perform well on environmental attributes.
- *Type B: untransformed landscapes with traditional agriculture.* This group includes countries in West Africa as well as some Amazonian countries that tend to perform close to their maximum potential on the environmental indicators because they are well endowed with natural habitats. But they do not perform as well on the economic indicator.
- *Type C: countries where geography is destiny.* This group, very close to the efficiency frontier, consists of a mix of countries that have large deserts, are close to the Arctic, or otherwise have inhospitable terrain. Common to this group are extreme climatic conditions that make agriculture difficult.
- *Type D: dense, transformed, and traditional agriculture.* These mostly low-income and lower-middle-income countries have high population densities, have converted large shares of their natural lands to economic uses, and lack intensified agriculture. They usually perform poorly across both the economic and the environmental domain.
- *Type E: low population density and moderate agricultural intensity.* This mix of low- and high-income countries tends to have low population densities and high amounts of uncultivated terrains, which may be heavily devoted to livestock production. Although some are wealthy, they are not particularly efficient at sequestering carbon or supporting biodiversity, nor are they maximizing economic gains.

Azerbaijan

Azerbaijan is a former Soviet economy that became independent in 1991 for the first time since 1918–1920. Sitting on the border between Europe and Asia, Azerbaijan is made up of the large flat lowlands of the Kura-Aras Basin sandwiched between the Greater Caucasus Mountains to the north and the Lesser Caucasus Mountains to the south. Technically landlocked, Azerbaijan has a long coastline on the Caspian Sea, and it shares borders with Armenia, Georgia, the Islamic Republic of Iran, and the Russian Federation. Azerbaijan also includes an autonomous enclave of the Nakhchivan Autonomous Republic, which is geographically isolated from the rest of the country.

Since achieving independence in 1991, Azerbaijan has seen its economy grow substantially, with per capita GDP rising from US$209 in 1993 to US$7,891 in 2014. Since then, income per capita has fallen to US$4,221, largely following declining energy prices. Agriculture is a relatively small share of the economy, contributing only 5–6 percent to GDP. However, it employs 36 percent of the total workforce and 42 percent of the female workforce, making it an important sector for both poverty alleviation and gender equity considerations. Major agricultural products of Azerbaijan include milk, wheat, potatoes, barley, tomatoes, watermelons, cotton, apples, maize, and onions. The yield gaps—the percentage difference between actual yields and potential yields—for staple crops are relatively large, including maize (15 percent), wheat (22 percent), and barley (23 percent).

Despite being a small share of the economy, agriculture accounts for 57.6 percent of land use, more than half of which is permanent pastureland. Forests account for just under 14 percent of land cover, a share that has been creeping steadily upward since independence, when it was about 10 percent. Land degradation from soil erosion affects 42 percent of Azerbaijan's territory due in part to heavy precipitation and flooding, but also overgrazing by livestock (Sartori et al. 2019; SSC 2021). Many areas experiencing soil erosion are adjacent to important cropland, particularly in the low-lying plains of the Absheron Peninsula, which contains Azerbaijan's capital and largest city, Baku, and 60 percent of the country's population.

Carbon emissions in Azerbaijan are dominated by the energy sector, which accounts for 83 percent of total emissions. More than half of energy-related emissions are fugitive emissions from oil and natural gas production. On a per unit of GDP basis, Azerbaijan is the largest producer of fugitive emissions of all major natural gas producers. After energy, agriculture accounts for the next largest share of emissions at 7.4 percent. Recently, emissions from land use change have been negative because carbon sequestration from land has been increasing. Azerbaijan's nationally declared climate commitment is to reduce emissions by 35 percent by 2030 relative to 1990 levels. This reduction would require, in turn, a reduction of about 38 percent relative to 2018 levels, or about 30.4 million metric tons of CO_2eq per year.

A spatially explicit analysis of the resource efficiency frontier can guide the types of investments needed and identify where they should be located. Figure 6.1 shows the current landscape for Azerbaijan, which lies well inside the efficiency frontier. It has many of the features of a type D country as described in chapter 3 and box 6.1—that is, a country with moderate to high population density and low-productivity agriculture.

Azerbaijan has achieved 70 percent of the economic production potential of its land—crop production, livestock, and forestry—that is possible without environmental losses (see the horizontal movement in figure 6.1 up to the efficiency frontier). This is labeled "Maximize production value, no trade-offs" in the figure. The map to the lower right of the frontier shows that this achievement would largely stem from intensifying agriculture in areas that are currently cropland, as well as converting grazing land to cropland. This process is perhaps better seen in the Sankey diagrams in figure 6.2, panel a, which shows how land area needs to transition from the current to the scenario where production value is maximized without trade-offs.

Significant improvements can be made in biodiversity and carbon storage without any reduction in monetary returns. Azerbaijan achieves about 69 percent of its full GHG sequestration potential without any loss of agricultural revenue—see the vertical movements to the efficiency frontier in figure 6.1. A vertical movement that holds economic production value constant while maximizing carbon sequestration would lead to an increase in CO_2eq sequestration of

FIGURE 6.1

Efficiency frontier and transitions of movements to frontier, Azerbaijan

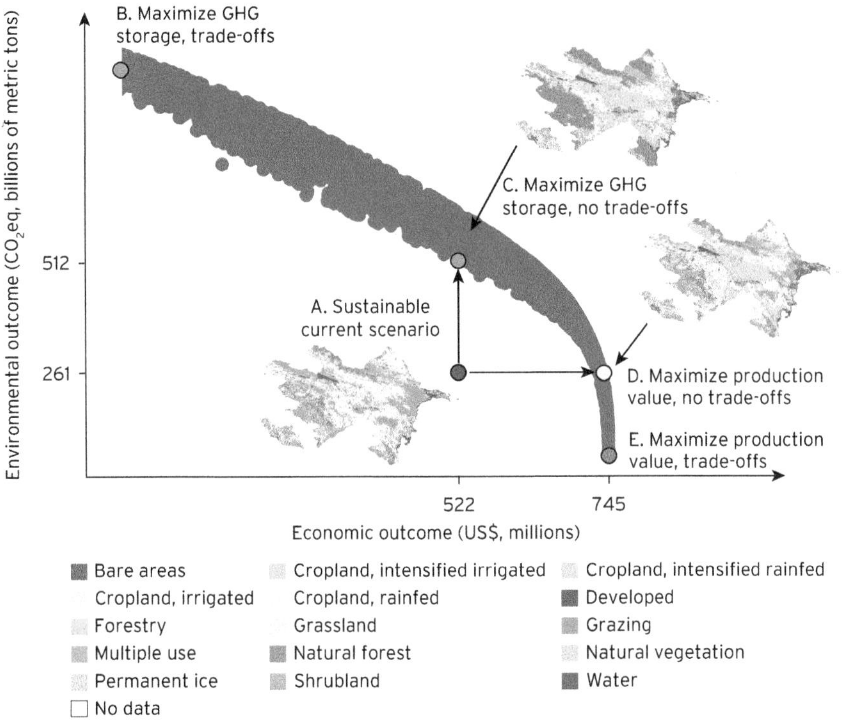

Source: World Bank.
Note: The blue dots trace the efficiency frontier. The interior (brown) dot shows the country's current position, and the various other dots represent achievable places on the frontier that maximize different objectives in the Pareto space. Moving vertically from point A to point C (blue dot), and horizontally from point A to point D (yellow dot), traces out the Pareto space, where improvements in the economic outcome, the environmental outcome, or both, can be made with no tradeoffs. The maps that surround the efficiency frontier show alternative landscapes and intensities of use for Azerbaijan that result in a more efficient use of its natural endowments. CO_2eq = carbon dioxide equivalent; GHG = greenhouse gas.

116 million metric tons, which is equivalent to about 1.5 years of emissions for Azerbaijan based on 2018 levels—see "Maximize GHG storage, no trade-offs" map in the figure. As shown in figure 6.2, panel b, these gains would be achieved by reallocating approximately 85 percent of grazing land, with a majority of it returned to natural land and the rest split between irrigated and rainfed cropland. In the highlands in the north and south of the country, most of that natural land must be returned to a state of natural forest, whereas the lowlands in the center of the country and near Baku are most productive as natural vegetation and grasslands. About 40 percent of the remaining cropland is intensified through irrigation investments (where sustainable and economical) and increased use of modern inputs. Such changes would help Azerbaijan progress toward its NDC.

For greater clarity, map 6.1 shows where these transitions occur geographically. Panel a in map 6.1 reveals the changes needed to reach the frontier to maximize

FIGURE 6.2
Land use land change transitions from current to Pareto max production value and from current to Pareto max GHG reduction, Azerbaijan

a. Current to Pareto max production value (ha)

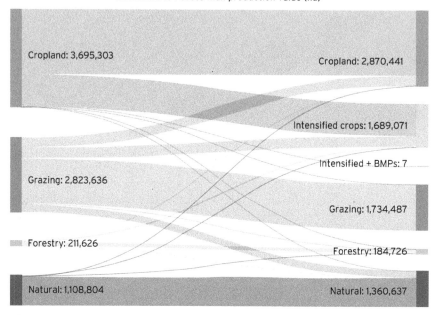

b. Current to Pareto max GHG reduction (ha)

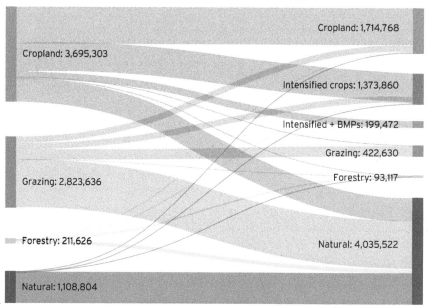

Source: World Bank.
Note: Minor land uses (such as urban and mixed use) are not included. BMPs = best management practices; GHG = greenhouse gas; ha = hectares.

MAP 6.1
Pareto production value maximization transition and GHG maximization transition, Azerbaijan

a. Production value maximization transition

b. GHG maximization transition

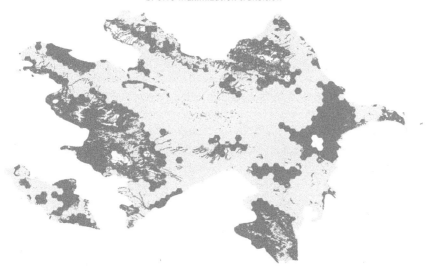

Source: World Bank.
Note: Maps depict the changes needed to reach the frontier to maximize economic gains without environmental losses (panel a) and the changes needed to reach the frontier to maximize greenhouse gas (GHG) sequestration without economic losses (panel b). Areas in brown indicate where a shift is needed toward greater intensification in agriculture, and areas in green involve restoring natural forest and vegetation.

economic gains without environmental losses. Areas in brown indicate where a shift toward greater intensification in agriculture is needed, and areas in green involve restoring natural forest and vegetation. Such Pareto changes would have no adverse net effects on GHG sequestration or biodiversity services, but they would lead to a significant increase in economic production through improvements in efficiency and the allocation of land and water.

Panel b in map 6.1 shows the location of transitions to maximize greenhouse gas sequestration without loss of economic output. Increases in forest cover and natural vegetation that maintain production value are concentrated in several areas. The highlands of the Greater and Lesser Caucasus Mountains can support significantly more forest cover, and the Absheron Peninsula in the east would benefit from more natural vegetation.

Although there is considerable scope for efficiency improvements in Azerbaijan, the challenge lies in finding the right policy mix to deliver these gains. For Azerbaijan, solutions can be categorized into those that encourage shifts away from livestock grazing and toward intensification of agriculture, and those that catalyze the desired land use changes. In practice, there are no simple policy panaceas. Hybrid approaches are needed, guided by cost, feasibility, distributional concerns, and the effectiveness of each policy instrument.

Table 6.1 is a nonexhaustive list of the options, with an assessment of the performance of each policy based on important criteria that can help guide the selection of the appropriate policy and investment mix in each subregion of the country.

Whether Azerbaijan pursues a path of maximizing economic production or environmental benefits, one result of the analysis is clear: a transition is needed from grazing to both natural vegetation/forests and intensified agriculture. Livestock grazing in Azerbaijan is both economically less efficient than crop production and responsible for significant soil erosion that reduces critical ecosystem services such as flood protection and land fertility. PES schemes or conservation land tenders, which incentivize restoration of forests in the Greater and Lesser Caucasus, are worth exploring. In addition to the carbon and biodiversity benefits they can generate, they can also help capture tangible economic benefits from forests for recreational use and ecotourism. Other policy instruments such as land protected area zoning and land taxes based on land use could also generate the desired land use change results, but may have harmful distributional consequences for landowners.

Agricultural total factor productivity, a measure of the ratio of overall outputs to overall inputs, has stagnated in Azerbaijan since 2005, whereas its regional neighbors have seen significant increases. This stagnation can be attributed in part to agriculture becoming more labor-intensive and less input-intensive. Land under cultivation increased by about 10 percent between 1986 and 2016, but total fertilizer use fell by more than 80 percent. Likewise, machinery use has fallen by

TABLE 6.1
Policy performance summary, Azerbaijan

Policy instrument	Cost	Design complexity	Implementation complexity	Distributional consequence	Effective in achieving aims	Suitability (high, medium, low)
Land use changes						
Payment for ecosystem services (PES)						High
Tenders to change land use	More cost-effective than PES					High
Zoning/planning						High
Subsidies						Low
Land tax based on use						Medium
Tenure and property rights					Tenure security is high in Azerbaijan	Low
Sustainable or nonconsumptive land use (forestry, tourism, etc.)						High
Certification schemes for sustainable products						Low
Intensification						
Sustainable irrigation						High
Seeds, fertilizers, etc.						High
Connectivity to output markets						High
Digitization						Medium
Extension services						Medium
Credit to smallholders						Medium
Insurance against crop losses						High
Tenure						Low

Less desirable consequence | Intermediate consequence | Desirable consequence | Uncertain/unknown

Source: World Bank.

30 percent, but at the same time active labor in agriculture has increased by about 80 percent.[7] Only some 30 percent of agricultural land in Azerbaijan is irrigated, which has remained constant since at least 2000. Thus, policies that incentivize the sustainable use of inputs such as fertilizers and improved seeds, mechanization of agriculture, and irrigation where it is economically and environmentally sustainable will be key to improving production efficiency.

Lao People's Democratic Republic (Lao PDR)

Lao PDR is mountainous and landlocked, surrounded by Cambodia, China, Myanmar, Thailand, and Vietnam. It remains among the less prosperous countries of the East Asia and Pacific region, with a per capita gross domestic product (GDP) of about US$2,600. However, its economic performance has been impressive; its growth averages about 7 percent a year. Although Lao PDR's economy is diversifying, it remains dependent on its natural resource sectors. Agriculture, dominated by rice cultivation in lowland areas, accounts for about 16 percent of GDP, 73 percent of total employment, and 72 percent of total cultivated area. Global Agro-Ecological Zones (GAEZ) version 4, a data product of the Food and Agriculture Organization (FAO), calculates that the gap between actual and potential yields stands at about 41 percent for dryland rice and 27 percent for wetland rice. Gaps of a similar magnitude affect other crops as well, suggesting considerable scope for improvements in productivity. According to the International Fund for Agricultural Development (IFAD 2018), the main factors limiting agricultural productivity typically are insecure access to land, farm inputs, and extension services, including lack of access to credit.

Lao PDR is situated in the heart of the Indo-Burmese Biological Hotspot, which is one of the world's biologically rich regions, is among the most endangered terrestrial ecoregions, and is one of the 10 most important global biodiversity hotspots. And yet forest loss and degradation remain high. Since 2000, Lao PDR has lost 21.5 percent of its tree cover. Some 80 percent of the country's land area, largely in the north, is mountainous. The remaining 20 percent is in a low-lying plain along the Mekong River and experiences annual flooding. The east of the country is sparsely populated and is likely to remain so.

A recent World Bank report by Sanchez-Triana (2021) found that nature-based sectors, such as agriculture and forestry, have strong links with the rest of the economy with high backward and forward multipliers. In addition, computable general equilibrium simulations show that investments in ecosystem restoration have higher value-added (GDP) multipliers than conventional (nongreen) investments in all plausible scenarios that were considered. This outcome reflects the positive externalities associated with ecosystem services and the limited substitutability between natural resources and other inputs. In summary, an investment in restoring natural capital, in the right place and of the right kind, not only improves environmental outcomes, but also can enhance economic productivity.

A spatially explicit resource efficiency frontier analysis can guide the types of investments needed and identify where they should be located. All data on land use are from the European Space Agency (ESA) because it is deemed to be a reliable source as it is based on satellite imagery (see the online technical appendix).[1,2] Figure 6.3 shows the current landscape for Lao PDR, which lies well inside the efficiency frontier. It has many of the features of a type E country as described in chapter 3 and box 6.1—that is, a country with low population density and moderate agricultural intensity, with a recent history of natural asset degradation.

Lao PDR achieves 56 percent of the full agricultural potential it could obtain without environmental losses. Figure 6.3 shows the country's horizontal movement toward the efficiency frontier. Much of this movement stems from the intensification of agriculture to close yield gaps, together with the reallocation

FIGURE 6.3
Efficiency frontier and transitions of movements to frontier, Lao PDR

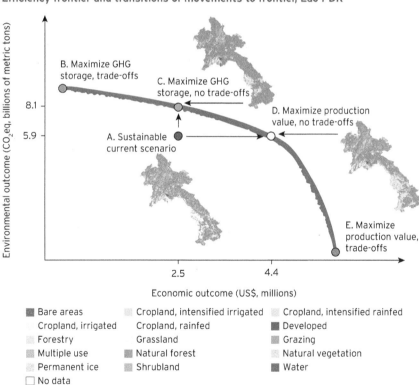

Source: World Bank.
Note: The blue dots trace the efficiency frontier. The interior (brown) dot shows the country's current position, and the various other dots represent achievable places on the frontier that maximize different objectives in the Pareto space. Moving vertically from point A to point C (blue dot), and horizontally from point A to point D (yellow dot), traces out the Pareto space, where improvements in the economic outcome, the environmental outcome, or both, can be made with no tradeoffs. The maps that surround the efficiency frontier show alternative landscapes and intensities of use for Lao PDR that result in a more efficient use of its natural endowments. CO_2eq = carbon dioxide equivalent; GHG = greenhouse gas.

of land to its most productive uses—"Maximize production value, no trade-offs" in the figure. Combining yield increases with movements of agricultural production to areas of high fertility and away from areas of high carbon storage or biodiversity conservation potentially leads to improvements in all dimensions: production value, biodiversity conservation, and carbon storage. Much of the gain is a result of shifting from lower-yield rainfed agriculture to intensified rainfed agriculture and intensified irrigated agriculture in pockets of the southern and eastern parts of the country.

Biodiversity and carbon storage can also be significantly improved without any reduction in monetary returns. Lao PDR achieves about 80 percent of the full greenhouse gas (GHG) sequestration potential that can be obtained without any loss of agricultural revenue (indicated by the vertical movements to the efficiency frontier in figure 6.3). A vertical movement that holds the economic production value constant while maximizing carbon sequestration would lead to an increase of 1.4 billion metric tons in carbon dioxide equivalent (CO_2eq) sequestered, which is equivalent to 51 years of emissions for Lao PDR based on 2018 levels—"Maximize GHG storage, no trade-offs" (Pareto max) in figure 6.3. These gains can be achieved by moving agricultural production toward areas with higher fertility and away from areas with high carbon storage and biodiversity potential and by intensifying agricultural production to increase yields so that crop production requires less area to produce the same amount of crops. Achievement of these gains also calls for restoration of some marginal cropland and grazing areas to natural lands. The remaining cropland would be intensified (with irrigation where it is sustainable and economic), and riparian buffers would be created to secure environmental gains. Such changes would help Lao PDR achieve its revised nationally determined contribution (NDC) commitment to an unconditional emission reduction target of 60 percent by 2030 relative to the baseline scenario.[3]

Map 6.2 shows where these transitions occur geographically. Map 6.2, panel a, shows the changes needed to reach the frontier to maximize economic gains without environmental losses. Areas in brown indicate where a shift is needed toward greater intensification in agriculture, and areas in green involve restoring natural forest or natural vegetation. Such Pareto changes (that is, a win without a loss) would have no adverse net effects on GHG sequestration or biodiversity services, but they would lead to a significant increase in agricultural output through improvements in efficiency and the allocation of land and water. Map 6.2, panel b, shows the location of transitions to maximize GHG sequestration without loss of economic output. Increases in forest cover that maintain production value are concentrated in two areas near the Thai border; one around the capital, Vientiane; and the other in southern Lao PDR in the provinces of Savannakhet and Salavan. In addition, forest habitat is restored in many other provinces.

The Sankey[4] figures of the Pareto efficiency improvements shown in figure 6.4 provide more details on the magnitude of changes and the transitions between

MAP 6.2
Pareto production value maximization and GHG maximization, Lao PDR

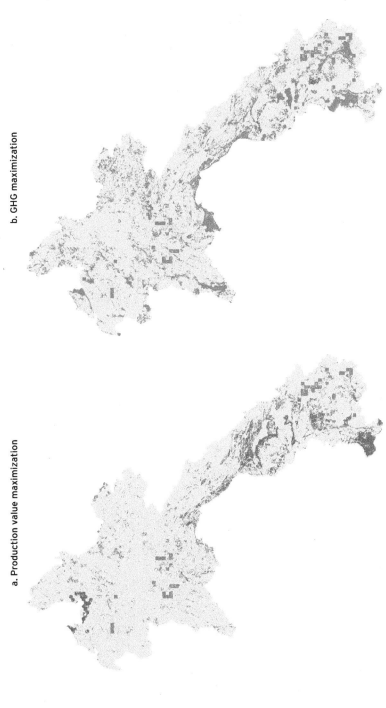

a. Production value maximization

b. GHG maximization

Source: World Bank.
Note: Maps shows the changes needed to reach the frontier to maximize economic gains without environmental losses (panel a) and changes needed to reach the frontier to maximize greenhouse gas (GHG) sequestration without economic losses (panel b). Areas in brown indicate where a shift is needed toward greater intensification in agriculture, and areas in green involve restoring natural forest and vegetation.

FIGURE 6.4
Pareto production value maximization and GHG maximization, Lao PDR

a. Land use land cover transitions to Pareto max production value (ha)

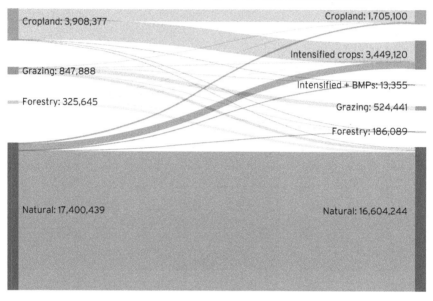

b. Land use land cover transitions to Pareto max GHG reduction (ha)

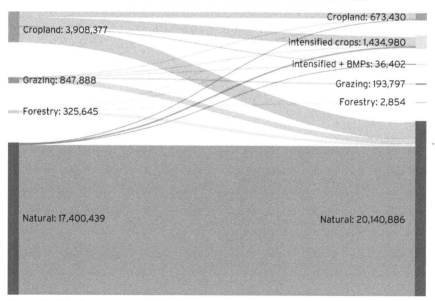

Source: World Bank.
Note: Minor land uses (such as urban and mixed use) are not included. BMPs = best management practices; GHG = greenhouse gas; ha = hectares.

the uses of land. A Pareto move that maximizes production value without environmental loss would call for:

- Shifting about 5 percent of relatively unproductive natural land (in terms of GHG sequestration and biodiversity) to either cropland, forestry, or grazing, which is more in keeping with the suitability of this land and thus yields greater net benefits;

- Reducing land devoted to low value-added grazing by 38 percent, which is shifted to more productive alternatives, including intensified crops, and the least productive areas are converted to natural land; and

- Reducing forestry by about 40 percent, with land converted to its natural state or cropland.

By means of all of these changes there is an overall increase in cropland, with over a third devoted to intensified but sustainable production and some involving best management practices.

Conversely, maximizing GHG sequestration without economic loss entails the following transitions:

- Increasing natural land (devoted to GHG sequestration, biodiversity, and nonconsumptive uses) from 17.4 million hectares to 20.1 million hectares

- Significantly reducing land devoted to low value-added grazing, with shifts to intensified agriculture or natural land

- Reducing forestry from about 300 million hectares to about 3 million hectares, with shifts to intensified cropland and natural land.

By means of all of these changes there is an overall reduction in cropland, with over a third devoted to intensified but sustainable production and best management practices.

Although there is considerable scope for efficiency improvements in Lao PDR, the challenge lies in finding the right policy mix to deliver these gains. For Lao PDR, solutions can be categorized into those that encourage intensification of agriculture and those that catalyze the desired land use changes. In practice, there are no simple policy panaceas, and hybrid approaches are needed, guided by cost, feasibility, distributional concerns, and the effectiveness of each policy instrument.

Table 6.2 is a nonexhaustive list of the policy options with an assessment of the performance of each policy based on important criteria that can help guide the selection of the appropriate policy and investment mix in each subregion of the country.

Because of constraints on public sector budgets, the lower-cost solutions and options that can generate wider economic benefits would likely be preferred. Nonconsumptive uses of land clearly fall into this category. Before the COVID-19

TABLE 6.2
Policy performance summary, Lao PDR

Policy instrument	Cost	Design complexity	Implementation complexity	Distributional consequence	Effective in achieving aims	Suitability (high, medium, low)
Land use changes						
Payment for ecosystem services (PES)						High
Tenders to change land use	More cost-effective than PES					Medium
Zoning/planning						High
Subsidies						Low
Land tax based on use						Medium
Tenure and property rights						Medium
Sustainable or nonconsumptive land use (forestry, tourism, etc.)						High
Certification schemes for sustainable products						High
Intensification						
Sustainable irrigation						Medium
Seeds, fertilizers, etc.						High
Connectivity to output markets						High
Digitization						Medium
Extension services						High
Credit to smallholders						Medium
Insurance against crop losses						Medium
Tenure						High

Legend: Less desirable consequence | Intermediate consequence | Desirable consequence | Uncertain/unknown

Source: World Bank.

pandemic, nature-based tourism accounted for a mere 4 percent of GDP, so there is room to expand this sector, especially given the country's natural endowments (Sanchez-Triana 2021). Lao PDR's forests are home to globally significant biodiversity, which can become a lucrative source of revenue for the country. For other nonconsumptive activities, partnering with reputable global organizations for certification would be another profitable way to increase the value added of the country's natural capital. In view of budget constraints, consideration could also be given to fiscal reforms by means of taxes on harmful externalities, which are a significant untaxed source of revenue.

In the agriculture sector, numerous diagnostics have pointed to the need to enhance access to key inputs. Although agriculture is the mainstay of the economy, farming is largely subsistence, and access to improved technologies is limited. Also affecting productivity is the declining soil fertility (IFAD 2018). Access to inputs is crucial for sustainable intensification, as is access to advisory services that can promote sustainable, adaptive, and integrated farming systems. Globally, investments in extension services produce high returns in agriculture, suggesting scope for further investments in knowledge and technology, despite the associated costs. The provision of credit where needed has also been found to be critical to boosting productivity and therefore may warrant closer scrutiny.

In general, although access to modern fertilizers has played a pivotal role in boosting yields globally, overuse should be avoided. Experience in other countries forcefully demonstrates how access to subsidized fertilizers has created a host of problems. Most notable are the health and environmental consequences of the excessive use of nitrogen fertilizer, which is associated with increases in colorectal cancer, blue baby syndrome, and stunting in infants. Likewise, although irrigation can have transformational impacts, examples abound of the unsustainable use, overuse, and inefficiencies resulting from a lack of appropriate management. These outcomes highlight the need for sound advice and appropriate extension services as an often essential complement to investments in physical inputs.

Liberia

Liberia, a West African country with a population of around 5 million, has, at US$632, among the lowest per capita GDPs in the world. Liberia was considered a fragile state up to 2021 and is striving to overcome the legacy of two devastating civil wars (1989 and 2003). The country's economic growth peaked in 2013 at 8.7 percent and has since slowed considerably. In part, this slowdown stems from Liberia's repeated crises: the Ebola outbreak, the collapse in the price of iron ore and rubber, and most recently the COVID-19 pandemic. As a result, per capita GDP declined by 12.3 percent cumulatively from 2014 to 2020, while the poverty rate had risen to an estimated 52 percent by 2021 (World Bank 2022b), erasing nearly half of the gains achieved in the first decade after the 2003 conflict.

Economic prospects are now brighter, and the World Bank estimates that Liberia's economy expanded by around 5 percent in 2021, driven by mining and external demand.[5] The World Bank projects that growth will remain positive in 2022, but will slow to 3.7 percent because of greater global uncertainty and the commodity price shock (World Bank 2022a).

Agriculture is the primary livelihood for 60 percent of the population and accounts for 31 percent of GDP. Agricultural yields are far below their physical potential. By some estimates, around 55 percent of rural households are food insecure (USAID 2017). Agriculture is central to Liberia's development strategy. However, smallholder farmers are engaged in predominantly unsustainable subsistence agricultural practices of low value food products. Efforts at commercialization of agriculture have been constrained by inadequate access to productive assets, viable value chains, and market access. Input markets are underdeveloped and access to credit is limited and therefore constrains the ability to expand production. For example, rice is a staple that accounts for half of all calories consumed in the country. Nevertheless, rice yields[6] (at 1.48 metric tons per hectare) are low in Liberia compared to neighboring countries, standing at roughly half those of Côte d'Ivoire (2.9 metric tons per hectare) and Ghana (2.9 metric tons per hectare) in 2020. The GAEZ model estimates that the yield gap for rice under conditions of low inputs and no irrigation is about 18 percent. Likewise, cassava yields are 10 percent below the yields in Guinea (9.0 metric tons per hectare) and 40 percent below those in Sierra Leone (14.5 metric tons per hectare). One consequence of low agricultural productivity is high levels of rural poverty.

Liberia was once well endowed with lush rainforests, rich biodiversity, and fertile soils. However, because of vicious cycles of poverty, indiscriminate natural resource degradation, and conflict, much of that natural capital has been degraded or destroyed. And yet despite decades of unsustainable exploitation, the country still is home to significant stands of forests. It possesses about 40 percent of the remaining Upper Guinean rainforest and hosts several other ecoregions, from montane forests to mangroves. Moreover, it has 2,000 species of vascular plants (including 225 tree species), approximately 140 species of mammals, and over 600 species of birds. However, Liberia is considered a biodiversity hot spot that is threatened with further pressures from conversion and degradation. Liberia's National Biodiversity Action Plan estimates that over 60 percent of the country's forested landscape is degraded, and the country ranks low in the 2019 Forest Landscape Integrity Index at 116th out of 172 countries. Since 2000, Liberia has lost 21 percent of its tree cover.

In short, Liberia is a type E country (as defined in chapter 3 and described in box 6.1) with low population density and agricultural productivity that is far below potential. In figure 6.5, the map labeled "Sustainable current scenario" shows current land cover and land use for the country. Much of the forests that make up the central part of the country have been removed for charcoal or degraded by shifting agriculture and now remain unproductive shrubland, or

FIGURE 6.5

Efficiency frontier and transitions of movements to frontier, Liberia

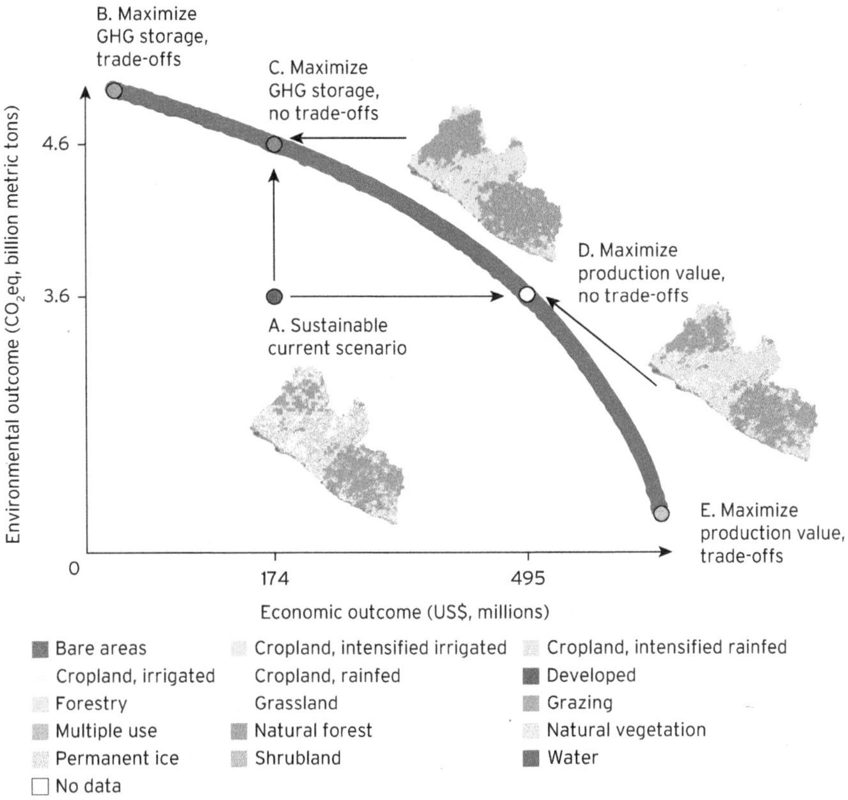

Source: World Bank.

Note: The blue dots trace the efficiency frontier. The interior (brown) dot shows the country's current position, and the various other dots represent achievable places on the frontier that maximize different objectives in the Pareto space. Moving vertically from point A to point C (blue dot), and horizontally from point A to point D (yellow dot), traces out the Pareto space, where improvements in the economic outcome, the environmental outcome, or both, can be made with no tradeoffs. The maps that surround the efficiency frontier show alternative landscapes and intensities of use for Liberia that result in a more efficient use of its natural endowments. CO_2eq = carbon dioxide equivalent; GHG = greenhouse gas.

grassland, or are utilized for low-intensity agriculture. A considerable amount of land is also locked up in concessions for oil palm and timber. In figure 6.5, the maps that surround the efficiency frontier (blue curve) reveal alternative land-scapes and intensities of land use for Liberia that would result in a more efficient use of its natural endowments. The map at the top left shows a world in which Liberia maximizes biodiversity by planting and conserving natural forests at the expense of most economic production in the country. By contrast, the map at the bottom right shows the opposite in which most forests and natural lands are removed and replaced with intensified, rainfed agriculture. In between lies an almost infinite set of alternatives that involve trade-offs and are perhaps of less interest in a world of both economic and environmental scarcity.

Meanwhile, the "Sustainable current scenario" map in the interior of the frontier reveals the significant opportunities for boosting agricultural performance without loss of forests by moving to the frontier. In fact, the country has achieved only 35 percent of its productive potential, implying that agricultural output could increase by improving efficiency and the allocation of land and water by 65 percent without loss of GHG sequestration or biodiversity—see map "Maximize production value, no trade-offs." Under this scenario, net economic production can be increased from US$174 million (the sustainable current scenario) to US$495 million. Thus an increase of US$321 million is possible without compromising the existing biodiversity or increasing greenhouse gas emissions. It is achieved through improvements in the efficiency of resource use and a better allocation of land to its most productive uses.

Likewise, GHG sequestration is at 77 percent of what could be achieved without economic loss—see map "Maximize GHG storage, no trade-offs" in figure 6.5. In this scenario, Liberia increases GHG sequestration by 1 billion metric tons of CO_2eq, from 3.6 billion to 4.6 billion. This amount represents over 83 years of business-as-usual annual emissions at the 2030 level (from Liberia's revised NDC of August 2021). It would also enable Liberia to meet the revised NDC target of reducing its economywide GHG emissions to 64 percent below the projected business-as-usual level by 2030.

Achieving these gains entails changing landscape uses and enhancing productivity through intensification. Map 6.3 shows where these shifts and land use changes would be located. Green areas involve restoring forests and natural habitats, while brown indicates cells in which agriculture should be expanded. These gains would be achieved through greater intensification of rainfed agriculture with riparian buffers or the conversion of land to sustainable forestry.

The Sankey figures of the Pareto efficiency improvements shown in figure 6.6 provide more details on the magnitude of changes and the transitions between the uses of land. A move that maximizes production value without environmental loss would call for:

- Increasing natural land cover from some 3.5 million hectares to 3.9 million hectares, together with significant intensification of cropland;

- Moving 178,000 hectares of land currently devoted to grazing mainly to intensified crops; and

- Moving 2 million hectares of land devoted to grazing to sustainable forestry.

There is a slight decline in overall cropland from around 3.1 million hectares to 2.8 million hectares. But agricultural value added still increases by well over 60 percent because over half of all cropland is converted to intensified but sustainable production, some with best management practices.

MAP 6.3
Pareto production value maximization and GHG maximization, Liberia

a. Production value maximization

b. GHG maximization

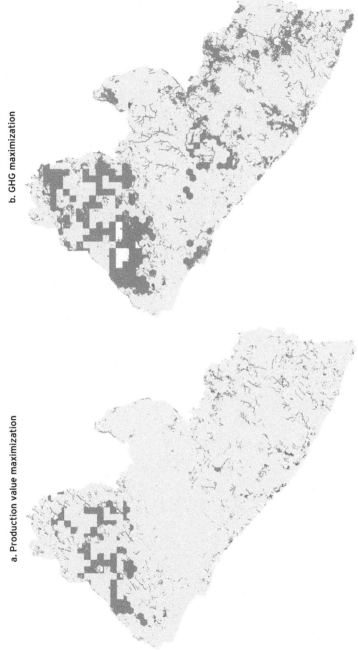

Source: World Bank.
Note: Maps depict the changes needed to maximize economic gains (that is, reach the frontier) without environmental losses (panel a) and the changes needed to reach the frontier to maximize greenhouse gas (GHG) sequestration without economic losses (panel b). Areas in brown indicate where a shift is needed toward greater intensification in agriculture, and areas in green involve restoring natural forest and vegetation.

FIGURE 6.6
Pareto production value maximization and GHG maximization, Liberia

a. Land use land cover transitions to Pareto max production value (ha)

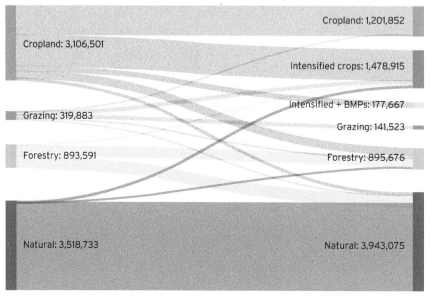

b. Land use land cover transitions to Pareto max GHG reduction (ha)

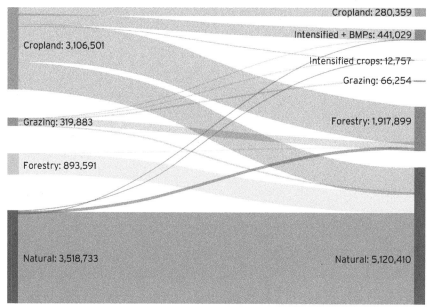

Source: World Bank.
Note: Minor land uses (such as urban and mixed use) are not included. BMPs = best management practices; GHG = greenhouse gas; ha = hectares.

Conversely, maximizing GHG sequestration without economic loss entails the following transitions:

- Increasing natural land (devoted to GHG sequestration, biodiversity, and nonconsumptive uses) by about 45 percent, from 3.5 million hectares to 5.1 million hectares

- Pursuing a significant 79 percent reduction in land devoted to low value-added grazing, from about 319,000 hectares to 66,000 hectares, which would shift to intensified agriculture or forestry

- More than doubling land in sustainable forestry from 0.9 million hectares to 1.9 million hectares.

There is a reduction in cropland from around 3.1 million hectares to 2.8 million hectares, with over half of that land devoted to intensified but sustainable production and best management practices.

Box 6.2 describes a recent World Bank project in Liberia that has successfully addressed deforestation and improved sustainable agriculture. Such a project exemplifies the type of action needed to reach the efficiency frontier and proves that change is possible in Liberia.

Table 6.3 is a list of some of the policies that can catalyze these transitions. In view of Liberia's low capacity and limited access to inputs, investments in basic inputs, credit, and extension services are a high priority for intensifying agriculture. Strengthening the regulatory environment to promote private

---

BOX 6.2
Sustainable forestry project in Liberia

Evidence of the current efforts to address deforestation and improve sustainable agriculture is the impact of the World Bank's Liberia Forest Sector Project. The project is funded by the Norwegian government in the form of a US\$37.5 million grant from a single-donor trust fund. The project's interventions supporting sustainable forest management and use have contributed to an expanded land area and improved management of protected areas, community forests, agricultural land use, land use planning, and livelihoods. The cumulative effect of these outcomes has led to socioeconomic development and reduced deforestation and degradation. Many of the project indicator targets for regularizing the protection of forests have been met or exceeded, which has positive impacts on long-term protection for sustainable forests in the face of the high rates of deforestation currently and in the future. Moreover, in achieving these targets the project has ensured that communities are at the heart of these reforms and that they have a voice central to the impacts. Beneficiaries include the youth and women in rural communities adjacent to existing and proposed targeted protected areas. The facilitation of existing and the creation of new small-scale, community-based, natural resource-based (including forest and nonforest products) enterprises that have a production or processing element will result in the gainful employment of youth and a lessening of the reliance on unsustainable forest resource use.

TABLE 6.3
Policy performance summary, Liberia

Policy instrument	Cost	Design complexity	Implementation complexity	Distributional consequence	Effective in achieving aims	Suitability (high, medium, low)
Land use changes						
Payment for ecosystem services (PES)/carbon markets						Medium
Tenders to change land use	More cost-effective than PES					Low (capacity and governance needs are high)
Zoning/planning						Medium (enforcement concerns)
Property rights						High
Sustainable or nonconsumptive land use (forestry, tourism, etc.)						High
Certification schemes for sustainable products						High
Intensification						
Sustainable irrigation						Medium
Seeds, fertilizers, etc.						High
Connectivity to output markets						High
Enabling conditions for value addition						Medium
Extension services						High
Credit to smallholders						Medium
Insurance against crop losses						Medium
Tenure						High

Less desirable consequence — Intermediate consequence — Desirable consequence — Uncertain/unknown

Source: World Bank.

sector participation in value chains can also boost the contribution of the agriculture sector to poverty reduction by enabling a move from subsistence to commercial agriculture.

At the same time, there is a need to halt the destruction of forests. Payment for ecosystem services (PES) schemes that tap into carbon market initiatives are worth exploring. Indeed Liberia, together with other West African countries, could jointly pioneer new approaches designed with the needs and constraints of the region in mind. Zoning, land use planning, and the establishment of mixed use as well as protected areas are also important, but they may not be effective where enforcement capacity is limited. Thus zoning could be accompanied by other policies that incentivize compliance. One such approach is nonconsumptive and sustainable harvesting of forest products. But as argued in chapter 4, to be effective such an approach calls for credible certification schemes, with independent verification and auditing. Establishing such systems would unleash the considerable potential of Liberia's natural capital.

Liberia has made much progress in clarifying and establishing land rights. In 2018, a Land Rights Act formalized "customary" claims to land. There may be less clarity about overlapping claims on oil palm and other concessions that cover approximately a quarter of the country's land mass. Addressing these residual concerns is important because of the number and geographic scale of concessions.

China and the Arab Republic of Egypt

Two additional brief country analyses are described in boxes 6.3 and 6.4. Box 6.3 applies the land use efficiency frontier methodology to China and discusses how nature-based solutions can play an important role in achieving both climate goals and economic goals. Box 6.4 applies the air quality efficiency frontier methodology described in chapter 5 to Egypt. It demonstrates that the methodology can utilize marginal abatement cost curves to prioritize policies and investments and make more efficient and sustainable air pollution decisions.

BOX 6.3
Land use efficiency in the context of China's quest for decarbonization: Using efficiency frontiers

China's 30–60 targets, along with its updated nationally determined contribution, set the goalposts for its long-term climate ambition. In 2021, China pledged that its greenhouse gas (GHG) emissions would peak before 2030 and it would achieve carbon neutrality by 2060. The scale of this net-zero challenge for the world's largest GHG emitter should not be underestimated. Achieving these goals will require a transition from peak to net-zero emissions within a faster timeframe and an emissions peak at a lower income level than those experienced by advanced economies.

Nature-based solutions (NbS) for climate change will play a key role in this transition. NbS refers to activities that protect, restore, and conserve ecosystems and natural resources to enhance carbon sequestration. These activities are afforestation, improved forest management, nutrient management and efficiencies in fertilizer use, improved grazing land management, soil carbon management, and wetland restoration, among others. Carbon sequestration via nature-based solutions is playing an important role in making the carbon neutrality goal achievable because it can be used to offset residual emissions in hard-to-abate sectors such as heavy industry and variable energy production. NbS can also provide co-benefits such as biodiversity protection, erosion control, and improved water quality.

By applying the land use efficiency methodology presented in this report (Figure B6.3.1), one can determine how and where emission reductions from landscape management are possible. The use of land for carbon sequestration must be balanced with the needs for

FIGURE B6.3.1
Land use efficiency in China, 2000–15

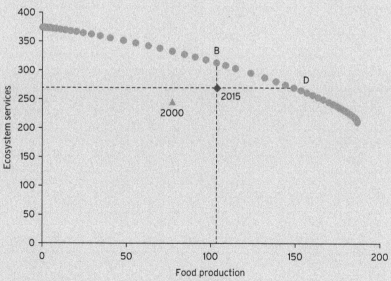

Source: World Bank.
Note: Figure is depicting the production possibilities frontier for China's ecosystem services and food production. Points B and D on the graph indicate Pareto moves that can improve ecosystem services or food production without trade-offs.

Continued

BOX 6.3
Continued

continued growth in food production and the economic development of rural areas. There are also opportunities to generate co-benefits. Spatial planning can be used to identify locations where trade-offs with livelihoods and food security are minimized and synergies with co-benefits generation are maximized. The World Bank and the Chinese Academy of Sciences utilized the spatially explicit landscape model described in this report to explore these possibilities in China. In the model, each point in the landscape generates carbon

MAP B6.3.1
Restoration and agricultural intensification enabling attainment of the efficiency frontier for carbon and food production, China

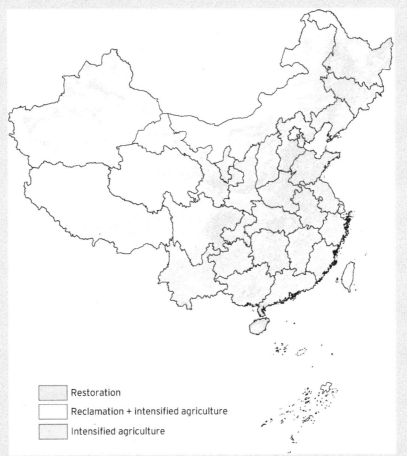

☐ Restoration

☐ Reclamation + intensified agriculture

☐ Intensified agriculture

Source: World Bank.
Note: Map shows the restoration and agricultural intensification in key locations that could shift China toward greater emissions reduction without loss of overall food production.

Continued

BOX 6.3
Continued

sequestration and other ecosystem services as a function of its ecosystem type, vegetation cover, climatic conditions, terrain conditions, soil conditions, biomass, and condition of the surrounding points. The model is calibrated using high-resolution spatial data from the 2015 national ecosystems assessment and used to test policy scenarios.

The results show that China has improved the efficiency of its land use, but substantial opportunities for carbon sequestration and other ecosystem services improvements remain. China's overall land use efficiency improved between 2000 and 2015, meaning that ecosystem services and food production improved in tandem. Figure B6.3.1 shows the transition using the efficiency frontier diagram, with years 2000 and 2015 labeled on the graph. The analysis shows that there are further opportunities for improvement through expanded use of NbS. Points B and D on the graph indicate Pareto moves that can improve ecosystem services or food production without trade-offs. In principle, China can increase land-based carbon sequestration by 34 percent with no net decrease in food production (transitions shown in map B6.3.1, previous page). There is also a high degree of synergy between carbon sequestration and other ecosystem services, with the biodiversity score (that is, the wildlife habitat) increasing by 28 percent, water retention by 31 percent, and soil retention by 4 percent under this scenario. The analysis was used to test policy measures that could contribute to this goal. Important measures included full protection of designated high-value conservation areas (China's "ecological redline" policy), habitat restoration on cropland on steep slopes, conversion of unsustainable and inefficient irrigation in arid areas to rainfed agriculture, and intensification of production through more efficient fertilizer use and irrigation rates.

BOX 6.4
Air pollution in the Arab Republic of Egypt: Identifying gaps and constraints

The annual average ambient concentrations of fine particulate matter ($PM_{2.5}$) in Greater Cairo over the last five years of available data suggest a value of 93 micrograms per cubic meter ($\mu g/m^3$)—see Larsen (2019). A variety of emission sources contributes to such high concentration levels. Notably, a significant fraction of $PM_{2.5}$ originates from wind-blown desert dust from the Sahara Desert and the Arabian Peninsula—perhaps as much as 20 $\mu g/m^3$ in Cairo. Large industries and transport sources also make significant contributions of about 15 $\mu g/m^3$ of $PM_{2.5}$.

The methodology described in chapter 5 is the basis for the air quality efficiency frontier for Egypt shown in figure B6.4.1. It demonstrates that Egypt falls into the category of type B countries—with high efficiency scores but low environmental scores—as defined in chapter 5. Indeed, the emission control measures adopted by Egypt place the country among the low-middle-income countries with the highest environmental efficiency scores. Controls of emissions from large industrial sources and basic controls of vehicle emissions are implemented in a cost-effective manner, reflected by an efficiency score of 85 percent. However, these measures address only a subset of the emission sources. As a result, the environmental score of 56 percent signals important potential for further air quality improvements.

Continued

BOX 6.4
Continued

To inform the selection of cost-effective measures, a marginal abatement cost curve ranks the available measures that could be taken (figure B6.4.2). A number of measures (especially for waste management) could reduce $PM_{2.5}$ exposure at negative costs. These are followed by low-cost measures, such as enhanced control of particulate matter and sulphur dioxide emissions at large industrial installations and power plants, further bans on the open burning of agricultural residue, and more efficient fertilizer application. More expensive measures include control of vehicle emissions. Together, these measures could reduce $PM_{2.5}$ exposure from Egyptian sources to about 38 µg/m³.

FIGURE B6.4.1
Theoretical air quality efficiency frontier, Arab Republic of Egypt, 2018

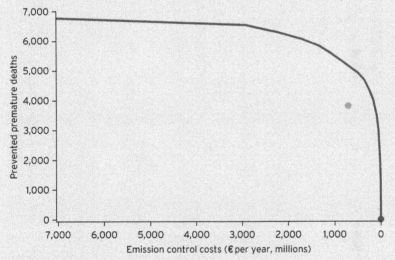

Source: GAINS model.
Note: Prevented premature deaths are based on various national measures. Point 0 (dark blue dot) indicates the counterfactual situation in which Egypt had not implemented any air pollution control technologies. The current situation is indicated by a light green dot.

Continued

BOX 6.4
Continued

FIGURE B6.4.2
Marginal abatement cost curve for reducing population-weighted PM₂.₅ concentrations, Arab Republic of Egypt, 2030

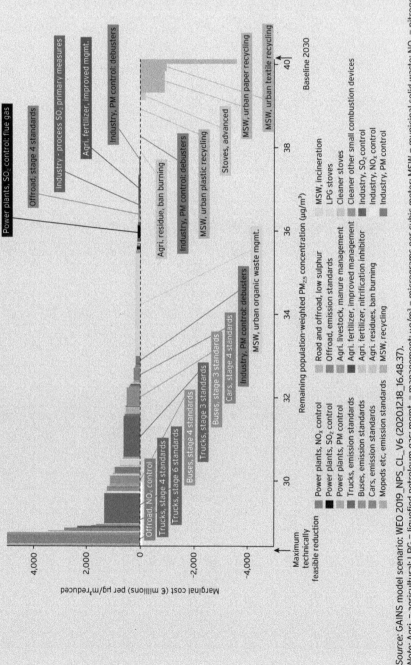

Source: GAINS model scenario: WEO 2019_NPS_CL_V6 (2020.12.18_16.48.37).
Note: Agri. = agricultural; LPG = liquefied petroleum gas; mgmt. = management; µg/m³ = micrograms per cubic meter; MSW = municipal solid waste; NOₓ = nitrogen oxides; PM = particulate matter; SO₂ = sulphur dioxide.

Notes

1. The online technical appendix (appendix B) is available with the text of this book in the World Bank's Online Knowledge Repository, https://openknowledge.worldbank.org /handle/10986/39453.

2. Large discrepancies can be found between sources of data. There are clear advantages to using ESA's remote sensing data over sources that use reported data. FAO gives several figures for agricultural area. According to FAO's *Statistical Yearbook 2021* (FAO 2021), Lao PDR had 1.719 million hectares of "agricultural area" in 2018. To that, FAO adds 0.675 million hectares for permanent pasture and meadow, for a total of 2.394 million hectares of agricultural area. The ESA data break hectares down into land class. Land class is, in turn, broken down into rainfed land and irrigated land as cropland (ESA categories 10, 11, 20), which amount to 2.4 million hectares. An additional 1.5 million hectares is mosaic land (categories 30 and 40). In the Sankey diagram (see note 3), this land is added to cropland for a total of 3.9 million hectares. Other categorizations will yield different values for cropland.

3. United Nations Development Programme, "Lao PDR," https://climatepromise.undp.org /what-we-do/where-we-work/lao-pdr.

4. A Sankey diagram is a visualization used to depict flows from one set of states to other states. The thickness of the arrows indicates the relative magnitudes.

5. Development Aid, Liberia Inclusive Growth Development Policy Operation 3 (P176993), Liberia Inclusive Growth Development Policy Operation 3 (P176993), https://www .developmentaid.org/tenders/view/858712/liberia-inclusive-growth-development -policy-operation-3-p176993.

6. Liberia's average rice yield is roughly half the regional average of 2.5 metric tons per hectare and far below the global average of 4.25 metric tons per hectare (FAO 2021).

7. Based on data from US Department of Agriculture, Economic Research Service, https:// www.ers.usda.gov/data-products/international-agricultural-productivity/.

References

FAO (Food and Agriculture Organization). 2021. *Statistical Yearbook 2021: Food and Agriculture.* Rome: FAO.

IFAD (International Fund for Agricultural Development). 2018. *Lao People's Democratic Republic Country Strategic Opportunities Programme 2018–2024.* Rome: IFAD.

Larsen, B. 2019. *Egypt: Cost of Environmental Degradation: Air and Water Pollution.* Washington, DC: World Bank.

Sanchez-Triana, E. 2021. *Environmental Challenges for Green Growth and Poverty Reduction.* Washington, DC: World Bank.

Sartori, M., G. Philippidis, E. Ferrari, P. Borrelli, E. Lugato, L. Montanarella, and P. Panagos. 2019. "A Linkage between the Biophysical and the Economic: Assessing the Global Market Impacts of Soil Erosion." *Land Use Policy* 86: 299–312. https://doi.org/10.1016/j .landusepol.2019.05.014.

SSC (State Statistical Committee of the Republic of Azerbaijan). 2021. "Environment in Azerbaijan." *Statistical Yearbook.* https://www.stat.gov.az/menu/6/statistical_yearbooks /source/environment_2021.zip.

USAID (United States Agency for International Development). 2017. "Assessment of Chronic Food Insecurity in Liberia." Washington, DC: USAID. https://fews.net/sites/default/files /documents/reports/Liberia%20Chronic%20Food%20Insecurity%20Report.pdf.

World Bank. 2022a. *Liberia Economic Update: Investing in Human Capital for Inclusive and Sustainable Growth*. Washington, DC: World Bank.

World Bank. 2022b. *Sub-Saharan Africa: Macro Poverty Outlook: Country-by-Country Analysis and Projections for the Developing World*. Washington, DC: World Bank.

CHAPTER 7

Conclusions

The study described in this report demonstrates that an efficiency-focused policy and investment approach to addressing economic and environmental problems is feasible, necessary, and more economically affordable than alternatives. With countries facing competing needs and stretched budgets, tackling inefficiencies remains one of the more cost-effective and economically attractive ways to achieve global sustainability goals. As global populations expand and the climate changes, pressures on common property natural resources will inevitably escalate, with worsening economic consequences. Using state-of-the-art techniques and new data, this study demonstrates that there are significant opportunities for using the world's scarce and valuable natural resources more efficiently. Doing so would stimulate simultaneous increases in economic productivity and improvements in environmental outcomes. Moreover, such a transformation is both achievable and economically desirable. Although it will entail demanding policy reforms, the cost of inaction will be far higher.

Conquering the headwinds to change

The modeling in this study demonstrates that gains in efficiency can mitigate or solve many of the challenges that face the world in the twenty-first century. More efficient landscapes can transform agricultural production to ensure that enough food can be produced to feed the estimated 10 billion people that will inhabit Earth by 2050. And by focusing on restoration of natural land, countries can succeed in sequestering nearly two years' worth of global emissions in landscapes, giving the world more time to achieve the carbon mitigation levels needed, while also restoring critical biomes for flora and fauna and reversing the trends in biodiversity loss. As for air quality, 366,000 deaths can be prevented each year—without the need for additional investments—by making current investments more efficient and effective.

Nevertheless, change will not come easily. Moving to the efficiency frontier may be difficult not just economically, but also politically and socially. In terms of economics, converting natural land to agricultural land and vice versa requires upfront spending on infrastructure such as irrigation dams and canals and transportation systems. Although the costs of such infrastructure are included in the modeling and the results presented are net of these costs, countries will still require financing in the short and medium term. Public budgets and international financing organizations such as the World Bank can provide some of this funding, but commercial financing will also likely be needed. Such financing will be particularly useful where legislation can create the enabling environment to signal that open access or common pool resources are scarce and thus should have a price that reflects that scarcity.

As with all major reforms, political and social challenges will emerge because change inevitably leads to winners and losers, and vested interests will resist change. The keys to solving these problems are communication to build support coalitions and compensation. The form of the coalition will depend on who benefits and who loses. For compensation, governments must establish credibility that they will follow through on their promises of compensation. This approach may require slow, stepwise reforms and transitions in which compensation is undertaken before reform. Indeed, the transition to the efficiency frontier will be slow and gradual. Thus, reforms and investments must also be gradual as these foundational issues are tackled.

Caveats, limitations, and future work

Compiling estimates of countries' current performance and efficiency frontiers for both landscapes and air quality requires pushing methods and data to the cutting-edge of science. As with any new global analysis, improvements will be needed in both data and methods, but, without a doubt, future advances will improve the accuracy and scope of this work.

The study described here relies on globally available data so that the analysis is consistent across all countries. However, reliance on such data does not allow incorporation of specific factors important in some countries that could be analyzed using more detailed local data. For example, in the landscape model land use and land management options are restricted to a relatively small set of 14 options. Thus one cannot model all land uses or land management practices that might be important in a particular country, resulting in conservative estimates of efficiency scores (in other words, allowing more options would result in still larger gaps). Even with this limited number of options, the employed models, together with the available data, are often at the limit of what could be reasonably predicted for all outcomes of interest (biodiversity, greenhouse gas mitigation, agricultural crop production, grazing, and forestry) under each management option. Although such limitations are binding in global analyses, country drilldowns like those presented in chapter 6 offer ways to expand and deepen the analysis through the use of more flexible and tailored models and data.

In addition, the modeling efforts here employ existing empirical relationships, which are adequate for understanding small perturbations of current conditions. However, large-scale changes in land use, for example, could cause major shifts in these empirical relationships, leading to large changes in outcomes of interest. Climate change is also likely to spur fundamental changes in ecosystems that will affect all outcomes of interest. Incorporating climate change is another frontier topic that deserves careful attention, but it is beyond the scope of this study.

Finally, the models examined the efficiency of only a small subset of the services provided by natural capital: crop production, livestock rearing, forestry, carbon sequestration, biodiversity support, and air quality. Arguably, for these services understanding of the science is most advanced and such modeling is most feasible. Future research may want to incorporate additional services such as water quality (as discussed in annex 2A) and water filtration, flood protection, pollination, and additional air pollutants. Currently, both the available data as well as the science behind these relationships are too sparse, but they are both likely to improve in the near future.

Concluding thoughts

Failure to steer economies toward greater sustainability may entail far greater risks and imperil economic and development objectives, and not just in the long run. Supporting a transition toward sustainability requires analytical tools to identify opportunities and policies that are feasible and implementable to bring about these changes. Empowering decision-makers with information about the range of opportunities and trade-offs between economic and nonmarket gains from different policies and landscape configurations is more likely to enable change by means of detailed assessments undertaken at the country level. That is the main objective of this cross-institutional endeavor, which has involved a partnership with researchers from the Natural Capital Project, the International Institute for Applied Systems Analysis, the World Bank, and leading academics.

Study Results by Country

This study analyzed 146 countries recognized by the World Bank that have a land surface area greater than 10,000 square kilometers. Table A.1 presents the full results by country for the landscape-efficiency score and its Pareto components. The following countries with a land surface area greater than 10,000 square kilometers were excluded because of data limitations: Arab Republic of Egypt, Democratic People's Republic of Korea, Djibouti, Fiji, Ireland, Israel, Kazakhstan, Kosovo, Kuwait, Kyrgyzstan, Qatar, Russian Federation, Tajikistan, The Bahamas, Turkmenistan, United Arab Emirates, Uzbekistan.

TABLE A.1
Measures of efficiency, by country

	Landscape efficiency score (%)	Geometric mean of individual Pareto scores (%)	Arithmetic mean of individual Pareto scores (%)	Environmental (carbon and biodiversity) Pareto geometric mean (%)
Afghanistan	75.6	57.2	57.3	59.8
Albania	96.1	63.7	65.1	57.5
Algeria	94.3	62.4	63.5	68.4
Angola	94.7	40.0	60.2	85.8
Argentina	86.0	53.5	57.2	70.2
Armenia	93.4	56.7	56.9	53.5
Australia	90.4	63.3	64.8	73.4
Austria	91.6	59.5	61.3	52.0
Azerbaijan	88.7	58.3	58.7	53.6
Bangladesh	68.7	40.1	46.7	33.5
Belarus	80.2	50.2	52.7	61.7

Continued

TABLE A.1
Continued

	Landscape efficiency score (%)	Geometric mean of individual Pareto scores (%)	Arithmetic mean of individual Pareto scores (%)	Environmental (carbon and biodiversity) Pareto geometric mean (%)
Belgium	96.0	53.8	59.5	41.1
Belize	97.3	50.8	65.2	89.7
Benin	83.2	50.7	54.7	66.5
Bhutan	96.4	45.8	65.2	92.1
Bolivia	93.4	48.9	60.7	82.5
Bosnia and Herzegovina	84.2	58.2	58.8	63.9
Botswana	98.0	70.7	71.7	75.5
Brazil	91.9	60.9	63.0	73.5
Bulgaria	92.2	70.6	70.8	68.1
Burkina Faso	85.6	50.6	51.1	51.8
Burundi	80.0	50.2	54.9	41.3
Cambodia	88.6	61.6	62.8	70.0
Cameroon	93.1	51.6	63.4	85.8
Canada	95.3	66.8	69.5	81.8
Central African Republic	97.4	27.5	61.9	91.6
Chad	81.4	50.6	52.0	60.1
Chile	88.1	58.8	60.4	69.3
China	81.1	53.8	53.9	53.1
Colombia	89.5	55.2	63.2	82.4
Congo, Dem. Rep.	95.5	39.2	62.4	89.9
Congo, Rep.	95.1	48.7	63.3	87.4
Costa Rica	89.8	51.6	60.2	79.4
Côte d'Ivoire	89.7	54.6	57.0	66.0
Croatia	79.7	57.1	57.5	58.4
Cuba	71.9	41.3	49.4	65.1
Czech Republic	91.6	62.6	63.9	55.9
Denmark	74.5	46.8	52.9	37.2
Dominican Republic	77.8	51.7	55.2	66.8
Ecuador	79.7	46.6	55.7	74.5
El Salvador	71.6	52.8	53.3	56.3
Equatorial Guinea	82.0	50.3	57.7	75.3
Eritrea	82.6	49.5	50.8	56.9
Estonia	70.9	40.3	43.8	53.8
Eswatini	93.7	62.6	63.0	59.0
Ethiopia	92.0	66.2	67.9	77.8
Finland	92.3	63.4	63.7	64.2

Continued

TABLE A.1
Continued

	Landscape efficiency score (%)	Geometric mean of individual Pareto scores (%)	Arithmetic mean of individual Pareto scores (%)	Environmental (carbon and biodiversity) Pareto geometric mean (%)
France	91.7	50.6	55.7	40.1
Gabon	93.2	45.2	62.8	88.3
Gambia, The	64.0	39.2	40.4	41.1
Georgia	84.0	50.8	52.4	60.2
Germany	95.6	59.9	63.6	49.8
Ghana	89.7	56.0	57.2	62.7
Greece	97.0	69.2	69.7	64.0
Guatemala	95.1	54.5	61.7	79.7
Guinea	95.9	45.4	58.2	80.0
Guinea-Bissau	79.3	33.5	49.4	70.2
Guyana	95.6	39.7	64.0	92.4
Haiti	61.8	31.8	35.9	39.8
Honduras	90.4	53.2	59.4	76.2
Hungary	87.1	57.3	58.1	54.2
Iceland	99.6	51.9	58.9	75.3
India	69.4	52.1	53.0	52.7
Indonesia	91.4	59.3	64.9	81.6
Iran, Islamic Rep.	88.5	65.0	65.3	63.1
Iraq	92.4	68.9	69.2	68.9
Italy	82.9	57.8	58.8	57.3
Jamaica	85.5	60.7	62.7	73.1
Japan	95.9	74.6	75.3	70.2
Jordan	91.5	58.0	68.1	90.2
Kenya	85.9	54.0	54.9	61.6
Korea, Rep.	97.5	74.9	76.3	68.2
Lao PDR	86.5	64.0	66.7	78.6
Latvia	73.6	45.3	46.8	53.3
Lebanon	94.7	59.9	62.0	50.3
Lesotho	77.5	47.5	49.7	52.3
Liberia	82.0	47.2	51.4	63.0
Libya	96.8	50.1	63.7	87.3
Lithuania	77.8	48.7	49.3	48.3
Madagascar	87.2	52.6	58.7	74.8
Malawi	81.4	56.1	57.9	55.4
Malaysia	95.0	66.2	69.4	83.0
Mali	84.5	60.1	60.3	62.9

Continued

TABLE A.1
Continued

	Landscape efficiency score (%)	Geometric mean of individual Pareto scores (%)	Arithmetic mean of individual Pareto scores (%)	Environmental (carbon and biodiversity) Pareto geometric mean (%)
Mauritania	87.5	60.2	63.2	74.4
Mexico	77.7	52.9	55.9	67.5
Moldova	84.0	51.1	52.2	52.1
Mongolia	74.2	45.6	47.7	50.2
Montenegro	96.5	63.9	64.8	71.5
Morocco	91.4	60.5	60.9	56.3
Mozambique	90.2	46.8	57.4	77.6
Myanmar	86.6	63.8	64.8	71.6
Namibia	95.6	69.1	69.3	70.3
Nepal	77.0	58.1	60.3	70.4
Netherlands	70.4	44.0	48.6	37.3
New Caledonia	97.8	47.7	60.4	82.5
New Zealand	82.6	53.9	54.6	56.4
Nicaragua	93.3	42.2	57.2	80.0
Niger	91.3	76.1	76.4	79.2
Nigeria	70.3	40.5	42.6	50.6
North Macedonia	93.0	63.7	64.4	61.0
Norway	94.8	54.0	60.4	76.5
Oman	97.7	62.1	71.9	94.3
Pakistan	64.0	57.7	59.3	65.0
Panama	95.1	60.9	66.8	84.2
Papua New Guinea	92.6	45.5	62.2	87.0
Paraguay	82.1	45.3	50.9	65.5
Peru	97.8	42.2	65.9	94.7
Philippines	90.5	63.9	64.5	66.9
Poland	78.5	54.3	55.0	56.3
Portugal	95.9	62.6	64.9	52.2
Romania	76.3	59.9	60.3	60.7
Rwanda	87.9	56.8	61.9	46.3
Saudi Arabia	94.5	54.5	61.5	41.5
Senegal	92.1	63.7	64.2	69.8
Serbia	84.9	58.3	58.5	60.8
Sierra Leone	67.5	45.2	48.5	58.1
Slovak Republic	88.5	63.9	64.2	60.7
Slovenia	87.1	64.9	65.3	61.0
Solomon Islands	87.4	48.4	56.1	73.8

Continued

TABLE A.1
Continued

	Landscape efficiency score (%)	Geometric mean of individual Pareto scores (%)	Arithmetic mean of individual Pareto scores (%)	Environmental (carbon and biodiversity) Pareto geometric mean (%)
Somalia	72.6	41.9	44.4	46.8
South Africa	86.2	56.1	57.5	59.7
South Sudan	89.1	52.5	59.1	75.0
Spain	93.5	61.5	62.3	56.7
Sri Lanka	77.8	60.4	62.3	71.7
Sudan	82.1	51.3	54.8	66.9
Suriname	97.4	23.3	64.8	96.5
Sweden	92.8	63.2	64.7	55.4
Switzerland	85.4	53.2	55.3	46.3
Syrian Arab Republlc	74.1	48.9	49.0	46.5
Tanzania	89.5	58.5	61.8	75.0
Thailand	82.1	59.0	60.7	57.9
Timor-Leste	84.7	46.4	47.7	53.8
Togo	84.6	41.4	50.6	68.0
Tunisia	87.0	45.8	49.4	39.5
Türkiye	92.9	58.2	60.5	49.0
Uganda	64.5	43.3	44.5	47.0
Ukraine	80.9	55.7	56.1	57.9
United Kingdom	87.0	44.1	51.4	31.9
United States	90.1	57.0	58.4	66.2
Uruguay	72.8	44.1	44.6	46.1
Vanuatu	98.4	39.2	63.6	91.9
Venezuela, RB	90.5	55.9	64.7	84.9
Vietnam	84.1	66.7	67.4	65.2
Yemen, Rep.	94.2	58.8	58.9	56.8
Zambia	95.2	53.1	61.8	81.5
Zimbabwe	81.6	44.8	50.2	64.5

Source: World Bank.